Retire in New York City—Even If You're Not Rich

"I've always known that New York is a swell place to retire, and reading this fine book is a great way to get you started."

ROBERT N. BUTLER, M.D.
President, International Longevity Center–USA

"The profiles in this book show us that retirement in New York City can be more lively than work ever was . . . and the Brooklyn profiles show that it can be even better here in Brooklyn! Kudos to Janet Hays for describing so many of the advantages of a New York City—and a Brooklyn—retirement."

MARTY MARKOWITZ
President of the Borough of Brooklyn

"What a delight—a book that makes the case so many of us know in our hearts. What better place to retire than in the city that is the center of the universe, with greater diversity, more options, and a livelier spirit than can be found anywhere else. Hays and Jensen not only remind us why we would want to be in New York; they also tell us how it can be arranged, providing guides as to where we might live, how to spend our time, and how to get involved in some of the many things that are happening every hour of the day."

RUTH MESSINGER
Former President of the Borough of Manhattan

Retire in New York City
—Even If You're Not Rich

New York City Can Be the Retirement Village
of Your Dreams, at a Price You Can Afford

JANET HAYS

With a Special Section on Housing by
RITA HENLEY JENSEN

Foreword by BETSY WADE
Former Writer, *The New York Times,*
"The Practical Traveler"

Bonus Books
Chicago and Los Angeles

06 05 04 03 02   5 4 3 2 1

Library of Congress Cataloging-in-Publication Data

Hays, Janet.
  Retire in New York City— even if you're not rich : New York City can be the retirement village of your dreams, at a price you can afford / Janet Hays ; with a special section on housing by Rita Henley Jensen ; foreword by Betsy Wade.
        p. cm.
Includes bibliographical references and index.
  ISBN 1-56625-175-3
  1. New York (N.Y.)—Guidebooks. 2. Retirees—New York (State)—New York—Life skills guides. 3. Retirement, Places of—New York (State)—New York—Guidebooks. 4. Moving, Household—New York (State)—New York—Handbooks, manuals, etc. 5. Cost and standard of living—New York (State)—New York—Guidebooks. I. Jensen, Rita Henley. II. Title.

F128.18 .H38 2002
974.7'1044'0846—dc21
                                        2002014337

Bonus Books
160 E. Illinois St.
Chicago, IL 60611

Printed in the United States of America

To my mother, Sara Caplan Ginsburg, whose courage, determination, and love have shown me that life can be meaningful at every age

CONTENTS

FOREWORD

by Betsy Wade

Former writer of the *New York Times* "Practical Traveler" column
Adjunct assistant professor, Hunter College, City University of New York

When they ask where I live, I tell my friends I live at the belly-button of the universe. Since they laugh and endure my arrogance, I guess I can say the same thing to you, even though I may sound like a *loca*, as we say in our first-level Spanish class. At my doorstep is the M-57 bus heading toward the art galleries of 57th Street; the M-72 heading through Central Park to the East Side and Hunter College, where I now teach a seminar in journalism and public policy; and the M-5 easing south toward Rockefeller Center and my adorable dentist, or past the vistas of Riverside Drive. One block over is the all-important Broadway–Seventh Avenue subway, which will bear me any place in the city I need to go, including the green-market at Union Square, where the authors of this book and I love to sniff the bread and tomatoes and buy flowers. It's one of the places in the city where I can buy the sausage without nitrates that my nephew the Emory professor can eat. And Union Square, in turn, is only a couple of L-train stops from fabulous Bedford Avenue in Brooklyn, my new favorite place for its used bookstores and rummage shops and cybercafés in which to sit and read my new old books.

For the first five years my husband and I lived here, the express subway whisked me to my job in Times Square. Now that I have retired, I still return to Times Square to continue my Spanish lessons, to go to the gym to work out with the area's svelte actors, and to meet old friends. But now I have my choice of the local, the bus, or a walk! In New York, unlike Beverly Hills, the cops don't ask where you think you're going if you're on foot.

When our grandchildren come to visit, I buy them Metro-Card "Fun Passes" and we visit bookstores, vegetarian restaurants, off-Broadway plays, the Bronx Zoo, and their aunt's Harry Potter emporium in SoHo, all for four dollars a child a day. Those of us grannies and grandpas who have driven squirming grands to some putative attraction in the outback really appreciate the kids' delight in inserting their MetroCards the correct way, swinging on the subway poles, pressing the yellow strip to get off the bus. (I often slip in a subtle lecture about automobiles and emissions, but others may skip that.)

And now, to make you really drool: The amazing Fairway supermarket, Citarella's fancy foods, the Levain Bakery, and a rather nice thrift shop are only a couple of blocks from my doorstep. I keep telling Janet and Rita they should forsake their stomping grounds in Inwood, the part of northern Manhattan where we brought up the grandkids' fathers, and come frolic with me. They don't believe me when I say that the local 72nd Street video shop, Fliks, delivers and picks up free, and it keeps in stock *Casablanca* and *Dinner at Eight* as well as *Babette's Feast*. The superette—don't you love the clash of images in that name—on my corner, the one I can see from bed, stays open all night, so if I have a fierce craving for cappuccino yogurt, I can pull on my running shoes, throw on a coat and pick a fix up at 2 A.M. Safe? Egads. The doorman is polishing brass, a superette employee is cutting flower stems, and the worst menaces in sight are the motorists speeding up West End Avenue in hopes of escaping us dangerous little old ladies and returning to Nowheresville, N.J. *Mi esposo*—notice how I am progressing—says I can be an insufferable snob, so forgive me.

When I moved here from the northernmost house in Manhattan, I could not believe the wealth of things at hand. But it took my younger neighbor to draw the mega-lesson clearly for me. The story is illustrative, so hang on.

We were standing in our little hallway, exchanging reports on our well-being. "I was looking for a place where my aunt and uncle could live comfortably in their old age," she confided. "I wanted a place where they would not need to be able to drive, where they could get meals delivered to them when they no longer felt up to cooking, where they could find intellectual stimulation, be visited by me and my brother and have healthcare easily at hand at all hours. I was thinking of someplace where everything was on one level in case they couldn't do stairs."

I leaned toward her, exuding the superior wisdom of my wonderful job as a travel writer, and the extraordinary resources I had accumulated. I replied, "Daphne, I have two books over my desk at the office: 'Best Places to Retire.' I'll bring them home and you can pick some places to look at."

She stared at me piercingly and repeated her thought: "Someplace where they would not need to drive and didn't have to walk upstairs." She pointed to the bell for the elevator, indicating the likelihood that the doorman Urbano Serna, known as Ito, could be on the spot in a minute, able to call a cab or a limo.

"I realized that what I needed to find was an apartment next door to me," she said.

Slow on the uptake, I am. But I rallied. "Listen," I said, "I have friends who are writing a book about exactly that. Maybe I should call them up and tell them you have figured out what they know and it's time to get on the horn to guide others."

And that is pretty much what happened. Janet and Rita's response was that I should tell you what I have told them, and here it is. Your pretty villages and retirement communities are okay, but in the Big Apple you do not need to rely on the kindness of friends. Or of strangers, for that matter, Blanche. Your transportation, healthcare, meals, gossip, books, movies, gyms, plays, shopping, friends, relatives, repair shops—Lord knows what all—are at hand. Haircuts? You can take a subway or bus to that most crucial place in our lives. Your transportation will cost you 75 cents a trip, transfers included. The city invites you: Welcome spring at Daffodil Hill on Eastern Parkway. Pace off the Onassis Reservoir path or cross the Brooklyn Bridge on foot. Subway and bus to Wave Hill in the Bronx and claim domain over the Hudson. The Shorewalkers club will walk you around Manhattan, the Bronx, and Staten Island, too, in case there's a spot you've missed. You can be independent and live the life you want. You should make the decision on the basis of what you hear inside you, not what you hear from the folks who brought you Disney World or the Marriott Hotels. So turn the page and see what awaits.

ACKNOWLEDGMENTS

Rosemary Armao conceived the idea for this book. She and I were driving home from a ski weekend in the Adirondacks, talking about how we hoped to live the rest of our lives. Snowflakes big as nickels were falling on the car. Rosemary thought about how New York City beckoned, and about how far she'd come from the days when she'd been afraid to drive across the George Washington Bridge. She said, "Why don't we write a guide to retiring in New York?" I wanted to do it. I knew that right away.

We first planned to write as a group, and we invited several friends to join us. But, after a few effervescent meetings, the enormity of writing a book while holding down full-time jobs led everyone except me and Rita Henley Jensen to drop out. Rita, in the face of job pressures that have multiplied by powers of 10 between then and now, stayed on to write the housing section and contribute a fresh, sensible perspective to the entire manuscript. Betsy Wade joined later to add the foreword. I'm grateful to both of them.

Retire rests on the shoulders of the men and women who are profiled and quoted in its chapters. And of the many others I interviewed but could not include in the book. Everyone answered my questions generously and offered perspectives that informed my thinking and writing. By telling me about their lives, my interviewees have expanded my life.

Mervin Block steered me to Bonus Books, answered ordinary and arcane questions, and taught me grammar I never knew existed. Audrey and Seymour Simon read chapters and offered thoughtful comments. Dottie Brier, Holly Butler, James C. Hall, Mary Holloway, Nancy Tomasello, James Weil, and Katherine Weissman listened to my problems, led me to others who could help, and guided me all along the way.

James C. Hall, Ariel Jensen-Vargas, and Michael Macioce enlivened the book with their photographs. Donna Macioce developed concepts for the cover design. New York City and Company also provided photographs; Maricela Herzog there was most helpful. I appreciate them all.

Devon Freeny, my editor at Bonus Books, made this book more classic, more graceful, more like what I'd always wanted it to be, than I was able to do myself.

I'm happy twice over to have had the continuing support and encouragement of my children, James, Joshua, and Andrew Adelson; Lisa Eisenberg and Nancy Allison. It's nice to receive their help. It's even nicer to see they've grown up to be the kind of people who offer it.

Before I dared let Bonus Books read one sentence of this manuscript, Julia Hall read every word. In our long editing sessions over the telephone, she made countless suggestions for rearranging and clarifying ideas, for omitting unnecessary text. "Net it out," she said. She plied me with relevant clippings, introduced me to potential interviewees, and pointed out aspects of retirement life I had overlooked. Julia was midwife. Without her, the delivery of this book would have been infinitely rougher.

JANET HAYS

I needn't say much more than Janet, except that I would like to thank Mary Hack, real estate management agent extraordinaire, for her careful reading of the housing section; my terrific daughters Ariel Jensen-Vargas and Shasta Jensen for their assistance and support; John Bracken, program associate for the Ford Foundation, for living in Sunnyside and loving it; and my best friend Sam, without whom none of what I have accomplished would have been possible.

RITA HENLEY JENSEN

Section One

Retire in New York City

CHAPTER **ONE**

Kaleidoscope

The Brilliantly Colored, Constantly Changing Lifetimes in New York

David Hays grew up poor in the South. He came north to college from Florida on a Greyhound bus. After riding all night, or maybe two nights, he woke up on a highway in New Jersey to see the sun rising over the Manhattan skyline. On the spot, he decided "That's where I want to live."

I met him in college. Long before we married he told me about his first awestruck view of the skyscrapers and his desire to live in New York. But not until we were over 50 did we move here. Dave died in 1995; I'm staying here.

New York City is a compelling city. No one can absorb all

that's happening. Even if I had unlimited time, unlimited money, and unlimited energy, I would have to make choices. Novelists give readings at the same hour my Italian class meets. Sometimes the Mets and the Yankees come up to bat on the same evening. Film festivals vie for attention with talks by Wall Street financiers, and the curtain rises on New York City Ballet and American Ballet Theater at the same hour. I can't run out of things to do. I can't get bored. I like it that way. I like having more available than I can ever do.

In New York, I can walk or take public transportation everywhere. Dave and I sold our car when we moved here. Before that we lived near Buffalo and had to drive everywhere we went. I couldn't wait to break out of that cocoon, my car. Every person I've interviewed for this book has singled out public transportation as a mainstay of life in New York City for older people. They all know retirees in Florida who curtail visits to friends and forgo concerts and plays because they can no longer drive at night. And then there are the people who are stuck at home, dependent on friends or hired help for rides because they can't drive at all. In New York, when you no longer have the strength to climb the subway stairs, you can still cover the city by bus. When it's too hard to mount that first step, the driver lowers the bus.

If you yearn to live alongside a golf course, New York City may not be for you. But if the prospect of a laid-back retirement bores you, think about living in New York. If you've enjoyed your visits to the city, imagine what it's like to live here permanently. You can open the newspaper any morning and find concerts, plays, ball games, operas, jazz—often at reduced cost, or free. And you can do more. This book tells you how you, yourself, can take part in the art, theater, and politics of the city. How you can attend workshops where you learn more about a play and its author, see dance troupes rehearse, sew costumes, and watch choreographers work out their routines. On a trip to New York, you can see St. Patrick's Cathedral; when you live here, you can visit the studios of artists who are restoring stained glass in churches all around the city.

Many books list the museums, historic sights, skyscrapers, and architectural gems of New York City. Newspapers and magazines tell you about the art and entertainment available here every day. This book is different. We concentrate on opportunities to *participate*—to sing in a chorus, show people around an historic house, study Talmud, or paddle a canoe. We show you how it's possible to create a new life here. A life that's as disciplined or as freewheeling as you want.

This book tells you where you can take courses or volunteer, and how to find part-time work if you want it. It talks about people who have made new friends and developed new interests and skills, people who have found a new sense of purpose in life after they initialed and sent their last office memo. This book profiles a retired salesman who goes to cooking school, a retired social worker who is now in show business, a retired union organizer who leads tours of the Cathedral Church of St. John the Divine.

Medical care is first-rate. The city has six major medical

schools with teaching hospitals, specialists, and specialized hospitals in virtually every field; research studies indicate that services for the aging are better here than in most places. One of my interviewees, who recovered from a stroke recently, told me that the system for arranging for home health aides works better here than in other places she's lived and that the quality of the caregivers is higher.

New York City is surprisingly safe—safer than many places where people retire. Look at the most recent FBI Uniform Crime Reports (year 2000) and compare the crime rates in New York with those in Phoenix and Scottsdale, Arizona; Palm Springs and San Diego, California; Naples and Orlando, Florida.[1]

- You are more likely to be murdered in Orlando and Phoenix than in New York.
- Your car is more likely to be stolen in Orlando, Palm Springs, Phoenix, San Diego, and Scottsdale than in New York.
- Of all seven cities listed, New York has the lowest level of burglary and the lowest level of theft.
- And when we compare the number of crimes per hundred thousand people for each of the seven cities, New York City has the second-lowest overall crime rate.

One night when I got home from a movie, I stepped out of the elevator to see a group of people clustered in front of my

---

1 For the FBI's detailed figures on safety, see the appendix.

apartment door. It was open. My adrenaline shot up. What was going on? It took a minute for me to figure it out because my neighbors come from the Dominican Republic, and my Spanish is poor. But gradually I understood. They had noticed my door was ajar and, having seen me leave a little earlier, thought something might be wrong. They checked and all was quiet. Yet they stood guard all evening, to make sure that my apartment continued to be safe!

Everything inside was just as I'd left it. Apparently I hadn't pulled the door completely shut when I turned the key, so the bolt hadn't engaged. Next morning I bought my neighbors a chocolate cake from a good bakery. Only a token reward, but how could I really thank them?

Despite the skyscrapers and crowds, New York City is remarkably human-scale. Somehow we don't feel dwarfed by the tall buildings or lost in the noisy crowds. We live in real neighborhoods, we walk to markets a few steps from our front doors, and we talk with our neighbors along the way. Even the very old and frail can go out to buy a couple of tomatoes on their own block. One woman told me, "I'm a city girl. I'm not used to jumping in and out of cars to buy a quart of milk."

All over New York we have stores that specialize in good produce, good meat, and good cheese. Hanging sausages and prosciutto tempt customers in the pork stores of Greenwich Village, and Indian grocers in Jackson Heights lure you with their spices. Pasta shops offer 20 kinds of ravioli and a profusion of sauces. Greenmarkets feature a dozen varieties of po-

tatoes and tomatoes with that summer garden smell. After
you've filled your refrigerator, you can find silks and diamonds on Madison Avenue, ceramics on Lexington, hand-
crafted leather in Greenwich Village, ribbons in the Garment
District.

New York City is not homogenized. You see more different
kinds of people here than anywhere else. You hear more languages, meet people doing more different kinds of work. My
New York friends earn their livings and work out the details
of their lives in astonishingly varied ways. Yesterday I had
lunch with a woman who supports herself writing literary
book reviews and teaching classes of seniors how to conduct
research on the Web. Only in New York have I found such acceptance of lives organized so idiosyncratically, such respect
for the person piecing a quilt of life.

One evening, after a flute and harpsichord concert at the
New York Public Library, I stopped for a late supper at a
sandwich shop across 42nd Street. The café was almost empty
and, when the few diners had been served, one of the waiters
sat down at a table near me, opened a notebook, and began to
write numbers. I assumed she was working on the restaurant
books. But, after a while, the pizza-maker from up front
dusted the flour off his hands and walked back to help her.
"Why don't you try solving that for the value of c?" he suggested. Not a typical bookkeeping operation. When I was
leaving, I stopped to talk with the pizza man, now back at his
station. Turns out he was tutoring her in calculus. "I love calculus, and I love helping young people," he told me. He does

it all the time back home in the Bronx. Do pizza-makers tutor calculus students in other cities?

Later that evening, while I was waiting on the subway platform, a big man in a big hurry stepped on the back of my ankle. I winced and bent down to rub it. A woman standing nearby asked if I was okay. "Not for nothing is it called the Achilles tendon," she commented. The concentration of knowledgeable people here delights me. And, contrary to popular belief, New Yorkers are not usually callous and indifferent. In fact, they are often attentive and thoughtful.

In much of America, people walking through expensive neighborhoods to look at homes and gardens risk being questioned by the police. In New York you can walk and look freely. You can stop and examine stone carvings, wrought-iron grilles, window boxes spilling petunias and geraniums, fanciful bridges, cast-iron façades, mosaic-tiled lobbies. Here such treasures aren't limited to wealthy neighborhoods; they can be found everywhere.

When you live in New York City you can:

- Breakfast on café-au-lait and croissants at a marble-topped table a block from home.
- Bike in Central Park.
- Walk your dog in Prospect Park.
- Dance on the plaza at Lincoln Center.
- Climb Bear Mountain or canoe Tom's River.
- Rent a boat and go fishing out of Sheepshead Bay.
- Get an apartment in a brownstone and garden out back.

- Vibrate to the beat of Brooklyn's West Indian Day parade.
- Ride the subway to cheer your favorite team: Yankees, Mets, Knicks.
- Join a flock of birdwatchers at Jamaica Bay or Pelham Bay, or in Central Park.
- Take urban walking tours led by historians, architects, sociologists, and writers.
- Enroll in a pastry-making workshop, learn to speak Italian, take a Ph.D. in art history.
- Grow zucchini on a neighborhood plot, plant daffodils at Fort Tryon Park, or prune, rake, and mulch at the Brooklyn Botanic Garden.
- Listen to chamber music at the Morgan Library, bandshell concerts in Damrosch Park, jazz on an East River pier.
- Lead tours at a major museum. (It may require months of serious study but you'll get nearly the equivalent of a master's degree. Free.)
- Quit raking leaves, shoveling snow, cleaning gutters.
- Free yourself from conformity.

Novelists and playwrights fill their notebooks with conversations they hear on the street. People who aren't writers enjoy just listening. My visiting teenage grandson was entranced with an umbrella vendor hawking: "It's a crime against humanity for anyone to be wet when I'm selling umbrellas for only three dollars!" Immediately the boy adapted the line to his own needs: "It's a crime against humanity for me to be hungry when they're selling ice cream for only two dollars!" His cousin, amazed to hear a religious orator calling him to God on the subway, asked me, "Is he trying to convert us?" "I think so." "Is that legal?"

One day, also on the subway, I overheard a young woman say to another across the aisle, "Ever since Grandpa went to the nursing home I feel you've been holding yourself back from me." A remarkably intimate conversation for such a public place, I thought, and began to listen. They continued to puzzle over family tensions until I heard the first one say again, "Ever since Grandpa went to the nursing home, I feel you've been holding yourself back from me." They were rehearsing a play!

Life in New York City is not always fast-paced and demanding. Sometimes I feel the city flowing quietly around me: On a soft summer evening when I'm strolling, skimming, almost floating over the hexagonal pavers on Central Park West between the crenellated apartment houses on my left and the park on my right; when it's snowing and I'm walking along the brownstones on West 87th Street watching the street lights blur and feeling the hush as the traffic sounds are muffled. Ten blocks downtown the blue planetarium globe shimmers through the flakes. On Saturday mornings in summer I walk under the leafy, arching locust trees on 16th Street on my way to the greenmarket at Union Square, where I buy corn and peaches and inhale the fragrance of basil and thyme.

When I was a child New York City was said to have more

Irish than Dublin, more Jews than Jerusalem, more Italians than Rome. Later people said there were more Koreans in Flushing than in Seoul. Today the city glitters with people from every continent, every religion, and just about every ethnic group in the world. A newcomer can find a comfortable "home group" of people with common interests within the diverse population of the city. Gays and lesbians say they feel more at ease here than in most places.

Money magazine ranks New York City as one of the best places in the country to retire. "Noisy and pricey but unmatched in its vitality," *Money* says. "No other city could equal its economy, vitality and culture." *Money*'s right. But living in New York doesn't have to be so pricey. If you want to live here but are stymied by the cost, this book will tell you how you can enjoy New York without going broke. The housing section, "Finding a New Home," explains how to track down an apartment you can afford. "Making a New Life" tells you where to find free and discount tickets so you can enjoy art, music, and drama without spending a fortune.

New York City is terrific for older single women. You don't have to be half of a couple to have a good time. Widows, divorced women, and women who have never married go everywhere, and no one looks askance. Single women are invited to dinner parties. We eat in restaurants on Saturday night without a man. We go to theater on our own, and on hikes. Robin Bahr, who moved to New York from San Francisco when she retired, notices that in New York age doesn't have the stigma it has in other places. "Older people aren't shuffled off to one side here. They're part of the whole community."

New York City is the place for retirees to celebrate a brand new life, if they want one. There's more intensity and stimulus packed into this sliver of land than anywhere else I know. And with the resources here, you can take up almost anything and explore it in depth. If you want a life with structure and focus, you can have it in New York. If you want friends and fun without schedule and commitment, New York's riches will last for the rest of your life.

When my brothers and I were in our 40s and no longer needed parental care and guidance, my mother said to me, "Dad and I realize that the most creative part of our life is over." I, too, feel that rearing my children was enormously creative, but I don't find my life less creative now. Here in New York City, thoughtful people challenge me with new ideas, and lively people keep me on my toes. Would I have taken the first ballet lesson of my life at 62 if I lived anywhere else? Would I have begun to write full-time? Produced this book? In New York City I can be myself. Better yet, I can continue to become myself.

CHAPTER **TWO**

Decision

New Year's Day 1980. It was mid-afternoon and I'd been restless, pacing in my kitchen just south of Buffalo. Suddenly the idea popped into my head: if we moved to New York I could do all the things I'd always wanted to do. I went to my husband, who was stretched out on the living room sofa. With no preamble I asked, "Do you think we could earn our living in New York City?"

Dave practically levitated.

In a flash we both knew we were ready to move. Dave had wanted to live in New York ever since that morning in 1947 when he first saw the skyline from the Jacksonville bus. For many years New York City had daunted me, but in the late

'70s I began to change. Every time we went to New York, I liked it more. So we thought, planned, and calculated to be sure we could make it work. For major decisions, the sequence that works best for me is to pay attention to my heart first to know what I really want. *Then* ask the practical questions: How will we do it? What will it cost? What will we be giving up? Can we handle it?

If you are considering moving to New York but have trouble wrapping your mind around so large an undertaking, focus first on knowing how you really feel about it. Set aside, for the moment, the practical questions: how you'll sell your house, the formidable moving job, whether you can afford to live here. Just ask yourself: "Does living in New York City appeal to me?" If you're not sure, read the *New York Times*, the *New Yorker*, *New York Magazine*, and other local publications. Read section 3 of this book, "Making a New Life." Visit your friends in New York and talk with them about their daily lives. New York is a particularly affective city. People either love it or hate it. Few are neutral.

When he was trying to decide whether to run for another Senate term, Bob Kerrey, former United States senator from Nebraska and current president of New School University, wrote out two statements—one saying he was returning to private life and a second saying he would run for another term. Kerry says, "The first one made me smile, the second one didn't."[2]

---

2 Quoted in the *New York Times*, article by Robin Toner, January 31, 2000.

If you're having trouble deciding whether you want to move to New York or not, you could compose two letters to a close friend—one saying that you're planning to move, another that you're staying put (or moving somewhere else). See how writing those letters makes you feel.

If you don't know how you could afford to live in New York, read section 2, "Finding a New Home," to get a handle on the biggest chunk of your budget. Maybe you don't know what you would do with yourself all day every day. Read the chapters on the arts, volunteering, education, sports and outdoor activities, and work. Maybe you love the city but don't have any friends there and worry about being lonely. Read "Promise and Challenge," the introduction to the "New Life" section.

Retire in New York City talks about where and how you can live and describes what older people here are doing with their lives. And we present some techniques to help you sort out the complexities.

"Retire in New York? It would be great, but who can afford it?" That's the refrain I hear when I tell my out-of-town friends about this book. It all depends.

Bob Kaplan retired at 56 after 35 years with IBM—many of those years in Europe. After Paris and London, Kaplan and his wife chose Manhattan over New Jersey, where they'd lived when their children were small. He feels that the financial planners who say you need less income in retirement than you did while working are wrong. "If you want to enjoy retirement, you spend significantly more," he says. When he first retired, the Kaplans spent more than his IBM take-home pay to go out to dinner and to theater, and to travel.[3]

But Georgea Pace enjoys her retirement in Manhattan on Social Security alone—$859 a month after Medicare deductions. Her rent is $607. Pace, who was introduced to me as a master of living on a modest income, goes out almost every day—to free concerts at Juilliard, lectures at the public library, Shakespeare in the parks, pay-what-you-will nights at the museums, meditation and Qigong at Riverside Church. She paints and writes poetry. Once in a while she gets a scholarship to a church-sponsored retreat in the Catskills.

Nancy Kigner, who lives on Long Island, wants to move to the city, but so far hasn't been able to find a place she can afford. She doesn't want to move here unless she can live within walking distance of Lincoln Center—just about the most expensive part of the city. Northern Manhattan, Queens, Brooklyn aren't for her.

My choice is different: I'd like to be able to walk to Lincoln Center too, but I can't afford to live that close. For me the choice between taking the subway and remaining in Buffalo was no choice. There's no right or wrong here; it's an individual preference. We provide the information; you figure out what you want to do with it.

Dave and I didn't know much about living in New York when we were planning our move, so we made mistakes. We

---

3 A year later the Kaplans find they are spending less money: Bob has gotten involved in long-distance walking and volunteer work, and September 11 has curbed their desire to fly.

came without a place to live and brought along (and put into storage) the gas range from our kitchen upstate. I'd figured we could rent a place for less if we already had a stove. I didn't know that New York City landlords are required to provide a stove, and that our monster model would never fit in the kitchen of an apartment we could afford.

Dave and I arrived separately because he was on a business trip. I was so excited when my plane landed at La Guardia I almost forgot to claim my suitcase. For a few days we stayed at the Lucerne Hotel, a faded *grande dame* now renovated, that was well known as a place where young musicians could stay cheaply. Then for three months we sublet from an Israeli professor away on sabbatical. The sublet, on Third Avenue at 24th Street, gave us time to get our bearings and find an apartment.

On New Year's Day 1981 we moved to our present place in northern Manhattan—a one-bedroom rent-stabilized apartment in a prewar building. Our rent then was $375 a month. With the allowable yearly increases, I'm paying $760 in 2002. The real estate agent had promised an apartment overlooking Fort Tryon Park, but 3G actually *under*looks the park. We're in the Broadway lowlands, just east of the rocky ridge that runs along the Hudson River. Lying in bed I can see the rocks and trees of the cliff on which the Cloisters stands. I can look up to the highest point in Manhattan—where George Washington held the British at bay for two months. When I was a young girl reading *Heidi*, I was enchanted with Heidi's lying in bed in her grandfather's cottage and seeing the mountain through a little round window. I thought it would be wonderful to lie in bed and look at a mountain, but not until I moved to New York City could I do that. It's not the Alps, but, from a supine position, who can tell?

My apartment pleases me. I have a good layout, nicely proportioned rooms, thick plaster walls, fairly high ceilings, ample windows and closets. The bathroom and kitchen are each only five feet by eight feet, but I've cooked for as many as 30 people in that small kitchen.

My building still has its original tile and terrazzo hallway floors. The original multi-paned front door had dark wood mullions and stars etched into the glass panels, but the replacement is one big pane of plate glass. When it got too scuffed, the fine old wood paneling in the elevator was covered with cheap plastic. The neighborhood is lively and often noisy and littered, but it's safe and friendly. Three food markets, two take-out restaurants, a post office, drug store, dry cleaner, laundry, beauty parlor, and newsstand are all less than five minutes walk from my door. The A train to Columbus Circle takes 20 minutes.

Most of the people I've interviewed have chosen to retire in New York City because they enjoy the vitality and excitement of the city. They like being overwhelmed by the choice of things to do. They like the street life and the ability to get around without a car. They like the paradox of anonymity and close contact with so many people. Though some worry about growing old and frail in this fast-moving city, they'd rather cope than leave.

By and large the people profiled in this book are financially comfortable but not especially wealthy. Before they retired they were social workers, high school and college teachers, advertising and public relations people, accountants, fabric designers, graphic artists, and writers. Some worked for large corporations, but few were at the top. Some were bankers, dentists, and retail merchants.

Each person's story is different. I talked with retirees who came to New York from small towns with little to stimulate them. And I talked with people from places as cosmopolitan as Chicago and as beautiful as Santa Barbara. I talked with people who had moved to Florida and returned to New York. Some of the people I met always knew they wanted to live here—or come back. Others came to that decision gradually— or suddenly—in middle age. Their stories may help you write your own.

Alice Marks[4] moved from a town where she was lonely to a city where she meets people whose outlook and interests are similar to hers. Her entire Gramercy Park apartment would fit into her children's playroom back in the Midwest. When her brother first visited, he offered to lend her the money to buy a

---

4 Not her real name. Every person interviewed was asked for permission to use his or her name. Those who declined have been given pseudonyms, and some identifying details have been changed. All such persons are noted in footnotes; all other names are real.

two-bedroom but she turned him down. "I've gotten rid of everything. I gave away two thousand books; I sold paintings and furniture. Now I have just what I want."

At 76 Marks is tall, angular, and elegant. On the summer day we met, she wore pale gray linen pants and a matching scoop-neck T-shirt; her well-coifed white hair was in a pageboy. She reminded me of Lauren Bacall.

Alice Marks used to run a tannery in the Midwest. She'd grown up there, graduated from law school and was admitted to the bar in 1945. But no firm would hire a woman. "We'd love to hire you," the partners told her, "but our clients would lose confidence in the firm if they knew we had a girl in the office."

When she married, Marks moved to the small town where her husband's family had run a tannery for several generations. A liberal in a conservative town, Marks didn't know any other Democrats; when she wanted to invite people to a fundraising dinner for Mondale and Ferraro, she had to consult the voting lists.

Marks began to work in the tannery when her husband became ill, and she continued after his death in 1966. Tanning is messy; it smells. Until Marks took over, no woman had worked in the plant itself, and the women in the office never ventured onto the tanning floor. Alice Marks went back and forth from office to plant several times a day, changing clothes completely each time. She hired women to work in the plant and took the office staff in to see how tanning is done. She hired the first female foreman and the first black foreman in her town.

But Marks was lonely. After her husband died, old friends seldom called. For 20 years she was at the plant every morning by eight o'clock, working until after seven in the evening. Socially, she hardly talked to a soul. "I had *one* friend who'd call sometimes at suppertime and say, 'Don't sit there eating canned tuna by yourself. C'mon over and eat with us.' She saved my life."

Marks came to New York often to sell her leather. She liked the city, and, in 1972, as a 50th birthday present to herself, she rented an apartment on Gramercy Park South. She used the apartment as a *pied-à-terre* for her business trips and bought her present apartment on the north side of the park in 1984. Five years later she liquidated the tannery and moved to New York permanently.

Coming into Marks's light, airy apartment from the dim corridor lined with oil paintings, I was so dazzled by the light from the big living room window that I didn't even notice I was walking through her all-black kitchen which also serves as her entry hall. Large abstract paintings on white walls give color to a living room minimally furnished in black leather, chrome, and glass. A window facing the park fills most of one bedroom wall; two walls are lined with floor-to-ceiling black bookcases. Pictures of her children, their spouses, and seven grandchildren are scattered casually in front of the books. Her bed, flanked by clear glass night-tables, stands against the fourth wall. The apartment, like its owner, is warm and striking, though spare; Marks's discipline, intensity, and intellectual rigor manifest themselves in the style and organization of her home.

Alice Marks felt only relief when she moved to New York. In her old town, single women weren't a natural part of community social life. Here she goes out with friends to eat and talk. She spends time with the people whose art she's bought, and she goes to concerts and restaurants with couples as well as with other single women.

A few years ago Marks began writing short stories. Some days she wakes up early to write; some days she eats a leisurely breakfast and begins to write late in the morning. And some days she starts at four in the afternoon and writes until 2 A.M. Her comfort with the non-schedule bespeaks her comfort with herself. Every other week Marks meets with a small group of writers to critique one another's stories, offering everything from general comments to line editing. Marks is the oldest member; the youngest is 33. They are serious and supportive of one another.

Marks intends to live in New York City forever. Her advice to would-be New Yorkers: "Come and stay and see how it feels. Rent a place for a year and see how it works."

A year after Roger died, Holly Butler, 65, decided to sell the Virginia beach house they'd bought when he retired. With-

out her husband, it was too big, too lonely, and "too full of
the life I wasn't going to have."

But where to go? Back to Weston, Connecticut—where
they'd lived for 38 years, reared their children, produced and
directed local plays, and championed candidates for political
office? Not necessarily. Maybe a college town. Butler thought
she could meet interesting people and would enjoy the cultural activities. She figured it would be easier for a woman to
go out alone and that she would be more welcome in a college
town than in a corporate town where most social life happens
in couples.

Butler looked at condos—gray clapboard townhouses in
Amherst, Massachusetts, and Saratoga Springs, New York.
(Condos were gray everywhere, it seemed.) And in both towns
she checked roads and timetables to see how long it took to
get to New York City. Saratoga, with Skidmore College and
the Saratoga Performing Arts Center, appealed to her: three
hours' drive to Boston, three to New York, three and one-half
to Montreal. But long snowy winters shorten the driving season, and trains are infrequent. How long would she be able to
make such a drive?

Swinging from Saratoga back toward Virginia, Butler
stopped in New York City to visit friends. They took her to
Moss Hart's *Light up the Sky,* a performance by the Actor's
Company Theatre, one of the city's many repertory groups,
and they capped the evening with a visit to a colleague who
lives 58 stories above Lincoln Center. "I'd never been there
before; I'd never met our host. But as I was saying 'Hello,' I

saw the World Trade Center lit up behind him. I brushed right past him—practically knocked him over—on my way to the windows. As I stood there gaping at the city at my feet, I thought 'There's Columbia down there. There's Barnard, and Fordham, and the New School. There's NYU and Hunter. . . . New York City is the ultimate college town!'"

"Every town I'd visited, I'd checked the schedule: 'How long will it take to get to New York? Where will I park my car when I go?' All of a sudden it clicked:

"Why not live at the interesting end of the railroad?"

Butler was cautious. "I met Roger the second day of my freshman year at Radcliffe. We were married 42 years. We both worked in advertising; we skied and sailed and brought up our children together. I'm not used to making decisions alone."

Being cautious, she moved to New York in three steps. She sublet an apartment at 73rd and Columbus for a month. "I got my Seniors MetroCard and a bus and subway map. When I visited New York, I always took taxis, but now I forced myself to ride the buses. The first time I rode the subway, a classmate took me."

Next, she borrowed a friend's apartment in Carnegie Hill to live in while looking for a place to rent. Her present apartment is a two-year sublet. After she missed a couple of places by not deciding fast enough, she grabbed this one as soon as she saw it.

On the 23rd floor of a Midtown building, Butler has light, air, and a wonderful view north to Central Park. The whole one-bedroom apartment would fit into a corner of the house in Virginia. All the furniture is her own and everything she owns is here—nothing in storage. Resisting any temptation to cram 12 rooms of furniture into three, Butler gave away or sold whatever she couldn't use.

Butler says that New York City has surprised her in some ways. Even though she'd visited many times, she had never even imagined the easy interchange with strangers she's found in New York

"When I'm feeling sad, the city rescues me in ways that Virginia never could," she says. People don't talk with strangers in Virginia or Connecticut, but here Butler talks to everyone—at bus stops, in the laundry room, at the theater.

Singing a duet on the bus with a man belting out "It's almost like being in love" until he tipped his hat and stepped off to the passengers' applause exactly on the final note; waiting for a bus and swapping stories about ophthalmologists with an 80-year-old woman who turned out to be a retired professor of Greek and Latin from Hunter College; interrupting coffee with a friend at an Upper West Side café to ask George Stephanopoulos (who was eating breakfast at the next table) what high-level Republicans and Democrats think of each other. It's these unexpected encounters with interesting people that excite and captivate Butler. "As soon as you engage people," she says, "they're delighted to talk with you."

Does she want to stay in New York? Although no other place appeals to her, she doesn't want to choose New York City "by default." Six months after our interview, at Christmas, she wrote, "Yes, I get lonely, and the city can be difficult. But I'd be lonely, minus Roger, anywhere on earth—and easy isn't interesting!"

What about buying an apartment? She doesn't know. It's easy to buy but it can be hard to sell if you need to. She likes the Upper West Side but worries about the cost. "If this apartment becomes available for another two years, I might stay right here. . . . I'm still feeling my way, figuring out what I want my life to be."[5]

Beri Greenwald, a 70-year-old graphic designer, splits her time between northwest Connecticut and New York City. Not wanting to give up either the beauty and solitude of the Berkshires or the drive and stimulus of New York, she's found a way to have both.

For a long time Greenwald owned a house in Connecticut, but by the mid-'90s she had tired of cutting grass, putting up screens, and shoveling snow. She took advantage of a good real estate market to sell and move into a two-bedroom rental house that required less maintenance work.

"Then I realized I really wanted to live in New York City, but it was too expensive, so I moved from the rental house to an apartment." It was cheaper and easier to care for. Now,

---

5 Two years later, Butler moved to Martha's Vineyard, where she bought a house. She visits New York frequently, camping with friends and splurging on theater.

with more free time and more money, she can live in the city part-time.

Greenwald resembles the loving grandmother in an old-fashioned storybook: an appealing dumpling with glasses, short gray hair, and a warm, friendly face. She smiles and laughs easily and looks as though she would have a soft, comfortable lap. Unlike the storybook grandmother, who is always pictured in a housedress, on the day of the interview Greenwald wore a light purple turtleneck and chino pants.

Until about 20 years ago Greenwald lived in New York City, designing books for large publishing houses. When she moved to Connecticut she bought a bookstore which she ran until she sold it a few years ago. She still designs brochures and newsletters for freelance clients.

She likes the trees and hills, the space and the quiet of her Connecticut home. She enjoys taking walks at night, driving along the country roads, going with friends to concerts in the Berkshires. Greenwald has an identity in town—she's "the book lady." But there aren't many singles around, and Greenwald doesn't play golf, or drink, or go to church, so she's not part of town social life.

She came to New York often and, from time to time over the years, felt a passing urge to move back. About three years ago, the pull grew stronger. Hesitantly, Greenwald started looking around for a place to live in Manhattan. She could only afford a studio apartment. Self-employed for many years, she'd always put a substantial chunk of her earnings back into her business and she has no employer pension. What money she has, she wants to keep liquid.

The studios she could afford to buy were mostly small and dark, so she decided to rent, at least for a year. She found some rentals she could afford now, but calculated that regular rent increases would make them too expensive in a few years. So she began to talk to people who had houses elsewhere and wanted to rent their New York City apartments part-time. A friend introduced her to a woman who worked Monday through Thursday in Manhattan and spent Friday through Sunday upstate. That woman also wanted an apartment in the city, so Greenwald suggested they search together. They soon found a studio on West 12th Street, but it was too expensive for Greenwald to pay a full half. The other woman offered to prorate the rent. At $1,400 a month plus one hundred dollars for utilities, each night comes to fifty dollars. Greenwald pays three hundred dollars and gets the apartment six nights a month. Three weekends each month she arrives Friday morning and stays until Sunday.

Though Greenwald offered to contribute furniture, the other woman furnished the place. Their tastes are similar. Greenwald keeps her own sheets and towels and some of her clothes and other belongings there. The two women get on well—they seldom see each other—and the arrangement works smoothly.

Of course, Greenwald spends more than three hundred dollars a month in New York: she goes to concerts, to the Joyce theater, to dinner with friends. But sometimes she just hangs out, doing nothing much, enjoying being in the city. Maybe she walks over to the river. Even going out Saturday night to get the Sunday *Times* is fun. She likes to feel alive, to have her antennae out, to see what's there and think about new directions in life.

When she grows frail Greenwald wants to live New York full-time. In Connecticut she volunteers for Women on Wheels, a group that drives elderly people to the doctor, the hairdresser, church. Greenwald knows that if she were on the other end of the equation, she wouldn't like having to depend on a service picking her up at a certain time, for a certain purpose. In New York City, with a cane, she figures she'll be able to get on the bus and go wherever she wants, whenever she wants.

But Greenwald is not frail now. She's enjoying her life and doesn't want to spend time thinking about frailty. Anyway, she cares more about mental activity than physical activity.

"As I grow older, I'm more determined to live the kind of life I'm supposed to live." And what is that? "I want to have experiences. Not just be a senior citizen in Connecticut."

Dick Leonard and Bernie Landou divide their time about equally between their 1790 farmhouse upstate and the apartment in the city they've rented since 1966. They're both retired—Leonard used to be a dean at City University of New York, Queensboro, and Landou had his own public relations firm. "We're pretty much of a mind that sooner or later we'll be in the city full-time."

Upstate they have a backyard, a pond, a guest house. They ticked off the reasons why, when the time comes that they can handle only one home, they'll sell the farmhouse and stay in the city:

- It's physically demanding to keep up the house and garden. They have to climb ladders, shovel show, pull weeds.
- In the country they get snowbound and have to depend on others; they have more mobility in the city.
- Healthcare is better in the city.
- They like energy, excitement, and intellectual stimulus of the city.
- And no driving! MetroCard and free transfers make public transportation much easier.

Dick Leonard is beginning to suffer from arthritis. His balance is off and he no longer walks their dogs. He still fastens the leashes, but Bernie Landou takes them out. And Leonard once left a big show at the Museum of Modern Art halfway through because he got too tired. As museum members and New York City residents, they can go back to an exhibit as often as they wish.

September 11, Leonard feels, has opened the option of living upstate when he and Landou can no longer maintain two homes. Landou wants to stay in New York, period, but Leonard is not so sure. Leonard says he's not afraid of a terrorist around the next corner and he has no fixed agenda of events that would cause him to leave New York. But he is concerned about the cumulative effect of a lot of small inconveniences (subway diversions, train cancellations) eroding the quality of daily life. They both prefer New York and have recently renewed their apartment lease, but Leonard can now imagine that someday life in the city will have changed enough to make him want to leave. Meanwhile, they're continuing with their regular life.

Richard Zuckerman had always planned to retire on his sailboat. Jamie Lintz,[6] his wife, had always wanted to move to Manhattan. Before they stopped working, Zuckerman and Lintz tried out places to retire. He scaled back his Long Island dental practice and for three years they spent January and June living in potential retirement areas in Arizona, California, Florida, and the Upper East Side of Manhattan.

That was stage 1 of their three-stage retirement program. Lintz did much of the planning. A banker and financial planner, she likes to think through details in advance. Zuckerman is more apt to take things as they come. Until they married 15 years ago, he'd never had a budget and she'd never known anyone who operated without one. Even though he found the idea of retirement scary—"Finances were scary. What I was

6 Not their real names.

going to do with myself was scary"—he generally left the planning to her. Lintz worked out their retirement budget and a detailed list of potential activities for herself.

Zuckerman has salt-and-pepper curly hair and a moustache. At 70, he's slender but muscular and looks like a man who'd be at ease hauling the sails. His voice is resonant and often conveys deep feeling. Lintz, 59, has a round face and curly dark hair. She's bouncier and more talkative.

In those "stage 1" years, they also traveled with Elder Hostel, where Zuckerman met other men who had already retired. "They survived," he noticed, somewhat reassured.

Lintz and Zuckerman liked California and Arizona in winter. Zuckerman liked the sailing in Florida, and he saw that men who retire there have more "playmates" (for golf, tennis, bridge) than men in New York. But neither Lintz nor Zuckerman wanted this routine year round. He says, "Without intellectual stimulation, your brain turns to cheese."

When they lived on Long Island, they'd come into Manhattan for weekends and, as they approached full retirement, New York City pulled them. They decided to rent here for a year. He doubted that he'd like it, but was willing to try. Looking for an apartment, they liked Greenwich Village but found it noisy and inconvenient for theater. Their month on the Upper East Side had convinced them that the East Side was too quiet. Eventually they drew a line from Zabar's to Lincoln Center, to Carnegie Hall, and looked at apartments from there to the river. They found few for rent but many to buy. In 1995 they sold their Long Island home and bought a one-bedroom unit in Lincoln Towers. The house brought in more money than they needed for the apartment, so they invested the balance. How was it to move from a four-bedroom house to a one-bedroom apartment? Well, they also have a three-bedroom apartment in the Berkshires, where they stay in the summer. It serves as very large closet!

Zuckerman and Lintz consider they're now in stage 2 of their retirement plan—active retirement. Zuckerman says New York City has worked out okay. It's not as expensive as he'd feared, and there are plenty of things to do. In fact, Zuckerman and Lintz are doing a number of things they'd never thought of before they moved to New York.

Lintz notes that she's had a life in New York from the day they moved in, but Zuckerman has picked up activities gradually as they came along and appealed to him. When he went to the Jewish Community Center to sign up for a computer course, he found he knew enough to teach in the Senior Net program. After visiting the Museum of Natural History, he applied to volunteer there. Lintz works at the museum too, but she'd planned it ahead of time. She studies painting at the 92nd Street Y. They belong to Manhattan Theater Club and Lincoln Center Theater. They ride their bikes in Central Park. They'd always wanted to live near a college and have a relationship with that college, so they picked Juilliard. For a contribution of about $150 a year, they can attend many free concerts. Last year Zuckerman and Lintz were summer parents for students at Tanglewood; one of their students will be at Juilliard this year, so the relationship will continue.

Zuckerman says his biggest difficulty in retirement comes from the conflict between wanting to have free time to do things on spur of the moment and his tendency to schedule in advance to be sure to have enough to do. So he doesn't have enough time for the spur-of-the-moment stuff. Back when he was working he imagined it would be heaven to read the whole *New York Times* every morning. Now he never has time. And he doesn't have as much time as he'd like to visit his grandchildren.

So Zuckerman and Lintz are trying to simplify their life. They simplified a lot in order to move here and they're still getting rid of stuff. They've simplified their wardrobes. He wears khaki pants—with sport shirts, a blazer, tee-shirts, whatever. She wears black. He says one of his goals is not owning anything with a motor.

Lintz's financial planning is paying off: "We're living on less than we have. We haven't had to dip into capital. I haven't told you yet," she announced to Zuckerman as we spoke, "but we're giving ourselves a raise."

Zuckerman and Lintz are vague about the third stage of their retirement. They mention a friend in an assisted living facility but don't dwell on the subject. The one thing they have decided is that when one of them dies or is incapacitated the other will buy a dog. Lintz says, "If everything were equal and we had our druthers, we'd spend spring and fall in New York City, summer in Berkshires, winter in a warm climate." But they don't want three houses. Zuckerman says he's suffering "sailing withdrawal," but he's "weaning himself away" from the sport. He sold his 34-foot yacht and scaled down to a 17-foot day sailor which he sails on a lake in the Berkshires. He misses sleeping on his yacht. To compensate, he's chartered a boat in the Caribbean for a trip with his children and grandchildren.

Grace Timberlake enjoys being overwhelmed by the choices available in New York City. She and her husband, John, moved here in 1987. They were both in their 50s when John's department at the *Chicago Tribune* was phased out, but a firm in New York offered him a new position. The Timberlakes spent a couple of months considering it and looking into other job offers, then moved here.

Grace thinks John might be equally happy in the Berkshires, but she wouldn't. In New York City, she feels free to be herself. Tall and angular, Grace leans forward when she talks, conveying the intensity she feels.

"I can say outrageous things when I want to. I like the character of New Yorkers. I like their openness. I can communicate with them. I know where I stand, and I can deal with them in the same way."

A new multiplex theater opened in Timberlake's neighborhood. She walked over as it was being completed and saw that instead of an old-fashioned marquee where you could see all the movies playing at a glance, this new theater had a moving digital "zipper." You have to stand there waiting and read the names one by one as they flow by. Timberlake has no patience for this. She walked into the lobby where she found three men in suits who obviously were involved in the project. "I hate your marquee," she told them. They recoiled. They cringed. Clearly, they were not New Yorkers. With New Yorkers, she could have said this, and a useful exchange of ideas would have followed. With outsiders, she has to be so much more circumspect.

Her admission surprised me. Grace Timberlake is an attorney and development officer for New York University Medical School. She works with prospective donors to arrange planned giving and bequests to the medical school. For that work, you need finesse. I told her I'd never heard her say anything outrageous. "That's because you're a New Yorker," she said. "It wouldn't seem outrageous to you. But if you lived in the suburbs of Chicago . . . it'd be a different story."

Chicago's a big city, Timberlake acknowledges. "If I'm really tired, Chicago appeals to me. It's more solid. It's quieter. It doesn't have an edge. Most of the time, I love that edge."

Right now the Timberlakes have a co-op in the Eagle Warehouse apartments near the foot of Brooklyn Bridge. It's convenient, but they have few windows and no view. When Grace retires and stays home more, she won't be able to stand it. They're definitely staying in New York, so they've bought a apartment in Prospect Heights across the street from the Brooklyn Museum of Art. Their new apartment has great space and a view across Prospect Park to New York harbor and New Jersey. Its equivalent in Park Slope or Manhattan would be far out of their price range.

Nunzio Pravata is 80. A tall, large-boned man with thick gray hair and a mobile face, Pravata is beginning to show signs of frailty—a pained expression sometimes, a side-tilting of his head as he talks. But a snowstorm and slippery sidewalks on the day of our meeting didn't faze him. When I called to suggest rescheduling he was already out of the house on a string of errands.

Pravata was born in Greenwich Village and has lived in New York most of his life. As a young man he worked for Arthur Murray, sometimes dancing in four shows a night at dinner theaters. Later, in his early 40s, when he was working in fabrics, he had an idea for a textile design and drew it on a paper bag. When he showed it to his superiors they liked it enough to have screens made. Cooper Union included it in their catalog of contemporary fabric designs, and he continued to develop his talents for design. For 18 years in the 1960s and '70s, Pravata and his late partner, Fred, ran a textile studio on Grand Street in Soho. Pravata created contemporary and traditional textile designs for silk screen; Fred made the screens, and they printed the fabrics right there. Through commissions from decorators they created original designs for various embassies, for the American Stock Exchange, for J.P. Morgan and Company, and for vice-president

Lyndon Johnson. Pravata won a national prize from the American Institute of Decorators.

Pravata and Fred moved to North Miami Beach in the early '90s when Fred became ill and needed a warm climate. After Fred died (they'd been together 53 years), Pravata returned to New York.

Pravata says, "New York City is the place for the gay group to unwind." You don't feel alone, neglected, or sneered at as in a small town, he said. Yet Pravata also told me that when a burly construction worker inquired about his SAGE button (Senior Action in a Gay Environment) he answered "Senior Action for a Green Environment." The burly guy approved.

Through SAGE, Pravata has seen at least one hundred plays since he came back from Florida. SAGE, and many other senior centers all over the city, call theaters on performance day to ask if they have any seats for seniors.

When I spoke with him, Pravata had just been accepted into an assisted living center on 93rd Street and Third Avenue in Manhattan. For a little over seven hundred dollars a month, he'll have a studio with kitchen, heat, and electricity, house cleaning services, laundry, meals, shopping help. It's called Enriched Senior Living—there's an income cap for eligibility. A number of these residences are scattered throughout the city. He found this one through a social worker at SAGE, and he spent a two and a half years on the waiting list. "The help is here. It comes through. You have to have the patience to fill out the forms and wait."

Would anyone leave Santa Barbara, California, with its Pacific breezes, white stucco missions and red tile roofs for the dirt and grit of New York City? Trudy Reece did. A westerner who grew up in Seattle and graduated from the University of California at Berkeley, Reece came here after she and her husband separated. They had visited New York with their kids, but now her son and daughter were grown and away.

Reece moved to New York City to come out as a lesbian, a move she didn't feel she could make in Santa Barbara. Even though she considers Santa Barbara a progressive university town, Reece feels lesbianism is not accepted there. In New York she can explore her sexuality.

She says she wants to experience New York's culture before she gets too old. She's been going to museums, and when I met her she had an appointment to try out for a jazz choral group the next day.

She likes the people in New York. Her friends here are different from her friends in Santa Barbara—more offbeat. She says people here have a certain feistiness, and they're more intellectual. Californians are more outdoorsy. In New York, Reece goes to the Cloisters with a friend; in Santa Barbara she went to museums alone.

A lively woman with a round face and short curly hair, Reece is still figuring out what she wants to do with herself. She's 54. She worked as a freelance writer in Santa Barbara, with a column in the local paper on senior issues. Her book,

The Parent Care Survival Guide, was published in 1993. She hasn't looked for writing assignments in New York, even though she suspects that if she had a stronger work identity her sexual issues would be easier to handle. But the plethora of choices in New York almost paralyzes her. She compares herself to her daughter, a college senior who's trying to figure out what career she wants. So many appeal. Reece advises her daughter: "Follow your passion. Go where your heart is. And talk to lots of people who are doing it. You can't figure it out by yourself." So far, it's been hard for Trudy Reece to take her own advice.

If your head is whirling with the different factors involved in deciding whether or not to move—Do I really want to sell my home? How often will I be able to see my children? Will I be able to go hiking easily? How will I find a new doctor? What will all this cost? Can I really pull it off?—a decision matrix can help you organize your thoughts. Or, if you're living in New York already and trying to figure out whether you want to stay here after you retire or settle in a smaller, quieter, warmer place, a decision matrix can help you sort things out. You can use a decision matrix to make sure you—or you and your partner together—get what matters most to you.

Start by writing down everything you consider important for your life and everything you've imagined doing after you retired. Things like: taking your grandchild out every week, learning to bake bread, living near a big medical center, a particular kind of weather. Don't censor, evaluate, or eliminate anything at the start. If you find yourself thinking, "I've always wanted to take saxophone lessons," resist the damper, "Oh, I probably couldn't do it." Write down "saxophone lessons." People who lead brainstorming sessions to help businesses develop new strategies have learned that they get better results when participants refrain from criticizing ideas as they come up. Write down every idea as you think of it. Later there'll be a time to assess them all.

Make your lists specific. Which sports are important to you? Skiing? Golf? Tennis? Which cultural activities? Experimental theater? Musical comedies? After you have your list, draw a big table and put all your items in a column on the left. Then make several more columns which you'll fill in shortly. We've put together a sample decision matrix to show how they work *(figure 1)*.

Your list will undoubtedly be different. You never play golf? Leave it out. Belonging to a synagogue is paramount? Put it in.

In the next column, rate each item on your list according to how important it is to **you**. Use a scale of 1–5, with 5 being the most important. In our sample decision matrix, we've figured that being close to family is very important. We give it a 5. Tops on our list: good healthcare, good theater, golf, and overall lifestyle. Each gets a 5. Beaches are not very important, so they get a 1. Our hypothetical couple love their home,

Figure 1—Sample Decision Matrix

Locations

Item	Importance Rank 1-5	Present Community		New York City		Phoenix, Arizona	
		Rating (1-5)	Score (Rating x Importance)	Rating (1-5)	Score (Rating x Importance)	Rating (1-5)	Score (Rating x Importance)
Housing							
Keep present home	2	5	10	0	0	0	0
Ample indoor space	3	5	15	2	6	4	12
Yard and garden	3	5	15	1	3	3	9
Close to family	5	3	15	4	20	2	10
Close to friends	4	4	16	2	8	3	12
Good healthcare	5	3	15	5	25	4	20
Good restaurants	4	3	12	5	20	4	16
Paid work opportunities	4	5	20	3	12	1	4
Cultural life							
Opera	3	2	6	5	15	3	9
Good theater	5	2	10	5	25	3	15
Join jazz group	2	2	4	4	8	2	4
Painting classes	4	2	8	5	20	3	12
Sports and outdoors							
Professional teams	3	1	3	5	15	4	12
Beaches	1	1	1	2	2	1	1
Hiking	4	4	16	4	16	2	8
Golf	5	2	10	3	15	5	25
Climate	3	3	9	3	9	4	12
Overall lifestyle	5	3	15	4	20	3	15
Total Scores			200		239		196

but it's too big now and they're ready to move on. They give keeping their home a 2.

The next six columns in our sample matrix are set up to compare three places to live: your present community, New York City, and another possible retirement community—in this case, Phoenix. After you've determined the importance of each item on your list, estimate how each of these communities rates with regard to that item. Again, we're using a scale of 1–5, with 5 being the highest rating. Close to family, for example, might get a 5 if you could visit your children easily and casually. If a visit requires an overnight stay, that item might get a 3; if you need a plane trip to see your family, that item would rate a 1.

When you have rated all the items on your list, it's time to calculate the scores. Multiply the importance figure by the rating for each community. Then add up the scores for each place you're considering. See how the different places shake out. No one would choose a place to live solely because it got a high score on the decision matrix, but it's instructive to see how well the place you're considering stands up to a critical analysis. The exercise can help you pin down the relative importance of one factor or another. You'll know better what kind of compromises you'll need to make as well as the good things you can expect.

Some couples prefer to fill out decision matrices separately, then compare them and talk about how best to satisfy the needs and caveats of both. They find that if one thinks that a walk along the beach every morning would be heaven and the other considers one Sunday a year plenty of time to spend at the beach, trying to agree on number for that item gets them bogged down very quickly. When the matrices are completed, areas of agreement and disagreement are quite apparent and the necessary adjustments become clear as well.

Other couples have told me that trade-offs come more easily when they work together, taking items one by one as they go along and not letting positions harden by assigning separate numbers. However you go at it, you may happen upon a place (like New York City!) that gives the beach person at least a 4 and the other a 5 for the chance to play in a jazz group.

If you do decide to move to New York City, you'll need a place to live. If you're a New Yorker already, you may want a different kind of place or a different location after you retire. Read section 2, a step-by-step program for "Finding a New Home" and evaluating it.

Section Two

Finding a New Home

by Rita Henley Jensen

CHAPTER THREE

Finding an Affordable
Apartment in New York

Some Fun and Games

One summer Sunday evening, on a lakeside in Vermont, after a day of water-skiing and a dinner of barbecue chicken and corn, a small group of friends settled down to a parlor game they had invented that very evening: "Name That New York City Asking Price."

The players included a physician in his early 60s from Cleveland, Ohio, who often travels to New York; a retired partner in a prestigious New York City law firm who owns a *pied-à-terre* on the city's Upper East Side; a personal trainer who had lived in three apartments in Manhattan before buying a co-op in Manhattan's Murray Hill; and a 31-year-old premed student at Brooklyn College who had lived in New York all her life and had rented two apartments and bought two co-ops at extremely reasonable prices.

This author served as moderator.

Tools required: the magazine section of the *New York Times*, where the most élite and expensive living quarters are offered for sale, and a piece of notepaper and pen to record the guesses under the players' names.

The moderator selected an advertisement and read aloud all the details available except the asking price. Players were permitted to ask questions, such as, What neighborhood did you say that was? Or, How many bedrooms was that? The players then guessed the asking price and the moderator recorded each person's guess and announced the actual asking price.

The results surprised everyone. Not only was nearly everyone wrong nearly all the time—the personal trainer came closest to the correct sales price on one of his guesses—but also all were wrong in the same direction. Over and over again, the players guessed in the millions when the price was in the five-hundred-thousand-dollar range—and these are the most expensive places to live in the city.

Try this game yourself with a group of friends and see if you don't confirm that most people have an inflated view of what apartments cost in New York.

One more example: Several weeks after the parlor game,

the front page of the Sunday *New York Times* real estate section—a must-read for anyone searching for housing in the
city—featured a story about a new school teacher who had
leased an apartment on Manhattan's Upper East Side for $427
per month. A broker specializing in low-cost apartments told
her about it but was too busy to show it to her. Impatient, she
rushed over to the apartment, found a workman who would
let her in, and discovered it was a real dump—but a salvage-
able one.

She took it on the spot, persuaded the superintendent to
put in a new floor and new windows, and found herself the
envy of all her friends.

Included in the story was a statistic, provided by a well-
known real estate firm: the average rent for a one-bedroom
apartments in non-door-staff buildings below 96th Street (the
border for Harlem on the East Side) was $2,967.

Nearly three thousand dollars for a one-bedroom in a nice
neighborhood!

However, if the reader happened to turn the pages to the
classified advertisements for one-bedroom apartments in
door-staff and non-door-staff buildings below 96th Street on
the East Side, one could hardly find an apartment that expensive. In fact, the prices hovered around two thousand dollars—and were often significantly less. The incredibly high-
priced apartments skew the averages, of course, and often
mask what the usual prices may be.

This *New York Times* feature reveals three truths about
finding housing in Manhattan:

- Some folks make their own good luck.
- Pick your desired neighborhood first, so you can move quickly when you see something that fits the bill in other ways.
- Even news reporters for the most prestigious news organization based in New York City would lose at the "Name That New York City Asking Price" game. Housing may not be as expensive as you think.

I say this not because I read the real estate section in the *New York Times* religiously—although I do—but because I have lived here since 1976, rather comfortably on comparatively little income. I never made much money—journalists usually don't—but I have found quite nice housing in Manhattan at a price I can afford. And, as it turns out, so has almost everyone I know.

Like many, before I arrived I had a wildly inflated impression of what it would cost to live in New York City. In 1976, after being accepted by Columbia Graduate School of Journalism, I traveled to Manhattan for the first time to begin my search for housing. Looking out the window of the commuter rail car bringing me into Manhattan from Long Island, where I was a guest, I took in a scene of row upon row of derelict buildings with boarded-up windows next to trash-strewn lots. I told myself that was where I would be living for the next year because I was not wealthy. I nearly wept.

I have learned a lot since that day—things I wish I'd known then. In these chapters, I'll pass those lessons along to you.

They draw on the wisdom of several top real estate agents, lawyers, and property managers, as well as more than two dozen people who have recently searched for and found housing in New York City.

Step One: Change Your Expectations about Space

Space is different for New Yorkers. We simply do not have as much as the rest of the nation—but we have resources that no other U.S. city offers. Many of us believe these unique amenities more than compensate for small rooms and too-few closets:

- We do not have our own front yards, but we do have an incredible system of parks.
- We do not have two-car garages, but we do have one of the world's best mass-transit systems. And just about every good and service can be delivered to our doors.
- We do not have guestrooms, but we do have inexpensive hotels and even a hostel.
- We do not have many walls on which to hang paintings, but we do have museums full of the world's finest art.
- We do not have big kitchens, but we do have thousands of neighborhood restaurants that prepare excellent food at reasonable prices and will most often deliver it free while it is still hot.
- Most of us do not have our own gardens, but we do have a multitude of public gardens tended by volunteers,

where we are free to plant and pull weeds with the best of them.

The rent or maintenance charges in New York pay for the area beyond the four apartment walls. They support the city's marvelous infrastructure, just as high property taxes in some suburbs pay for high-caliber public schools.

Step Two: Consider Your Expenses

This new approach to space can have a significant impact on your potential monthly expenses. Compare the costs of New York apartment living with home ownership in other cities— and be sure to include other current expenses that you will no longer need to pay if you move to New York. Take out a sheet of paper and begin to do the math:

Your current mortgage and
  property tax payments $ _____
Homeowners insurance $ _____
Home maintenance and repairs
  (monthly average) $ _____
Landscaping (monthly average) $ _____
Heating (included in most New York housing) $ _____
Car payment (you won't need a car anymore) $ _____
Car insurance (ditto) $ _____
Car maintenance (ditto) $ _____
Gas and oil (ditto) $ _____
Total $_____

Compare that with the average rent paid by New Yorkers according to the Census Bureau. The most recent data available, from 1999, places the median monthly housing cost for renters in the New York City metropolitan area at $684 and, for owners of co-ops, condos, and homes, $980.

These are the medians for the entire region. If you want an apartment within walking distance of Lincoln Center, be prepared to pay substantially more. The point is, affordable housing *is* available.

And, of course, if you're selling your present home, you can invest the proceeds in a co-op or condo. Several people we interviewed for this book paid less for their new city apartment than they received for their suburban home.

Step Three: Look Around— You Will Have a Great Time Doing It

Now that you are beginning to daydream about long walks in Central Park and the stuff you should toss out, with space expectations lowered and with budget in hand, you are prepared to begin searching for an apartment in New York.

The search for housing in New York City will require you to use every skill you have picked up in your adult life. You will have to be savvy, persistent, patient, cautious, and assertive. It may take more time than you thought possible; you might meet real estate agents who you are convinced should be in jail. You may make a lifelong friend while you search.

But if you spend some time at it, you will find a convenient and attractive place to live where you can feel safe.

(Subsidized moderate- and middle-income housing does exist in New York City under the name of Mitchell-Lama—almost four hundred different rental and limited-equity cooperative developments. As the Mitchell-Lama Web site explains, many waiting lists are closed and each development has its own income requirements and application procedures. When the waiting lists open—sometimes for as little as two weeks in a 20-year period—the development must advertise in local newspapers. Obtaining one of these apartments is a process beyond the scope of this book.)

New York is not a big city. Certain areas give that feel—Rockefeller Center, Wall Street, Times Square—but most likely you won't end up living in those places. Many of us who live here now experience the city more as a mélange of tiny villages and neighborhoods, each with an identity, culture, history, and land ownership patterns, connected by a common government and a vast public transportation system.

If you are not familiar with the city—except perhaps the theater or business districts—spend a day on my favorite bus, the No. 4 leaving from Penn Station. Ride it all the way uptown to the Cloisters and back again. Hop off anywhere along Madison Avenue as it goes north; poke your nose into the shops, or walk a block west toward Central Park to Fifth Avenue and go to a museum—Metropolitan, Guggenheim, the City of New York, the Jewish. Get back on the No. 4 and, as you cross the top of Central Park, look to the north and view

Harlem along 110th Street. It's a busy place with kids walking to school, shoppers scurrying to stores, and, at this writing, building after building being renovated. Go up past Columbia University and Barnard, and the lovely neighborhoods that surround these institutions, then through Spanish Harlem—filled with discount stores, tiny restaurants, and shops where the patrons make long-distance calls home to Latin America.

When you get to the Cloisters, spend an hour not inside, but outside, walking its fabulous grounds with panoramic views of the Hudson River, the George Washington Bridge. Stroll through the neighboring communities. To the immediate south of the Cloisters is Hudson Heights, one of the premier affordable communities in Manhattan. (Its chief claim to fame is that Dr. Ruth Westheimer lives there—and heads up the local YMHA.) To the north is a less expensive, Latin-dominated neighborhood with excellent housing stock; it's home to a widely diverse population of schoolteachers, actors, dancers, cab drivers, social workers, and journalists. (Columnists for the *New York Times* and the *Daily News* live in this neighborhood).

On your return trip, hop off at 116th Street, Columbia University, and wander south on foot, by bus, or by taxi. Falling in love? Wander through the wonderful Upper West Side, officially from 96th Street to 72nd Street. This is the epicenter of affluent, liberal New York, full of lovely small shops and bookstores, and the home of Zabar's and Fairway—places to find the delicious fresh food New York is known for.

On another day, try taking the No. 7 train to Shea Stadium

in Queens. The trip was made famous by a rude Atlanta base-ball star who disliked the diversity among people who use the line. But those who live in New York, or wish to, enjoy the fact that the line is a little United Nations. Immigrants from all over the world have settled in Queens. Take the No. 7 any-time and stare at the gorgeous silk saris, marvel at the jewelry, and listen to the sounds of many languages. Get off in Flush-ing and look around. Smell the wonderful cooking aromas from across Asia—from Afghanistan to Japan.

Or take the Metro-North train from Grand Central Termi-nal to New York Botanical Garden in the Bronx. Take a taxi to the Belmont section of the Bronx—the borough's Little Italy—and stop in at the restaurant of your choice for the some of the best Italian food anywhere. Attend an event at Brooklyn Museum of Art and walk around the surrounding neighborhoods, including Park Slope. Take the Staten Island Ferry and the bus to Snug Harbor Museum. Cruise over to Hoboken on yet another ferry. The only way to find a place to live in New York is to get there and look around.

New York has ocean beaches and river palisades; it has cobblestone streets lined with 19th century townhouses; it has modern skyscrapers with elevator banks and attentive staff standing at the ready by the door.

You may prefer to be within an easy walk of Museum Mile. In that case, you will look almost exclusively on the Upper East Side, and you should be prepared to spend on the high end of what you had planned. Perhaps you always dreamed of having a key to Gramercy Park. Or you want to see Lincoln Center out your window and walk to shopping and all major subway and bus lines. Or, you may want a view of the Statue of Liberty—try looking in Battery Park City. Like lots of green outside your door? Try the area near the Cloisters.

If you can find nothing in your price range in these areas, it is time to look in the wonderful boroughs. Like Manhattan, each of the outer boroughs is composed of neighborhoods. The Bronx, thought of nationally as the center of gangs and drug traffic, is actually the location of the one the few places in the city that has three- and four-bedroom brick homes, comparable to the most élite neighborhoods in any city. This section is known as Riverdale, because it overlooks the Hudson. It is easily accessible by subway and car, and is surrounded by two spectacular parks—one of which offers horseback riding, a pool, and a golf course. Queens, Brooklyn, and Staten Island have equally distinct and inviting neighborhoods with affordable prices, city services, and easy access to Midtown.

Step Four: Research

Spend a week reading the newspapers and looking online. Beginning on a Saturday evening, buy all the big daily newspapers published in New York: the *New York Times*, of course, but also the *Daily News*, the *Post*, and *New York Newsday*. You should do this even if you intend to use a broker—before you go shopping, you should know a little about what to expect.

For example, on the weekend the "lucky teacher" article appeared, classified advertisements in two other daily newspapers covering the city—the *New York Daily News* and *Newsday*—featured apartments in neighborhoods not included in the *Times*, for much more reasonable rents. Try these publications, especially if you are interested in living in Queens or Brooklyn.

Throughout the week, pick up the weekly papers; the apartments advertised therein tend to be less expensive. There's the *Riverdale Press*, an award-winning weekly covering news in the affluent West Bronx; the *Amsterdam News*, the weekly covering news in Harlem and other predominantly black neighborhoods; the *Irish Voice*, covering news of the Irish-American communities; and the *Jewish Forward*, covering news about the city's Jewish communities. All had real estate classified advertisements, some of which, while not the bonanza found by the schoolteacher, were less than one thousand dollars a month, or one-third the declared average. If you consider yourself a member of an ethnic group, the city more than likely has a newspaper published at least weekly for your group that includes classified advertisements for rental apartments. Be sure to check there.

Also, try *Loot*, the newspaper composed only of classified advertisements. Several friends have had good luck relying on it.

Online searches are becoming more popular and certainly

have many advantages, but they have distinct disadvantages as well. You cannot mark up a database that is online and carry it with you, for example. And printing it out sometimes yields a sheaf of paper much too large to wade through. Nevertheless, be sure to give online resources a try.

And be sure to include *www.newyorkmetro.com/realestate* in your Internet search. It has an authoritative, yearly guide to 26 New York neighborhoods.

If you have access to a periodical library, consult the September 2000 and 2001 issues of *New York Magazine*. These issues featured profiles of affordable neighborhoods; the magazine regularly carries features about housing in the city.

Now that you have done your reading, you should have a firm grasp of the price ranges and amenities available.

Step Five: Explore the Possibilities

Now you are ready to begin actually looking at apartments. Call one or two apartments that are advertised and make appointments to see them. If you like the neighborhood, return to it and walk around. If you see a storefront real estate office, stop in and tell them what you are looking for. You might get lucky. Always be vocal about what you don't like. This is not considered rude in New York; it's considered ordinary business conduct.

Recently I overheard two different people in two widely disparate situations mention that a neighborhood in Queens called Sunnyside was the new place to live. A quick drive-through revealed tree-lined streets near shopping, and mothers pushing baby strollers. A check on the subway map showed that Sunnyside was on the No. 7 subway line.

This being the sum total of my knowledge of the neighborhood, I set off one Saturday morning to see what I could find. I hopped on the No. 7 leaving Times Square and I timed my ride. To my surprise, 12 minutes later I was standing in front of the Sunnyside arch. Walking a few steps down Queens Boulevard, I noticed a wonderful medley of eating places, all lined up next to each other, from Mexican to Turkish, from Irish pubs to Colombian steakhouses.

Within 10 minutes, I found myself speaking to a homeowner sweeping the sidewalk in front of her three-family brick Tudor home. She loved her neighborhood, she said, and she told me which real estate agent to use—the one who has been in the neighborhood the longest. And, she wanted me to know, the Museum of Modern Art was opening MOMA Queens soon, and, of course, the neighborhood was the home of P.S. 1, the experimental art gallery in a former public school. As I walked farther, I discovered streets sheltered by tall, arching trees I could not identify but that filled me with a sense of safety and calm. I asked a young male passerby for the name of the tree. He stopped to chat with me about the beauty of his neighborhood's sycamores.

I took a bus to Manhattan and back just to check the time. (A half-hour each way.)

Back in Sunnyside, I continued my walk, taking notes of what was available:

- Greengrocers, butchers, and fish stores—as well as a larger, general-purpose food store.
- A wide variety of restaurants with entrées priced less than $10.
- Several pharmacies.
- Several banks.
- A public library.
- A gym.
- A healthcare clinic and other medical service providers.
- Two well-tended and recently renovated parks with working restrooms (not only nice to visit but indicative of a politically active community).

My last stop in Sunnyside was the tiny office of Patrick O'Malley, then a Democratic candidate for city council. He subsequently failed to win the primary, but I was impressed. A former schoolteacher and an assistant district attorney in Queens, he was in the office that day with his two school-age children, preparing to attend a local event. He was full of knowledge about Sunnyside, explaining that it was a NORC—and stopping to explain to his children what a Naturally Occurring Retirement Community was—before giving me the percentage of registered voters who vote in every election.

I was completely charmed by O'Malley and what he reflected about the community: deep roots and commitment to maintaining the quality of life in his hometown. I knew then that, given the people I had met on my short visit to Sunnyside, I would indeed enjoy living there. Just to be sure, I found a Mexican restaurant and grabbed a quick bowl of delicious Mexican chicken soup—I think it's the touch of cilantro that makes it stand out so.

If I were not so happy with where I live—in Northern Manhattan—I would have picked up and moved immediately.

Step Six: Find an Apartment

Once you have found a neighborhood and know your price range, it is time to begin looking in earnest. Use whatever method works for you—newspapers, real estate office, referrals from friends—and begin viewing apartments.

Jackie Archis is a slender, tallish woman in her mid 50s, a highly organized performance manager at the Metropolitan Opera, who lives with her cats within walking distance of her employer in a moderately priced first-floor studio with a small rose garden outside her window, door staff at her beck and call, and a place on the roof of the building where she and her neighbors sunbathe. She was not born to such luxury. She hunted it down with the type of determination one might need to organize, for example, an opera performance.

In the summer of 1987—when the real estate market was at its peak—Archis moved from Poughkeepsie into a share of a two-bedroom apartment in New York. She sublet for 10 months and began teaching at the Professional Children's

School. The following February she started looking for a permanent residence. An apartment with two levels would be terrific, she thought. She also wanted a garden, a place that allowed cats, and a space to sunbathe. Since she was living on a teacher's salary, she thought she would look for a share.

Archis scoured the *New York Times* and the *Village Voice*, contacted local real estate agents, and even put up a sign where she worked and at the Met, where she had a part-time job ushering. The apartment she liked was too expensive; the others were too flawed.

She did find one that had a winding staircase. Staring at the narrow steps leading to the basement, she asked herself if she really wanted to be climbing a winding staircase when she was 70. The answer was no, so she moved on to look at single-level apartments in brownstones—the city's classic townhouses that are often converted from single-family residences.

But nearly all brownstones have stairs leading to the first floor, and once again she decided that was not for her.

A high-rise, perhaps? Maybe I need door staff, she thought. Up and down she rode, looking at apartments in the best and not-so-best buildings. The large apartments were not affordable; the smaller ones were just too small. She came to another conclusion: "I did not want to live in a box."

She also realized that the most important element was that she wanted to feel safe. How could she tell a building was safe? She did not know, but it just had to *feel* safe. When she walked down the street at night, it just had to feel safe.

So maybe she did not need a one-bedroom. Perhaps a studio would do. Off she went, looking at studios, again in brownstones, high-rise buildings, and garden apartments. With the clock ticking, she was invited to a cocktail party at a colleague's Midtown apartment. Archis saw the beautifully kept, art-deco doorman building and knew she could live there forever. But, nothing was available. She kept hunting, now comparing each apartment with the gold standard of her colleague's building.

Suddenly, it was mid-May, and her sublet ended June 1.

"Now, I was getting scared," Archis says.

She gave a one-thousand-dollar deposit to an attorney who was renting out his first-floor renovated garden studio on Riverside Drive at 83rd Street. But the place smelled, and on the way home she realized that the odor was mildew coming up from the building's basement. She cancelled the lease and lost her deposit.

With 10 days to go, she had a breakthrough idea: Her colleague's Midtown apartment still beckoned, so she asked for and obtained the names and phone numbers of all the real estate agents who had ever rented apartments in the building. She called them all, explaining she really had to have an apartment in that specific building.

Within days, the school principal entered her classroom and tapped her on the shoulder: You have a phone call.

"I never ran faster in my life."

The price was right. She signed the lease and, on moving

day, her new next-door neighbor asked her two questions: How many cats do you have? And, Do you like the ballet?

The questions were "icing on the perfection cake. . . . We had two critical things in common," and a warm friendship was born at that moment. When the building was converted to a co-op, Archis bought the apartment, where she intends to spend the rest of her life.

Once you locate the apartment of your dreams—or even one that will do for a while—several other hurdles remain before you can move in. If you are looking to rent an apartment (or sublet a condo or co-op apartment), you must be aware of three things:

- Brokers in New York usually charge 15 percent of the first year's rent as their fee—and the tenant pays it. Most, but not all, apartments are rented through brokers. New buildings, however, often have in-house rental agents.

- Many people find apartments in which they wish to live by making friends over time with a building's superintendent and frequently asking if any apartments are available. If they end up renting an apartment on behalf of the landlord, the supers often receive the equivalent of a broker's fee from the prospective tenant. This is sometimes referred to as "key money," and it's officially illegal but the accepted practice, nevertheless.

- Landlords usually require good credit references and a month's rent as security plus the first and last month's rent paid at the signing of the lease.

One last caveat: Don't tie the knot with an apartment you love without asking the "20 questions for renters" or "20 questions for buyers" outlined in the next two chapters.

CHAPTER **FOUR**

Twenty Questions to Ask Before You Rent an Apartment in New York

The New York City rental market is one of the most highly regulated in the United States. It's also one of the most competitive. You'll need all the background information you can find, and all the wit and energy you can muster, to locate and secure an apartment you like. But there *are* apartments, and you have many protections. For information about the regulations applying to tenants and landlords, look at *www.housingnyc.com* for the *Tenant's Rights Guide* put out by the office of the New York State attorney general. You can also consult *What Every Landlord and Tenant Should Know*, a five-dollar booklet prepared by the Citizen's Housing and Planning Council, for a clear presentation of the laws and requirements pertaining to landlord and tenant relationships. (Call 212-286-9211 to order.) *Tenant's Rights Guide* presents information about both regulated and unregulated housing; *What Every Landlord and Tenant Should Know* deals principally with regulated housing.

The mayor's office maintains a Web site, *www.nyc.gov*. Scroll down to *Services* and click on *Housing* to find definitions and descriptions of many kinds of apartments. The Web pages explain what's required of landlords and of tenants and give you access to a database of every building in New York City with a list of every violation cited against it. It offers information about housing for seniors and lists places available now or upcoming. For quick access to these and other features, select *I Want To . . .* from the Housing Directory menu.

Another Web site, *www.oasisnyc.net*, has mapped out the entire city, showing the location of and information about every building, and highlighting open spaces and green spaces.

These resources amplify many of the answers to the questions below. The material here is for orientation only, not legal guidance.

1. *Is This Apartment Rent-Stabilized?*

Rent control and rent stabilization offer many protections to tenants. *Rent-controlled* apartments are those built before February 1, 1947, and continuously occupied by the same tenant since June 30, 1971. When that tenant moves out, the apartment usually becomes rent-stabilized. Since this chapter is principally for people moving into New York City apartments now, we will not deal further with rent control.

Rent-stabilized apartments are those in buildings with six or more units that were constructed after February 1, 1947, but before January 1, 1974. In these buildings, rent increases are established by the Rent Guidelines Board; each year the board approves percentage increases which govern all lease renewals. (In recent years, allowable increases have ranged from 2 percent to 6 percent.)

When a rent-stabilized apartment becomes vacant, the landlord is entitled to a 20 percent vacancy increase plus ¹⁄₄₀ of the cost of any capital improvements. When the stabilized rent reaches two thousand dollars or more *and* the apartment is occupied by persons whose total annual household income exceeds $175,000 for each of the two preceding calendar years, the landlord may apply to have the apartment removed from rent stabilization.

Caution: Some buildings are rent-stabilized because the landlord has received a tax abatement for new construction, for complete rehabilitation of an older building, or for conversion from another use. In these buildings, which may have been built after the 1974 cutoff date, rent stabilization continues even when the rent is above two thousand dollars. But if the landlord follows tenant-notification requirements properly, the apartment rents can go to market rate when the tax-abatement period ends. If you are looking at a rent-stabilized building, ask if the controls stem from a tax abatement. If they do, check all details carefully.

In unregulated buildings—i.e., those not subject to rent stabilization or rent control—the lease may or may not have an automatic renewal clause, and the landlord is free to charge any rent agreed upon by the parties.

2. *What Is the Landlord Required to Provide?*

Every residential building in New York City and every person living in one must comply with New York City's Housing Maintenance Code. Landlords are required to keep buildings livable, safe, and sanitary; to provide hot water year-round and heat from October 1 through May 31; to make timely and competent repairs inside and out; to paint each apartment every three years; and to maintain the apartments and the building in other ways that are clearly specified.

3. *Is There a Written Lease?*

A written lease clarifies the responsibilities of both landlord and tenant and is highly desirable. The landlord of a rent-stabilized apartment is required to issue a vacancy lease to a new tenant and to offer a renewal lease at the end of the original and all subsequent lease terms. If you aren't offered a lease, ask for one, and if you don't receive it in a reasonable length of time, contact the New York State Division of Housing and Community Renewal (DHCR).

If you're living in unregulated housing without a lease, you are considered to be renting on a month-to-month basis. Payment of each month's rent entitles you to live in the apartment for another month. Renters whose plans are in flux may prefer this.

Read your lease carefully. Be sure it lists the name and address of the landlord. Be sure that every item you agreed upon orally has been written down—including the rent—and that the lease specifies the alternatives you have when it expires. Check to see what utilities are included in the rent and if there are any special rules regarding pets, home businesses, sublets, or other issues of concern.

4. *What Happens to My Security Deposit?*

New tenants are usually required to place one or two months of rent on deposit. The deposit will be returned when you move out if the premises are in good condition, showing only normal wear and tear, and if no back rent is owed.

When the rent goes up, you will be asked to add the amount of increase to your deposit so that it equals the current rate. The landlord must keep security deposits in a separate bank account, and the interest belongs to the tenant (less 1 percent of the deposit, which the landlord may keep for administrative expenses). You may ask for the interest to be paid to you each year, applied against rent payments, or accrued to be added to the amount eventually returned.

5. *How Safe Is This Neighborhood?*

Newcomers to New York City may not be accustomed to so diverse a population and may feel uneasy among people who speak a strange language or follow unfamiliar cultural patterns. It helps to remember that almost all of these people are working very hard to establish themselves and have no interest in bothering anyone. You will quickly learn to spot signs of trouble.

Check out a neighborhood to be sure you like it before you look at specific apartments. Generally speaking, an active neighborhood is a safe neighborhood. Muggers and pickpockets like to work where they are not observed. And when residents feel comfortable on the street, they're more like to be out and about. Ask if there's a beat cop who walks by regularly.

Visit at different times of day and look around. At 8 A.M. do you see people dressed for work hurrying to the subway? Mothers taking their children to school? At 11 A.M. do you see older people, perhaps with walkers or companion helpers, en route to the senior center? None of these people are going to harm you. Nor are the young women fresh from the beauty parlor on Saturday afternoon, the fathers taking their sons to First Communion, the old couples walking arm in arm on Sundays.

Come back at night and see how you feel about the neighborhood then. Come by subway. Who gets off? People carrying theater programs? Musicians with instruments returning from gigs? Families holding pennants from a Knicks game? If it's lively and the people you see move purposefully and are absorbed in their own concerns, you can feel quite safe.

Loitering teenage boys and young men sometimes make me apprehensive. I don't worry about the lively ones jousting with their friends on the sidewalk (even though they may annoy me with their noise and obliviousness). I become suspicious of drug activity—the center of most of the non-family violence in the city—when I notice a car stopping and a young man who had been leaning against a building approaches the car for a short conversation before the car quickly drives off. This could be innocent, of course, but if it happens several times, it also could be a sign of commerce in illegal drugs. Broken windows? Abandoned buildings? Trash-strewn empty lots? Tread carefully!

6. *How Safe Is This Building?*

Is the door staff up front, or can you walk in without anyone noticing? If no door staff is on duty, the building's front door should be locked. Buildings are required to have self-closing, self-locking front doors with secure locks opened by key. Look at the door. Do you see signs of tampering? Does it look as though you could push it in? Check the front door to your own apartment. It should be strong, with at least two well-working locks, a chain closure, and a peephole.

All buildings are required to have well-lighted lobbies, stairwells, and halls, and mirrors in the elevator so you can see who is there before you enter. Does yours comply? Test the intercom from the apartment you're considering. Can you hear a visitor clearly?

And look at the people in your building's public areas the same way you looked at the people on your street. Are they busy, involved in the regular pursuits of everyday life?

7. *How Many Elevators Are There?*

Elevators have a way of breaking down, and tenants may find themselves walking more often than they wish. A building with more than one elevator offers a buffer against elevator breakdown. But check to see where the shafts go and whether there are upper-floor connections between different wings. Ask how many times and for how long the elevator was out of service in the last six months, and decide whether you can walk up and down to the apartment of your choice if you need to. Remember that sometimes you'll be carrying groceries, laundry, suitcases, even a grandchild.

8. *What Common Spaces Are There in the Building?*

Some buildings have no lobby, only a direct entry to hallways and stairs leading to apartment doors. Lobbies range from small and simple to large and lavish. You need not rule out a building with a small or non-existent lobby; the apartment may be quite nice.

Most buildings have laundry rooms and some have basement storage. Higher-priced buildings may also have health and fitness club rooms, pools, and party rooms. Look at the common rooms even if you think you won't use them. They are one clue to the level of building maintenance. Do all the washers and dryers work? Is the basement storage secure? Can you lock up your stored items or do you keep them in a large common room? Do you have to pay extra to use any of these spaces?

9. *Where Can I Park My Car?*

If you want a car, you may want a building with a garage. Ask how much it will cost to keep your car there. Is it staffed around the clock or will you have to park it yourself sometimes? If you park it yourself, how is your safety protected while you're in the garage?

If there is no garage in the building, there may be one nearby. Or you may want to park on the street—saves money but adds hassle because you will be required to move your car regularly to comply with alternate-side-of-the-street parking regulations.

10. *How Is the Building Staffed?*

All landlords must provide janitorial services. If a building has nine or more apartments, janitorial services must be provided 24 hours a day, and the superintendent must live on the premises or within a block or 200 feet. Janitorial staffing levels for larger buildings are also specified.

Many people are willing to pay the higher cost of living in a building with door staff for its convenience and the feeling of safety and welcome. Door staff receive and hold packages, screen visitors, call taxis, and perform many other helpful services. Luxury buildings may employ a concierge or deliver mail to your door. Your budget will no doubt be your guide.

11. *Will This Apartment Be Noisy?*

Noise is a serious problem in New York City. The flip side of living in the city that never sleeps is that you may not be able to sleep either. Ambulance sirens, car alarms, and loud conversation can wake you at any hour. And, within your building, people may play music at too high a volume, or mount shelving just when you are trying to work. But there are some things you can check out in advance:

Prewar buildings generally have thick plaster walls which block sound; newer buildings may have sheetrock which transmits more of it. New windows can dramatically decrease the amount of street noise that enters the apartment. If you have air-conditioning, you are more likely to keep your windows closed in summer, when there is the most street noise. Are there trees in front of your building? Trees muffle sound too. And ask if you're required to have rugs; many leases require the tenants to cover a certain percentage of the floor area (usually 80 percent) in order to control noise.

Check your block for noise potential. If there's a discotheque, it's likely to be roaring well after midnight. Theaters and restaurants, which can make the neighborhood lively and attractive to you, also generate noise late into the evening. (And check to see if a restaurant's exhaust fan is under your rear window.) Is there a subway exit at your front door? Convenient, but you may have a crowd going by every seven minutes. Is there a hospital in the next block? Count on sirens.

Lately there's been increasing public pressure to control noise in New York. Life here may quiet down a bit if and when the city government puts weight behind the effort.

12. *May I Have a Pet?*

Many leases prohibit pets, except for guide dogs for the blind and deaf. If you have a dog or cat or bird, or are thinking of getting one, you'll want to know. If you have a more exotic pet, check out any special restrictions that may pertain to it. If your pet can't walk the stairs or is too big for you to carry, ask if it can ride in the elevator.

Even if your lease prohibits pets, if you house a pet in the apartment for three months, and have not hidden it or received any indication that the landlord objects, then you are allowed to keep your pet. If the landlord objects before the end of three months, you may be forced to get rid of your pet or move out. If you refuse, you can be evicted. (The attorney general's Web site says that for the no-pet clause to be waived the tenant has to keep the pet "openly and notoriously" for three months, and the owner has to know it and not complain.)

Pet protection does not apply if the animal causes damage or seriously interferes with other tenants.

13. *How Well Is the Building Maintained?*

Landlords are required to keep a building clean and free of vermin and rodents, perform repairs, and maintain the premises in safe condition. Look the building over, inside and out. If there are plantings, are they well tended? Are the window frames neat? Is the brick in good condition? Inside, are the halls and stairways clean, the floors waxed, the plaster neat and smooth? Or do you see litter, cracked window glass, peeling paint, graffiti?

As mentioned above, the city housing Web site at *www.nyc.gov* lists the complaints that have been filed against every building in the city. You can see the date a problem was reported, the nature and hazard rating of the problem, and the date the landlord fixed it.

14. *What Major Improvements Have Been Made over the Last Five Years? What Are the Plans for Further Improvements?*

A major capital improvement is a substantial, building-wide improvement that benefits all tenants and is needed for proper maintenance and operation of the building. If your landlord has made major capital improvements—a new roof, new boiler, re-piping, pointing of the brickwork, new windows—

or is planning to do so, you know that he or she is taking good care of the building. Even though you are not an owner, it is nicer to live in a well-cared-for building, and you are less likely to be inconvenienced by breakdowns.

However, major capital improvements can lead to rent increases. To offset the cost of such improvements, the landlord of a rent-stabilized building may apply to DHCR for an increase in rents, but tenants do have an opportunity to challenge the increase. Rules for these procedures are detailed in *What Every Landlord and Tenant Should Know*. A major capital improvement increase becomes part of the base rent on which subsequent increases are calculated. But in no case can major capital improvements on a rent-stabilized building add more than 6 percent to the rent in a single year. Larger increases are phased in over a period of years.

15. *What Will You Do to This Apartment before I Move In? What Am I Allowed to Do to Make It the Way I Like It?*

Most landlords repaint and spruce up an apartment when a tenant leaves so a new renter will find it attractive. They may install new kitchen and bathroom fixtures, or new appliances; in a rent-stabilized apartment, $\frac{1}{40}$ of the cost of capital improvements may be added to the base monthly rent. If the fixtures and appliances are not new, find out when they were bought. Ask if the air-conditioner works or the radiators leak.

If there's any way to adjust the heat. Turn on everything. Run the faucets, flush the toilet.

If the apartment needs fixing up, ask what they'll do and what you can do. Can you install an air-conditioner? Refinish the floors? Buy the paint and have the landlord paint it in the colors of your choice? New fixtures may be cheaper if you install them yourself, but you may not be allowed to. The landlord will want the permanent increase to the base rent.

16. *What Are My Responsibilities toward Maintaining the Apartment?*

Tenants are responsible for paying the rent on time, for respecting the building and the other occupants, for keeping their own apartments clean and in good condition.

Ask what you do with your trash. Does the building have working chutes or do you have to carry your trash to the basement yourself? What do you do with items that are too big to fit in the chute?

Ask what kind of exterminating service the building has, whom you should call to get a leaky faucet or a burned-out socket repaired, and whom to call if your leaky faucet isn't fixed in a reasonable amount of time.

17. *Are There Any Special Protections for Seniors in This Building?*

People 62 and older living in rent-stabilized apartments, whose income is $20,000 or less, may be exempt from rent increases under the Senior Citizen Rent Increase Exemption Program (SCRIE). And seniors moving into a residential healthcare facility, subsidized low-income housing, or other senior-citizen housing may terminate a lease without penalty. Check to be sure you meet the time schedule required for notification.

Tenants over 62 years of age in a building undergoing conversion to a cooperative or condominium may stay on as renters.

18. *Is There a Tenants' Organization?*

Tenants have a legal right to form a tenants' organization in order to secure their rights. Such organizations can be effective in situations in which landlords drag their feet about repair or maintenance. When a landlord files for conversion to a cooperative or condominium, tenants often organize in order to negotiate more favorable terms.

19. *Are There Plans to Convert to a Co-op or Condo?*

Conversion is a complex process, subject to many laws and regulations. If the apartment you are thinking of renting is in a building undergoing or slated for conversion, talk with the Council of New York Cooperatives about the specific plans, read the next chapter, "Twenty Questions to Ask Before You Buy an Apartment in New York," and consult your attorney before you decide to rent. Conversion protections for tenants older than 62 may not cover people who move in after the process has begun.

20. *Will You Introduce Me to Another Tenant So That I Can Ask That Person about the Building?*

An insider will give you a different perspective. Ask your potential neighbor to amplify general answers—"The super is terrific"; "This building is never clean"—with concrete examples so you can judge for yourself.

CHAPTER FIVE

Twenty Questions to Ask Before You Buy an Apartment in New York

Many retirees buy apartments for the tax advantages—similar to those of home ownership—and the added sense of control over their living space. And over the years New York real estate has consistently proved to be a good investment.

Buying a co-op apartment: Actually, you cannot buy a co-op apartment. What you purchase are shares in a corporation that owns the building. As an owner of these shares, you are permitted to live in the apartment under the provisions of the proprietary lease. As a shareholder, you assume a portion of the corporation's debt—that is, the underlying mortgage on the building—so forget, for a moment, about the view from the living room, and focus on the long-term outlook for the corporation.

Buying a condo apartment: In this case, you *do* buy the actual apartment, and you and your neighbors pay common charges for the overall maintenance of the building. Your purchase price will include a proportional share of the building's mortgage.

Which you buy depends on basically one question. Both will provide good housing and most likely accrue in value. Co-ops are less expensive up front, while condos have lower monthly fees. Yet the critical distinction for most apartment hunters is the power of the board of directors. Co-op boards keep tight control over who buys and approves all sublets—usually a rigorous process with tight time limits. Condo buyers are usually permitted to sublet at will and even to treat the apartment as an investment.

Buying into a New York co-op or condo apartment building may be the biggest investment you will make in your entire life. Moreover, you actually reside in this investment. If the company is poorly managed and your apartment or shares become worthless, not only do you lose money, but also the place where you live may not be maintained properly.

As you search for an apartment to buy, you may go through a similar experience as you would if you were looking for a rental apartment. However, once you have selected a co-op or condo, and are prepared to make an offer, the process becomes a bit more complicated than for a rental.

The following questions will help you manage the process. You may want to make a tentative offer (you should know the market value of the condo or the apartment's shares by now) pending satisfactory answers to these questions. Watch out for the danger signs, which will be marked as *red flags*.

1. *How Many Apartments Are in the Building?*

This is a key question for co-op and condo owners alike. If there are only eight owners, you may be expected to carry quite a bit of the workload required to run the building—from calling vendors to putting out the recycling. On the other hand, heavily populated high-rise buildings can seem impersonal, and you will have little say in major business decisions.

2. *How Many Apartments Are Owned by the Sponsor? By Investors? By Tenant-Shareholders or the Condo's Resident-Owners?*

a.) The *sponsor* is usually an entity with a name that reveals little, such as "30 Fifth Street Corp." (a fictional example). This entity owned the building before it became a cooperative or condo, and therefore owned all the building's shares or apartments at one point. In a co-op, the sponsor sells its shares to either investors or tenant-shareholders. In a condo, the sponsor sells to resident-owners or investors. In both cases, generally speaking, buildings with a large percentage of apartments owned by the sponsors should be avoided. The sponsor probably controls the board and the building will be run to enhance its profits, not the lifestyles of the people living in the building. *Red Flag: More than 20 percent owned by sponsor.*

b.) In most cases, *investors* buy apartments occupied by rent-regulated tenants paying rents lower than the monthly maintenance charge the investors must pay to the co-op or condo corporation. The investors' purchase prices are often significantly lower than the price of an unoccupied apartment. Under current New York law they may not evict the tenant. Instead, they play a waiting game, collecting their rent and hoping their apartments will become vacant soon. When their apartments do become vacant, they may either rent them out at market rates (without board approval in both co-ops and condos) or sell them at a large profit. Some believe this is one of the more ghoulish practices of New York City real estate, because the most common way such valuable apartments become empty is through the deaths of their tenants; the apartments' owners are often likened to greedy relatives, eagerly awaiting the end. Buildings with a large share of apartments owned by investors should be avoided. Investors rarely maintain their apartments well and rarely contribute to the overall well-being of the building. *Red Flag: More than 20 percent owned by investors.*

c.) *Tenant-shareholders* are persons who live in the co-op apartments they own; and *resident-owners* live in condos they own. Banks will often refuse to lend money to buy an apartment unless more than half the apartments in the same building are owned by tenant-shareholders or resident-owners. The reasoning is simple: owners will take better care of the building. You should refuse to buy an apartment in a building with fewer than half tenant-shareholders or residents-owners unless the apartment is a true bargain and you are confident that the building will soon cross over to the 51 percent mark. However, if the building is 100 percent owner-occupied, the price may be so high as to be prohibitive. *Red Flag: Tenant ownership is less than 51 percent.*

3. *If the Sponsor Holds More Than 10 Percent of the Shares or Apartments, Who Is the Sponsor, Really?*

Who are the actual human beings who own the entity that is called the sponsor? What are their names and business addresses? Write them down and check with the New York office of the attorney general, real estate division, to ascertain whether the office has brought any enforcement proceedings against them. The enforcement office is understaffed and only goes after the most egregious cases. *Red Flag: Any enforcement action, no matter how insignificant it appears.*

4. *Has the Sponsor Been Late on Maintenance Payments to the Co-op or Condo Corporation for the Apartments It Owns?*

Ever? Last year? This year? Not only does the sponsor's financial stability affect how the building is maintained, tardy

payments indicate that the sponsor may be in financial difficulty and preparing to default on its obligations. *Red Flag:
Tardy sponsor payments.*

5. *Do Investors Control Apartments?*

If so, how many investors are involved? That is, does one person or entity own all the investor apartments, or are there several investors? Who are they—their actual names? Who lives
in the investor apartments, rent-regulated tenants or market-
rate tenants? Beware if an investor is renting to market-rate
tenants. That means the investor is basically running a for-
profit apartment rental business under the roof of a nonprofit
building you want to call home. Not good.

Have the investors been late on their maintenance to the
co-op or condo corporation? If they have been, they too might
be heading for default. When was the last time the investor
was late? Six years ago, not a problem. Last six months, big
problem. *Red Flag: More than one investor is behind on
maintenance, or one large investor is not current.*

6. *Of the Apartments Owned by Tenant-Shareholders
or Resident-Owners, How Many Are Sublet?*

A large number of sublets may indicate that the apartments
are difficult to sell for reasons that may not be readily apparent. Moreover, renting subletters simply do not care for a
building the same way that owners do. Lastly, absentee

owners are seldom in the business of managing rental proper-
ties and usually have no interest in doing so. It is no surprise,
then, that they do a poor job of it. *Red Flag: More than 5 percent of apartments are sublet by owners.*

7. *What Is the Corporation's Sublet Policy?*

Most condos permit unregulated sublets—a feature attractive to some. In most co-ops, the board must approve all
sublets—a feature attractive to others. For co-ops, a too
loose policy may indicate that the apartments are difficult
to sell. A too strict policy may mean that you can't sublet
while you take an extended journey or need a stay at a
rehabilitation center. The usual policy is to allow one-year
sublets with a one-year renewal, upon request to the board.
*Red Flag: In co-ops, no sublets permitted or no sublet
regulations.*

8. *What Capital Projects Are Currently Planned?*

Most of the housing stock in New York City is, at minimum,
30 years old. Usually, a building will have one of the following major repairs underway: pointing of the exterior bricks,
roof replacement, garage steelwork replacement, window replacement, boiler replacement, electricity service upgrade, re-
moval of asbestos in common areas, elevator modernization,
fuel tank replacement, or entrance renovation. *Red Flag:
None of these are underway or planned for, and the co-op or*

condo corporation has failed to set aside funds to make major repairs.

9. *What Is the Expected Source of Funds to Pay for Major Repairs and Projects?*

A well-run co-op or condo corporation should have anticipated the need for major improvements and set aside funds or
borrowed money without raising the owners' monthly maintenance fees. **Red Flag:** *A reserve fund less than 15 percent of
annual revenue.*

10. *Is an Assessment Contemplated?*

An *assessment* is basically a surcharge over and above your
monthly maintenance bill to pay for a specific expense. Many
co-ops and condo corporations have had to resort to assessments, but more than one such charge may indicate that the
board is not planning properly to pay for improvements and
repairs. In other words, if the board paid for new windows
throughout the building through a combination of its reserve
funds and an assessment, that may be an example of good
planning. If, however, the board is using an assessment to pay
for such routine and relatively inexpensive maintenance as
painting the fire escape, a maintenance increase may be
needed. If the building has an assessment, get all the details
you can. What is it for? How long will it last? What portion
of the overall expense was financed through an assessment?

How was the assessment allocated to the shareholders or apartment owners? Have there been other assessments as well? *Red Flag: Repeated assessments may indicate that the board is ducking the need to raise maintenance or has not taken the time to find other, less onerous means of financing repairs and improvements.*

11. *How Long Has the Current Maintenance Charge Been in Effect? What Was the Most Recent Increase?*

Does the board expect to raise maintenance charges to meet its obligations? Different co-op and condo boards have different philosophies. Some believe that the annual revenues are elastic and should be increased to cover whatever expenses arise—including discretionary spending. Others feel constrained to keep expenses within expected revenues. *Red Flag: Frequent increases may indicate bad planning. No increases may indicate lack of proper building maintenance.*

12. *What Is the Board's Late-Maintenance Policy?*

Some co-op and condo boards insist on late fees after the 10th of the month. Others whisper discreetly into the ears of late payers. Some rush to court. Others would never think of suing to recover back maintenance. *Red Flag: A lackadaisical approach to collecting unpaid fees.*

13. *What Are the Specifics of the Building's Mortgage?*

For co-op buildings, what proportion of the monthly maintenance fee is consumed by the building's mortgage and interest payments? Too high a percentage indicates that the corporation is spending too much of its revenues merely to meet the monthly mortgage payments. For condo owners, what is the total amount of the building's indebtedness, of which you are buying a portion?

Other questions about the underlying mortgage for both condo and co-ops are:

- What is the interest rate? Is it competitive?
- Who holds the mortgage? The sponsor or a bank?
- When does the mortgage come due? The co-op or condo corporation might have to refinance the mortgage and, if the number of tenant-shareholders or resident-owners is relatively low, the corporation may find it difficult to find financing. In general, the higher the percentage of tenant-shareholders or resident-owners, the less risky the investment and the higher the initial costs. Also, be concerned if sponsor holds the mortgage; it gives the entity enormous control over the building's finances.

Red Flag: For co-ops, more than 33 percent of co-op maintenance fees goes toward paying mortgage and interest. For condos, the terms of the building's mortgage are not market rate.

14. *Is the Building Currently Involved in Litigation?*

All residential building owners are subject to lawsuits in the ordinary course of events. However, boards have been known to go off the deep end and engage in prolonged and fruitless lawsuits against irksome shareholders or owners. Boards have also been negligent and failed to sue shareholders or owners behind in paying their maintenance. *Red Flag: Any lawsuit against the building beyond ordinary "slip and fall" nuisance claims brought by individuals who claim they suffered a personal injury as a result of the building's negligence; no lawsuits against owners for failure to pay maintenance. (Maybe all the owners are perfect payers, but you should ask.)*

15. *Are the Superintendent and Other Staff Proficient in Their Duties?*

If you can, walk down the building's stairs from the top floor to the basement. Stroll by the place where trash and recycled materials are stored. Peek into the courtyard behind the building. Look out the building's windows. *Red Flag: The trash area is smelly on a Monday afternoon. (All of them are smelly on Monday morning.)*

16. *How Many Tenant-Shareholders or Resident-Owners Are Members of the Board?*

The board should have at least five such members—this indicates that owners are interested in running their building and getting the necessary work done. Also, ask if any tenant-shareholders or resident-owners are long-term members of the board. *Red Flag: Too few board members—or board members with too little experience—puts too much work and power in too few hands.*

17. *How Many Board Seats Do the Sponsor and/or Investors Have?*

Red Flag: More than one investor or sponsor representative on the board of a co-op or condo may give real estate professionals too much influence.

18. *What Have the Recent Sales Prices Been in the Building for an Apartment of Similar Size and Location to Yours?*

Sales prices vary dramatically within co-op and condo buildings, and the seller won't want to tell you if an apartment just like the one you love recently sold for $20,000 less than you're paying. But, do your best to get this data. Check the laundry room or other public spaces for a bulletin board advertising other apartments for sale, including asking prices. Chat someone up in the laundry room. Ask the management agent. Inquire of the super. Check with another neighborhood real estate agent. You may be willing to pay more for a highly prized apartment, but you should at least know how much more.

Red Flag: The price for the co-op or condo you are think-ing of buying is either dramatically lower or dramatically higher than other sales. Maybe the seller is in a rush to leave town to accept a great job. Or maybe the seller undertook ex-pensive renovations you will have to redo. You should know the reason for the price differences.

19. *What Banks Offer Individual Mortgages to Residents of the Building?*

Knowing which banks have already done business in the building may speed your own mortgage search. You should check with at least three banks and compare rates offered to those published in the newspapers or online. *Red Flag: Only one bank is offering purchase-money mortgages.*

20. *Last and Most Important: How Soon Can You See the Past Two Years' Financial Statements?*

NaBors Apartments co-op[7] posts its annual audited reports on its Web site, making them publicly available to all poten-tial buyers. Other co-ops and condo corporations treat their financial statements as if letting prospective buyers see them would jeopardize national security. If you have not read the annual report before you place a bid, make it clear to the buyer that you may change your mind after reading the re-port. When you read the report, read the footnotes—always—

---

7 The apartment complex managed by the author of this section.

and compare the answers given to you verbally to the ones in writing in the report. *Red flag: Deficit spending and footnotes you cannot understand.*

Digest all this information, talk over the answers with your lawyer, ask any additional questions that may arise, and then make your best offer.

After You Decide to Buy

Once you have entered your bid and it has been accepted, you may need to arrange for a loan to finance your purchase. Each co-op and condo has its own policies about how large a percentage of the purchase price may be financed, and some even insist on all-cash transactions.

In a co-op, you will also need to be approved by the board. Again, each board has it own process, but, in general, you will have to provide the board with a completed application detailing your finances. It is usually during this process that you may ask additional questions about the building's policies on pets and move-in hours. You should review one final document at this stage: the house rules. Usually appended to the proprietary lease, the house rules regulate when move-ins are permitted and whether amplified music can be played after 11 P.M. Some are silly and rarely enforced. However, one common rule is almost always enforced: rugs must cover 80 percent of the floor space. It is usually the downstairs neighbors who see that the rule is abided by. Failure to follow the rules could lead to eviction—even if you pay your monthly maintenance fees—so read them carefully.

Gathering Documents

Most co-op boards ask for the following documents and review them before an interview is scheduled:

- Tax returns plus recent W2s and 1099s
- Letter from employer stating salary
- Business and personal reference letters—two each
- Most recent pay stub or other proof of income
- Most recent bank statement and brokerage account statement
- Proof of other income, assets, and liabilities, if any—for example, copy of deed and mortgage obligations for other real estate owned, or documentation of rental income or child support obligations.

If you wish to speed the approval process along, be sure to ask the seller if other documents are required.

The Interview

Co-op board interviews can sometimes be unpleasant; however, many are meetings of potential good friends with much in common. Not only do you and the board members share an appreciation of the building and the neighborhood, but also, because the board learns where you work and often even your hobbies, board members with similar interests may strike up a conversation about shared loves.

The stakes are high, however, on both sides of the table. Boards are usually made up entirely of volunteers who are not real estate professionals and aren't trained to ask appropriate questions. All they really want to know is if you will be quiet, considerate, and tidy—including whether you will dispose of your trash properly or muzzle your dog in the elevator (if the building allows pets). You may be uncomfortable at first. You, the applicant, are facing a group of strangers, with your entire financial portfolio open for perusal.

Like a savvy job hunter, prepare for the interview as best you can by asking the seller what the key issues are that the board is facing, and what the differing views are. Once in the interview, armed with this knowledge, wear a suit and a smile, state often why you want to live there, describe your quiet lifestyle, and avoid expressing strong opinions on the issues you know to be controversial. Reply factually, briefly, and politely to all questions and remember: most board members are as eager to get this over with as you are. Once you are approved, the building's management agent should provide you with your move-in instructions and help you arrange a closing—a meeting at which the shares to the apartment are transferred into your name and the loan documents are signed.

You will need to find a real estate attorney to handle your closing. This person may charge you a significant (four-figure) fee, but he or she usually earns every cent of it by protecting your interests in this vastly important transaction. Like real estate brokers, many attorneys have represented many buyers in a single building. Ask the seller and the building manager for a list of names of attorneys who have represented other purchasers—this should save both time and money.

The final "do not forget": Treat yourself the night of the closing. You have accomplished something wonderful!

Suggested Reading on Co-ops and Condos

Basic Information

Binder, Neil. "The Purchasing Journey: An Overview of the Home-Buying Process." *The Cooperator*, May 2001. Available online at *www.cooperator.com*.

HSBC Holdings. *Owning a Co-Op*. 2000. Available online at *us.hsbc.com/personal/mortgage/co-opguide*.

Office of New York State Attorney General Eliot Spitzer. "Before You Buy a Co-op or Condo." 1998. Available online at *www.oag.state.ny.us/realestate/physical_aspects.html*.

Books

The following books can teach you practically everything you need to know about how to buy shares in a co-op and how to live as a condo owner.

Binder, Neil. *The Ultimate Guide to Buying and Selling Coops and Condos in New York City*. 2001.

Chesler, Vicki, ed. *Co-op and Condo Ownership: The Complete Guide for Apartment Buyers, Owners, and Boards.* 1995. Out of print; may be available from used bookstores.

Friedman, Jack P. and Jack C. Harris. *Keys to Purchasing a Condo or Co-Op.* 2000

Irwin, Robert. *Tips and Traps When Buying a Condo, Co-op, or Townhouse.* 1999.

Shapiro, Sylvia. *The Co-Op Bible: Everything You Need to Know about Co-Ops and Condos: Getting In, Staying In, Surviving, Thriving.* 1998.

Thomsett, Michael C. *How to Buy a House, Condo, or Co-Op.* 1996.

Woodson, R. Dodge. *The Condo and Co-Op Handbook: A Comprehensive Guide to Buying and Owning a Condo or Co-Op.* 1998.

After you've moved in, maybe even before you've unpacked all your boxes or hung your pictures, you'll be eager to start your new life as a New Yorker. Turn the page to discover the opportunities that await you.

Making a New Life

CHAPTER **SIX**

Promise and Challenge

The Born Loser reprinted by permission of Newspaper Enterprise Association, Inc.

Retirement is the freest and least structured of all the major life passages. In that freedom lie its greatest promise and its greatest challenge.

Think about earlier life passages. A teenager getting ready for college spends the last two years of high school preparing: SATs, application essays, visits to colleges, interviews. These tasks do more than get the student into a college; they absorb some of the student's anxiety, and they prepare her to grapple with the personal and academic demands coming up.

Think about getting married. Wedding decisions—whom to invite, formal or informal, church or garden, dancing—evoke deep-seated beliefs about how to live and may highlight unrecognized or unexamined differences between the bride and groom. Planning the wedding can help them know each other and shape their new life together. Wedding guests—all the family and friends who come to see the bride walk down the aisle and toast the couple with champagne are showing the newlyweds that they care, that they're behind this marriage, that they want it to succeed. Their support helps the couple over the inevitable rough spots to come.

Think about trying to get a new job. You revise your résumé, find out as much as you can about a prospective employer, and figure out how to apply your experience to the new company's needs. You think about which tie to wear to the interview. By the time you start the new job, you're on your way to doing the new work.

Now think about retirement. Society's demands and rituals are thin. No comparable set of built-in tasks helps get us ready. Many of the major decisions about retirement were made years ago when we set up our pension plans and decided how much to invest in our IRAs. At 65 we file for Medicare and Social Security, but compared with the work of our earlier transitions, filing is just paperwork. It doesn't stretch us. Maybe our company hosts a party. Maybe close colleagues invite us to a farewell lunch. These affairs can be heart-warming, but they do little to prepare us for the days and years ahead.

Part of the problem comes from how we think of retirement. Look up "retire" in the dictionary; the definitions imply passivity and withdrawal. In other life transitions, we expand ourselves, anticipate new experiences, take on new responsibilities. Society has structured these passages to help us succeed. We learn to rely on this guidance, and, when it comes time to retire, we must adjust to life without it.

What about those who never grew accustomed to society's assistance, who didn't move along a prescribed life path? Or bask in the support of family and community? Those who left home, chose a line of work, or married in the face of indifference or even serious opposition? Some men and women with successful careers fell into them, almost by accident. Some tended to hop-scotch through life and found that serendipity served them well. Do these people have an easier time at retirement? I don't know. It would be interesting to find out. But even people who took giant steps alone had models to follow. We saw our parents' marriage, our aunts' and uncles'. We saw people ahead of us in school getting jobs and going to college. Everyone who ever bagged groceries on Saturdays or started out in the mailroom saw a little of how the work world works. But active retirement is brand new. Up until now, retirement was thought of as . . . ? Nothing. Just rest, well-deserved rest after a lifetime of hard work. We don't need to prepare to rest. Or do we?

This is not your parents' retirement. For the first time in history, large numbers of men and women reach their 50s, 60s, even 70s with a reasonable expectation of living a few more decades in good health. If we have energy and even a modest income we can suddenly find ourselves with a heady freedom. Without the responsibilities of rearing children and earning a living we can explore new and longtime passions, reinvent ourselves, or develop our old selves as we never could before. All of a sudden we have years to do exactly what we want. How many of us want to rest for 20 years?

With fewer external demands, we make more of our own decisions. Do we want a schedule, or not? Do we want to commit to outside obligations—even one hour a week—or not? Now that I no longer go to a job, I sometimes think about becoming a ski bum for a winter. Back in the '50s, just out of college, I was too serious, too intent on my future "real life" to drop out—even for a few months. Now I could do it, but I haven't tried it—yet. It's a little scary. Of course, I could take my laptop with me . . .

Many of the people I've talked with tell me they never want a nine-to-five job again, never again want to hear the alarm clock ring before sunrise. They are vehement. Yet a lot of these same people wake up early. And many have taken on demanding volunteer work or class schedules. But not all. Some leave themselves open to follow spur-of-the-moment whims or brainstorms.

Retirees, especially new retirees, can feel unmoored. With unlimited free time and nobody wanting the expertise they've spent a lifetime developing, they may find it hard to answer the question, "What do I really want?" Retirement forces you to examine yourself, to understand your own needs, desires and personality more fully than you may have done before. Maybe you've always wanted to paint but never could because you had to earn a living. Are you brave enough to try it now? Was it only a fantasy, not compelling enough for a serious investment? If you are going to fashion a gratifying new life without the bulwark of outside demands, you need the courage to look inward first. You need the courage to risk failing.

"Face it Ragnar—we're retired! The life plan we made for ourselves in our 20s and 30s has been used up."

Ragnar Naess's friend was telling him that it was time for a different life. For years Naess, a potter, had been making production-quantity runs of his own designs, a strenuous operation that grew harder as he grew older. So, for the last few years, Naess has been reorganizing his studio, his living quarters, and his finances to free himself to work on individual art pieces.

Jane Lattes, former director of volunteer services at the American Museum of Natural History, met many retired people in the course of her work and saw some of the problems they confronted after they left their jobs. For some, retirement connoted aging and loss; some wouldn't even use the "R" word. The more that people have defined themselves by their jobs, Lattes said, the more they have to struggle with feelings of a loss of self-worth. She found that a lot of people imagine their retirement will be Nirvana, and, indeed, with new leisure that first year can be magical. But then they get bored; they panic; the need for structure reasserts itself.

Lattes noted that people who were dissatisfied with their jobs are often dissatisfied with retirement as well. They believed they only worked for the money, but now they begin to sense their paid work also filled emotional needs. Structure, for instance. People talk about loss of job or loss of spouse, but few think about loss of structure. Retirees who no longer want the discipline of a full-time job still may need some sense of order.

To a degree, Steve August exemplifies the pattern Lattes described. Some time after he retired, August realized that working out and playing tennis were not enough for him. He began to feel nervous. Not long after, he saw a poster for the Institute for Learning in Retirement, checked it out, and signed up to teach there. August says knowing that he has to be at ILR at certain times on certain days—and that he has to be ready to teach when he gets there—gives him a sense of purpose.

Building a new life is not always easy. Many of the people profiled in the coming chapters have gone through difficult transitions: Mary Louise Smith spent entire days surfing the Net. Franz Alt taught himself to repair cars, to cook, and to use a sewing machine, but, after about three years, all that busywork fell flat. Norma Globerman had plenty of activities to fill her time but felt a void she couldn't quite fathom.

Grace Timberlake, who was still working when I talked with her, worries about life without a job. "When I've had no structure, I find it's one o'clock [in the afternoon] and I'm still reading the morning paper." In her head she hears her aging father asking, "What good are we?" Her father, a carpenter who took pride in his ability to walk faster and lift more than anyone else, felt useless when he grew too old and weak to work and was spending his days watching TV. So Timberlake feels she must continue to be "productive"—which to her means creating something tangible, offering something to others. When she retires, Timberlake expects to volunteer in a capacity similar to her present job. "In a way, I envy someone who doesn't have these feelings."

Many retirees speak of the need to be "productive" in Timberlake's sense of the word. But not all. Not everyone needs tangible results from a day's activity; not everyone wants structure. Another way to look at the question might be, "What makes you feel your time is well spent?"

Beri Greenwald says her time is well spent when she feels alive, when her antennae are out to see what she can take in, or give, when she's thinking about some new direction in life. Trudy Reece feels her time is well spent if she's "living in the moment," completely absorbed, not thinking of what she'll be doing in an hour or what the next step might be.

"My time is well spent if I'm doing things that lend to my creativity," Jamie Lintz says. Lintz paints. If she goes to a museum, or sees something in a new way as she walks along the street, that's time well spent. Repetitive chores—laundry, dishes, bed-making—she resents.

After she retired from her job, Julia Hall decided *not* to make long-range, scheduled commitments but to leave herself open to do what seemed most important, or necessary, or interesting, or fun at any given time. When she was younger, Hall was always measuring herself in her mind. How many pages (of her unpublished novel) did she write today? How many sheets of cookies (*not* uneaten) did she bake? Then suddenly she made a total switch. She says she's "no longer concerned with improving every shining moment" but thinks about what would make her life feel rewarding right now. So, on one day, she and Grace Timberlake explored the Red Hook section of Brooklyn, and on another they attended a performance of Japanese drummers at the Brooklyn Botanic Garden. More than once, Hall was able to stay at the hospital with a friend having surgery. And when I asked her if she'd help me by editing this book, she agreed instantly—and very likely has spent more time on it than she ever anticipated.

"When the people Angela and I met on trips asked what I did, and I told them I had a Mercedes dealership, that was good," Mike Sclafani told me. "In the first place, I was proud of it. And then it always led to conversation. Everybody knows Mercedes. Everybody has had their own experience with car dealers. It was a terrific ice-breaker. We made a lot of friends." Now, when Sclafani tells people he's retired, the conversation stops. It's a nothing. "And even though I'm content with what I do now, that bothers me," he says.

He's not alone. Karl H. Klaus, founder of the nonfiction writing program at the University of Iowa and author of a perceptive memoir, *Taking Retirement*, says "What am I if I'm not a professor of English?" Finding a way to think of oneself, to describe oneself to others, can be difficult. Saying you're a retired Mercedes dealer, or English professor, or social worker may not cut it. Most people want to talk about the present.

I asked a few people what they say to the question "What do you do?" and, at best, I got skimpy answers. "I do lots of things," several people told me. My sister-in-law tells people she was laid off from Digital (even though that was 10 years ago). Julia Hall ducks and says she's a practicing hedonist.

Many resent the question and assume the person asking simply wants to place them on a hierarchy of success, or decide whether they're worth bothering with at all. Some questioners do want to rank you, but not all. Some may be looking for a point in common with a new person. Some are interested in another person's viewpoints, skills, talents, and interests. In having a more fully-developed picture of that person.

Our past jobs are not just history—over and done with. For better or for worse, the work we did for so many years has shaped the way we think, the way we relate to others, our views on personal and world issues, the details we notice when we look around. Still, if asked what we do, most of us want to say something current. And active retirement is so new, the problem hasn't been solved yet.

People moving to New York usually want to make friends here. Retired New Yorkers may want to meet new people too; their own circle may be shrinking. I find that, as I grow older, friends become more and more important to me. With Dave gone and my children immersed in their own lives far away, I need my friends more than ever. Most of us would agree with retiree Karen McAuley, who says, "I think the most important thing is to feel connected. Not like a leaf blowing in the wind." Yet finding friends isn't always easy, especially for older people. Young people moving to New York may gravitate to one another, but, by the time we're 60, it can seem as though everyone else is already happily set in a tightly bound circle, too busy to notice a newcomer.

Some of the people profiled in this book speak to strangers everywhere they go and seem to make new friends without even trying. At a conference, Jeanne Turner met an agent who introduced her to a young singer getting started in a show business; from there, Turner, a retired social worker, developed a second career managing young singers and dancers trying to "make it" in New York. More than a few have become long-term friends. Blossom Carron and another woman joined the couple standing next to them at the Museum of

A sightseeing boat circles Manhattan Island (NYC & Company, Inc.)

Opposite page top: Statue of Liberty, New York Harbor (James C. Hall)

Opposite page bottom: Times Square (NYC & Company, Inc.)

Above left: Chrysler Building illuminated at night (NYC & Company, Inc.)

Above right: Bryant Park, looking toward the Empire State Building (NYC & Company, Inc.)

Opposite page top: Radio City Music Hall (NYC & Company, Inc.)

Opposite page bottom: Apollo Theater, Harlem (NYC & Company, Inc.)

This page, clockwise from lower left: West Indian Day parade, Brooklyn (James C. Hall)

Downtown Dance Festival, Manhattan (James C. Hall)

Sculpting at a street fair, Brooklyn (James C. Hall)

Japanese dancer at the Cherry Blossom Festival, Brooklyn Botanic Garden (James C. Hall)

Face to face at the Metropolitan Museum of Art (James C. Hall)

Top: Watching a radio-controlled model boat in Central Park (NYC & Company, Inc.)

Right: Outdoor food markets in Chinatown, Manhattan (NYC & Company, Inc.)

Bottom: Central Park in winter (Janet Hays)

Clockwise from upper left: Residential
street, Upper West Side, Manhattan (Janet
Hays)

Brownstones, Sterling Place, Prospect
Heights, Brooklyn (James C. Hall)

Neighborhood stoops, Brooklyn (NYC &
Company, Inc.)

Brooklyn Bridge, pedestrian catwalk
high above the traffic (NYC & Company, Inc.)

Modern Art in scoffing at the installation of paint rags they were all viewing. Afterwards, the four went out for coffee, and a few weeks later those same museumgoers invited Carron and her friend to a party where Carron met the man who became her second husband.

Other people find it hard to talk to strangers. Some of us could visit a museum once a week for a year and never find a new acquaintance to go out with afterwards. We could nod to the same people in the elevator every morning and nothing would ever develop. One way around this problem is to join an organization or take a class in something that interests you. Or volunteer to help a cause you believe in. You'll meet people who are interested in the same thing you are, and you'll have something to talk about right away.

The setup, informality within a structure, helps. Conversations start more easily in the dressing room after swimming or around a table stuffing envelopes. Common interests alone may not be enough for a deep friendship, but among people whose interests overlap yours, you may find a few whose personality and outlook also click with yours.

Sometimes it's hard. Robin Bahr was disappointed to find that, in New York, her friendships are fragmented. She sees dance friends at dance class, book group friends at book group. In San Francisco, where she lived before, Bahr had a circle of friends that did everything together. Here, "people are friendly within a little world but not in an overall world." She feels people here are friendly enough at class or meetings but too busy to arrange social occasions at other times.

Perhaps Bahr needs a little more time. For me it took a while, but now I do sometimes go out to lunch after class with other women in my ballet group; last year, four of us went to see our teacher perform in *Nutcracker*. Gradually my classmates are becoming a bigger part of my life. People often hesitate to suggest moving beyond the structured encounter, but almost everyone is happy to be asked to have coffee after a meeting or to attend a related activity. Out of tentative beginnings, solid friendships have developed.

Or form a group of your own. Not long after Sharon Walsh moved to New York, she spoke to a few people she knew about starting a book group and invited those who were interested to her apartment for a first meeting. Those people invited others. Pretty soon we had a lively bunch gathering monthly at one another's apartments to order up supper and talk about the book. Now book-group members are hiking together and going to movies together between meetings.

Many of the people I spoke with thought that the transition to retirement would have been much harder if they hadn't developed outside interests during their working years. They felt that those whose lives consist only of work have a tougher time at retirement.

I have a slightly different take on the situation. I've always believed that the best way to prepare for the next phase of life is to immerse myself in the present phase as fully as possible. I got that idea years ago when I was looking for a nursery school for my son Josh. Talking with other mothers who were also investigating nursery schools I often heard the question, "Will this nursery school prepare my child for kindergarten?" As if the children were supposed to spend the nursery school years on watered-down kindergarten exercises. But I thought the best thing to do was to make the nursery school experience as rich as possible. If the school engages my child deeply in play at three and four, he'll be ready to do the work expected of him at five.

Yes, my approach is idiosyncratic. Different people have vastly different ways of integrating the interests and demands of their lives. But focusing on one thing at a time has worked for me. I stayed home with my children when they were growing up, but found I could handle a regular job when I needed to. And I worried about being bored when I retired from my job, but it hasn't happened yet. I like what's on my plate now, and I have more than enough. So, if you've been too immersed in your job or bringing up your children to pick up activities on the side, you shouldn't worry about having a fulfilling retirement.

Of course, there are exceptions. If you want to enjoy the later part of your life, it helps to put away some money in advance. It helps to take care of your health. If you've focused on work to the exclusion of family and friends, you've risked a lonely old age. And if you've learned some new things along the way—playing the cello or serving on your co-op board—then you know for sure you are capable of learning something new in the future. But there's no need to take up painting or sailing when you're 30 or 50 *just so* you'll have something to do when you retire.

What enables you to move happily into this new phase of life depends more on your attitudes toward yourself and the world than on actual skills or developed interests. Think of yourself in a fluid way. Think, I'm a person who can generate new ideas; I can meet situations creatively; I can commit myself to a piece of work and do it well; I can form loving ties with family and friends; I can grieve over sorrows without being crushed by them.

If you have that kind of confidence in yourself, and you know that the world is marvelous and needful of your efforts, you will craft a rewarding retirement.

The five chapters of "Making a New Life" introduce retired people who, in remarkably different ways, have grasped New York's bountiful opportunities and created new lives for themselves.

CHAPTER **SEVEN**

The Arts

Part One: The Scene

New York City retirees smile when they talk about the Broadway shows, the opera and ballet, the museums and galleries only a subway ride away. I have yet to meet a sated New Yorker. The city is a glorious repository for the traditional arts and a crucible in which new work bubbles up every day. Living here you can enjoy these cultural gems on multiple levels and from various perspectives. You can look at sculpture and listen to music. You can learn to dance, sing in a choral group, paint, pot, or quilt.

After a lifetime working in classrooms, offices, banks, and labs, the retirees profiled in this chapter are immersing themselves in the arts. Many are encouraging long-dormant artistic yearnings to flower; others are discovering talents they never knew they had. It's not only the resources of the city that make it possible to take up watercolors or tap dancing in your 60s; it's also the culture, a culture of curiosity and experimentation. New Yorkers know you're not limited to what you did before. They don't laugh at people who move outside their own molds, even if they fail. New Yorkers know that risking failure is part of growth. The people in this chapter have discovered that tiptoeing or plunging into the arts in later life can be as rewarding as that special seminar in college or that first really good job.

The Scene: Performing Arts

When I was a teenager in Ohio, before I'd ever visited New York City, I dreamed about going to Broadway shows and to glamorous nightclubs where men in tuxedos bought martinis for women in slinky dresses. The Stork Club is gone now, clothes are seldom formal, and we all buy our own martinis. But Broadway still dazzles us with light, song, and drama. Glancing over New York's cultural diamonds, we find symphonies, chorales, and string quartets at Carnegie Hall, dancers leaping across Lincoln Center stages, and Pavarotti singing at the Met. You can hear Brahms and Beethoven at Avery Fisher Hall and Phillip Glass at the Brooklyn Academy of Music.

But Carnegie Hall, Lincoln Center, and BAM aren't the

only gems in the city. Music, drama, and dance burst from theaters, lofts, studios, churches, and even storefronts in all five boroughs. Take the HB Theatre in Greenwich Village. Every year HB commissions a collection of one-act plays, each by a different writer. All the plays are set in the same locale. The first time I went, I saw eight short plays in one evening, all set in an airport; last year, the action took place in a funeral parlor. During the Christmas holidays I took my visiting granddaughters to HB's *St. George and the Dragon at Christmas Tide*. Sitting in the front row, the girls could almost touch their favorite character, the prancing Hobbyhorse. Performances at the HB Theatre are usually free.

Ticket prices in New York can max out your credit card, but savvy theatergoers know less expensive ways to see and hear many good performances. Send a self-addressed stamped envelope to the Juilliard School and you get the season's roster of free concerts. Subscribe to Club freeTime (a monthly paper listing free and low cost events in the city) and you're entitled to special low-priced tickets for high-priced events. Seniors can join the Theater Development Fund (TDF) and order reduced-price tickets to many Broadway and off-Broadway plays. And small theaters often provide free tickets to people who are willing to usher.

Look at the daily fare available in New York at little or no cost. On a single Thursday in November, *freeTime* listed 44 events: 12 lectures and talks, 9 concerts, 7 films, 3 theatrical performances, and a smattering of walking tours, book signings, receptions, and symposia. Of the 44, 2 were pay-what-you-wish and 4 carried a charge of seven dollars or less. The rest were absolutely free.

Maybe you want to do more than look or listen. Franz Alt, 90, has been playing the viola since he was a boy in Vienna, and he still plays regularly with four or five amateur chamber music groups. Grace Polk[8] took her first cello lesson after she retired from teaching kindergarten. Yvette Pollack worked on an amateur theater group's newsletter for several years before she dared try acting.

And dancing! I started ballet when I was 62. Hooked from the first *plié* at the *barre*, I now take class three times a week. Dance studios around the city have a surprising number of gray heads in their tap, jazz, flamenco, ballet, and modern classes. Folk and square dance groups meet regularly. Retirees who jitterbugged to the big bands when they were in high school can swing on the plaza at Lincoln Center in the summer and at the Swing Dance Society on Saturday nights year-round; if you want to brush up on your steps, come an hour early for a lesson.

Sometimes I wonder if the choreography of the streets, the way the people on the sidewalks all move to their own rhythms without bumping one another, stimulates the outpouring of dance in this city. Meandering tourists with their faces turned up to stare at the building spires, Wall Street pinstripers buying and selling stocks over their cell phones as they walk, delivery guys pushing, head down, through the

---

8 Not her real name.

crowds to get pizza to architects-on-deadline while it's still hot, models with scarves floating behind them dashing in high heels to photo shoots. They all race, run, stride, or stroll along the pavement in a spontaneous ballet. And, in many neighborhoods, older people leaning on walkers or supported by aides join the throng. No wonder Broadway Dance classes are jammed. No wonder toddlers and seniors pull on leotards at Ballet Academy East.

New York City was, perhaps still is, the music capital of the United States, maybe even the world. The world's most renowned musicians compose and perform symphonies and concerti, pop songs and jazz. Amateur players in all five boroughs play trumpets, harpsichords, and synthesizers. Seniors and teenagers are forming Klezmer bands, early-music groups are building and playing baroque instruments, immigrants from India and Pakistan play the sitar, and in the summer account executives and computer programmers leave their offices early to join the sing-in's at CAMI Hall, just across the street from Carnegie Hall. The Web site of the Guild of Community Music Schools, *www.nationalguild.org,* lists 21 certified community music schools in New York City, and *www.van.org* (Vocal Area Network) describes over 140 choirs in the greater New York area. Whether you want to play or sing, listen or compose, whether you choose the tuba or the piano or the bass drum, whether you've been playing for 80 years or are just beginning, you can find a teacher, a class, a group that's right for you.

The Scene: Visual Arts and Crafts

New York City's art museums—the Metropolitan, the Modern (MOMA), the Guggenheim, the Whitney, the Brooklyn Museum—can keep art lovers rapt. Retired New Yorkers often prefer to go on weekday mornings when the galleries are quieter, or on evenings set aside for reduced entry fees. When you live here you can see one exhibit at a time instead of trying to cram medieval armor and Monet haystacks into the same morning. When you live in New York, you can hear a lecture about a current show at the Met one day and chamber music at the Frick another. Summer weekends you can hear contemporary music in the MOMA sculpture garden.

Museums aren't the only places to look at art. There are special exhibits all over the city. Lobbies of office buildings feature murals by well-known artists, and even elevator cabs in some skyscrapers are worth a detour. Art galleries are open to everyone, and gallery-hopping is an honored New York pastime. If you sign the guest book you'll receive announcements of future shows, and, if you follow the reviews or read the arts publications available in public libraries, you can gradually educate yourself in contemporary art.

Visiting studios is a good way to learn about the techniques artists use to achieve their effects. Around the Christmas holidays many artists and craftspeople hold studio open house, and throughout the year community centers such as the 92nd Street Y offer studio tours. Visiting a glassmaker's studio on a Y tour changed the way I see stained glass. The artist showed us his tools and explained some of the techniques of the craft; then he took us to two nearby churches where he pointed out how earlier stained glass workers had applied those same techniques to create their brilliant windows.

The next part of this chapter, "The People," profiles nine retired New Yorkers who are working in the arts. A few told me they took up art "out of the blue" with no earlier interest. But most of them have felt a lifelong passion for the arts, a passion they often suppressed in order to fulfill practical responsibilities.

The men and women in this chapter differ in certain ways from the ones you'll read about in the chapter on volunteering. People who want to continue using their work skills often volunteer in a related capacity: retired science teachers prepare specimens at the Museum of Natural History; retired businessmen join SCORE to help new entrepreneurs get started. But, by and large, the people in this chapter have stepped away from their careers to tap a core self that had lain fallow for decades.

The third part of the chapter, "The Opportunities," lists some of the places where you can hear music, take lessons of all kinds, get free or low-priced tickets to quality performances. "Opportunities" also gives you Web addresses where you can tap into well organized information about the performing and visual arts in New York. No single book can list everything in the city. But we hope to get you started.

Part Two: The People

Cornelia Hansen

On March 3, 1988, Cornelia and George Hansen closed their design shop. On March 4, Cornelia Hansen began drawing classes at the Art Students League of New York. She drew six days a week for an entire year to prepare herself to paint.

Forbidden by her father to study art in college because he felt she'd never earn a living painting, Hansen became a teacher, shifted into decorating, and vowed that as soon as she was free she'd paint full time. Now the Art Students League of New York is her studio; she's there at her easel two or three days a week.

No other school runs like the League, she points out. You can sign up for any course, with any instructor, in the morning, the afternoon, or evening and at your desired frequency. No admission requirements, no exams. Tuition is prorated and even beginners get serious attention from some of the finest artists in the United States.

Hansen paints in watercolor. She began with flowers, landscapes, and street scenes. From time to time she gets stuck, but her instructor moves her along. "If you don't get out of landscapes, you'll never do anything else," he told her. Gradually she began experimenting with new styles, abstracting her forms. Visiting museums and galleries to see current work keeps her alert.

The Hansens live in a modern apartment with light, bright walls and furnishings. A zebra rug on the floor, an abstract painting over the couch, her own watercolors of flowers and Spanish towns. All blend in airy lightness. The Hansens' home looked so fresh, I was amazed to learn they'd lived there 38 years.

At 78, Hansen is full of energy. She speaks emphatically and every time she laughs, which is often, her face crinkles up and her eyes almost close. I needed woolen pants, a turtleneck, and a sweater on the cold day we met, but she moved around freely in loose, silky black pants and a short-sleeved shirt. She told me that, with more traffic and more buses, New York City gets physically harder for her every year. But she finds ways to cope.

She showed me the *New York Times* Spring 2000 Home Design Magazine with George Hansen's picture on the cover. When he was a young man, George designed the wall-mounted swing-arm lamp—an icon of modern lighting that can be found in the Lyndon Johnson presidential library in Texas, the Carlyle Hotel in New York, and in suburban bedrooms all over the United States.

Ever since George contracted with a Spanish firm to manufacture his lamps, the Hansens have been spending half of each year in Barcelona. They've made friends with townspeople there, and Cornelia belongs to a painting group that puts on well-received exhibits in the studios of a retired Barcelona architect.

Hansen was introduced to art by her aunt, who told her, "Don't ever give up painting. It's your friend for life." On her

92nd birthday, two days before she died, the older woman was working on two canvases at once.

Hansen feels the same way. "I wasn't searching for something to do. Painting was there and I had to do it. I'll be doing it till I die."

Marilyn Henrion, Mary Louise Smith, and Gwendolyn Grant

Marilyn Henrion, Mary Louise Smith, and Gwendolyn Grant all became serious quilters after they retired. Each has, to some degree, arranged her life around quilting. But they work in different ways, and they use their quilts for different purposes.

All the years Marilyn Henrion was working as a placement counselor and teaching career planning at Fashion Institute of Technology she hungered for the visual arts. She'd taken up quilting in 1976, and in her last two years on the FIT faculty she was champing at the bit to quilt full time. In 1989, when she said goodbye to her colleagues, she told them they'd better phone her occasionally or she might disappear into her studio and never be seen again.

It didn't turn out quite that way.

She began to exhibit her work. Instead of disappearing into her studio as she had predicted, she found herself lecturing, writing articles, running workshops on quilting, and giving interviews. Ten years after retiring from FIT, Marilyn Henrion had achieved prominence in her new career: her quilts have been shown all over the world and bought by corporations, museums, and institutions. Two years ago, at 68, Henrion stopped her time-consuming teaching and lecturing to focus entirely on quilting itself, often working in her studio all day, and sometimes until midnight or 2 A.M.

Is she lonely?

"Lonely? I don't know that word. Solitude, yes; loneliness, no." After bringing up four children in a small New York City apartment and working in a busy office every day, Henrion finds solitude heaven. But she's not at all aloof.

Henrion and her husband, Ed, live in a Mitchell-Lama apartment in Greenwich Village, not far from New York University. "Mitchell-Lama makes it possible for people like us to be in Manhattan," she told me. Spacious without feeling bare and comfortable without being cluttered, their apartment has large windows with views north to the Chrysler building. Her quilts, Ed's paintings, Japanese fabrics, and works of other artists cover the walls.

Henrion spends about two-thirds of her time in the couple's country house in northeastern Pennsylvania, where she has enough room for a studio and the solitude she needs to create her designs. The Henrions don't operate according to any particular schedule but make the two-hour trip between their country house and city apartment whenever they wish.

The architecture and geometry of the New York City are embedded in Henrion's psyche and influence her work. Grids appeal to her; pastoral themes do not. In New York she draws on the museums, galleries, fabric shops, and a network of other artists to enrich her work. But she finds it takes a lot of energy to be in the city. "I'm wiped out by the end of the day." In Pennsylvania she can work far into the night. Henrion finds New York City enriching and depleting at the same time and doesn't see letting go of either the country house or the Manhattan apartment.

Ed's retirement is different from his wife's. He's totally *un-driven*. After teaching art at Erasmus High School in Brooklyn for 30 years, freedom is key for Ed Henrion—freedom to do whatever he wants, whenever he wants. Since 1987 he's been spending about 95 percent of his time in the country where he reads scientific books and plays chess. He may go to a movie or take a nap—on a whim.

For 10 years Marilyn Henrion was content to sew traditional quilt blocks and be one of a long line of women quilters carrying forward the old skills and the old designs. Then she took a design class and immediately began to create original quilts, often incorporating visual images from her travels all over the world. Now, in the third phase of her quiltmaking, Henrion designs quilts that embody her own ideas and feelings. The shapes she cuts and stitches so carefully are metaphors. Her newer quilts include circles that float up like soap bubbles. To Henrion the circles represent the fragile, fleeting nature of our lives.

After September 11 Henrion found she could not continue the serene designs she had been stitching the day before. She began a new series. Only after they were completed did she recognize their turbulence and chaos. Henrion takes comfort thinking that through her quilts her ideas will live on after she's gone. She sees herself joining the continuum of quilt-makers, known and unknown, who have left their marks.

But it's not about personal fame and recognition. Exhibits, sales, publicity, and marketing are fun and a challenge for Henrion, but not deeply significant. "It's nice to have affirmation, but for me it's not essential. I know when I do good and when I don't." She says she's a happy person. And she looks it. Her regrets come only when thinks about not having time in life to do everything she'd like to do. "I could have been an astronomer," she says.

~

If you like quilting, but aren't as fond of solitude as Marilyn Henrion is, you can find quilt groups everywhere. Gwendolyn Grant and Mary Louise Smith belong to Quilters' Guild of Brooklyn, to Quilters of Color Network of New York, to Empire Quilters, and to other groups. I talked with Grant and Smith at an exhibition of miniature quilts at the Lefferts Homestead in Brooklyn, where both women had works on display.

Gwendolyn Grant has traveled to quilt conferences in the United States and to Australia, China, and South Africa with quilt groups, seeing exhibits and attending workshops the host quilting guilds arranged for their American visitors. In South Africa she traded fabrics with a quilter she had met earlier on the Internet. "Quilting is a worldwide addiction," she says.

Quiet, self-possessed, with finely chiseled features and a gray ponytail, Gwendolyn Grant projects elegance even in jeans and a parka. She retired in 1991 as a lieutenant in the New York State Department of Corrections. She says she had no problems about retirement. Rather, she'd been eager to leave her job at the prison. In 1992, she and her sister traveled across the country and up to Alaska in an RV. They spent months on the trip, roving without a timetable. She continues to operate without a schedule—doing what she wants, when she wants to.

Grant makes quilts mostly for her children, her grandchildren, and her great-grandchildren. She doesn't sell her work because she doesn't want to be held to the level of perfection that sales would require.

Years ago, when she saw a display of quilts at a Long Island fair, Grant was attracted to the craft. But she could only do a little while she was working. Now design ideas come into her head faster than she can finish her quilts, so she has a growing stack of patchwork tops waiting to be quilted.

~

Mary Louise Smith was president of Quilters of Color for four years. She teaches quilting at Medgar Evers College and conducts workshops at senior centers and churches in Brooklyn, and at the American Craft Museum and the Museum of American Folk Art.

But when she first retired Smith woke every morning feeling lost, not knowing what to do with herself. She'd been managing the international money transfer department at a major New York City bank, using five computers to oversee the transfer of $33 billion a day. By comparison, staying home seemed pretty tame. And, even though she'd seen an exhibit of Japanese quilts at the Brooklyn Botanic Garden in 1990 and decided she wanted to try quilting, it took her a while to get going.

One morning after breakfast, Smith began to surf the Internet. Before she knew it, the day had passed and it was 5:30. There she was, still in her nightgown, looking at archeological sites in Mongolia when she heard her husband coming through the front door. Smith jumped into bed, dove under the covers and told him she was sick—hadn't been able to get out of bed all day. Smith's husband caught on pretty quickly. "Get a life!" he said.

Back at the bank she'd done mental work. Now she wanted handwork. After a stab at making porcelain dolls, Smith went to a nearby community center where she soon found herself in a room with 21 Bernina sewing machines, teaching a group of men how to make themselves dashikis. When a quilting teacher came to the center, Smith found her calling.

Smith is outgoing and talkative. A heavyset woman with a round face and curly blond hair, she's the center of attention in any group. You can see the influence of her French mother in her love of life and of her Caribbean father in the themes and colors of her quilts. One quilt commemorates the eruption of Mount Pelée—the volcano that destroyed her grandparents' hometown in Martinique.

Smith has sold a few of her quilts, but mostly she keeps them to show in juried and invitational exhibits. As her pile of quilts grows larger, she plans to sell more. She figures that the documented history of exhibitions will increase the value of her work.

Quilting, with its small stitches and thread often matching the background fabric, can be hard for older eyes. At one point, Smith feared she was going blind. When her doctor told her she needed an operation, she astounded him by responding, "Oh, thank goodness." On the operating table, just before going under anesthesia, she cautioned the surgeon, "Don't forget, Doctor, I'm a quilter!"

Mary Louise Smith made an excellent recovery.

Jack Poggi and Robin Bahr

When Broadway Dance Center showcased student work, Jack Poggi and Robin Bahr were two of the Tapnuts, who "celebrate the joy of tap-dancing in later life." Poggi started tapping at 65 and Bahr took her first tap lesson after she retired from a career in marketing.

As a child, Jack Poggi couldn't sing on key. His second grade teacher told him to move his lips when the class sang but not to let any sound come out. By high school, Poggi thought of himself as a klutz. Now, at 72, he's singing and dancing in his own solo cabaret shows in Manhattan. Tapping is a big part of his life. He finds it playful, expressive, and one of the things that keeps him in New York City. Without it he might move upstate where his son lives.

As a young man Poggi was an actor. Then he taught acting at C.W. Post College on Long Island for 20 years. When he retired Poggi and his wife moved back to New York City, and he took up the acting career he'd left behind. A slender, muscular man with white hair and bushy white eyebrows, a long, narrow face, and blue eyes, Poggi is lithe and dynamic. When we met for lunch before his tap class at Broadway Dance, he was wearing a yellow turtleneck, chinos, sneakers, and a black leather cap.

He told me that, since he's retired, the nature of his acting has changed. Now he works more on whole body movement. He takes ballet and tap classes; he studies yoga and Tai Chi. "I'm a walking catalog of Open Center classes."[9] Later that day he would be meeting with a new voice teacher who combines singing with body movement. As he grows older Poggi finds he can use his body in ways that he never could when he was young. He's no longer a klutz; he sings on key.

All his retraining has culminated in three cabaret shows—monologues interspersed with dances and songs. Poggi's first show was about his high school days: he combined songs that were popular then—"There Will Never Be Another You," "Polka Dots and Moonbeams," "Goodnight Sweetheart"—

---

9 See chapter 9, "Continuing Your Education," for information about the Open Center.

with a monologue that contrasted the romantic life portrayed in the songs with his real life as a lonely, self-conscious adolescent. The second cabaret, *Confessions of a Mostly Unemployed Actor*, featured stories about the difficulties of the acting business, the auditions, and the constant need to look for work. In his third show, *Me and Fred*, Poggi sang "Puttin' on the Ritz," "Cheek to Cheek," and other Fred Astaire songs, and drew ironic parallels between his life and the life of Fred Astaire.

Poggi came to New York City as a young man because it was the place for actors. It's still the place for him. He likes the theater and the cabaret, likes going to auditions even when he doesn't get the work. He meets people, he keeps his skills sharp, he's part of the acting world. His book for actors, *Monologue Workshops: From Search to Discovery in Audition and Performance*, is in its fifth printing, On Saturdays he teaches a course in monologues at the Actors Connection, and a few students come to his apartment for lessons.

His Zen studies have helped him to enjoy his life in the present more than he once did. Immediacy doesn't always work for him but, in general, he takes pleasure in what he's doing at a any given moment and thinks less than he used to about where it might lead or what he should do next. And he observes that you have to do this when you're 72, because there's not so much future left.

"I'm finally at the point where I don't have to prove anything to myself or anyone else." Poggi no longer defines himself in terms of his work or position, or thinks he has to achieve something special to feel worthwhile. He prefers a phrase from a workshop he once attended: "Who I am is an emerging possibility."

~

Robin Bahr had never danced. When she retired and moved from San Francisco to New York, she never thought of dancing. Then suddenly she knew wanted to tap dance. She knew it would be right for her. "I made a beeline for it."

Bahr is a small blonde dynamo. When I met her, right after her class at Broadway Dance Center, she was wearing black tights and a black tunic with a multi-color design on the front. Her hair is a little spiky. For a woman who grew up in a suburb of Detroit and worked in San Francisco until 1997, she's remarkably New York: she moves fast, she talks fast, she doesn't waste time. After the class she changed into street shoes and, unwilling to wait for a slow elevator, she led me down the service stairs of the Broadway Dance building.

Bahr says tap dancing was hard for her at first, that she was bad at it. "I was always very good at what I did. I had a good position; people listened to me, respected me. And then to come here and be bad at what I was doing . . ." She was very discouraged, but that didn't stop her. "I'm a persistent type. I'd give it up if I lost interest. But not because I wasn't good. That's contrary to my nature."

Until she was 45, Bahr took care of her three children and served on the boards of the Junior League and other community organizations. She began paid work when she saw that her marriage was failing, and she realized would soon have to support herself. Over the years she moved up to become director of sales for a large hotel in San Francisco. When she retired, Bahr moved to New York because her two daughters live here. She says she can't really compare her life in New York City to her life in San Francisco because in San Francisco life was all work—at least 11 hours a day.

Bahr found her New York apartment in record time. She came east for a weekend and, with her daughter, looked at two places advertised in the paper. As they left the second one, a man approached them and invited them to look at another apartment for sale on the same block. They looked. And Bahr bought it in half an hour.

By the time she performed in Tapnuts, Bahr had two solid years of tap behind her. She says tap has made her fit and very aware of what she's seeing at dance performances. But performing scared her. She isn't sure she'd do it again. Her teacher had high standards, and Bahr didn't want to let her down. And she was afraid that if she made too many mistakes she might not be allowed back in the class. Of course that didn't happen. Friends of mine who saw her perform say she was great.

Franz Alt

If you should be carrying a musical instrument on the A train—especially if you get off at 190th street in Manhattan and take the elevator up to Fort Washington Avenue—you might meet a slender, gray-haired man with an elfin look about him. If he were to spot you with your instrument case, he might ask you if you play classical music—and if you'd like to join a quartet or an ensemble. Franz Alt recruits wherever he goes.

At 90, Alt travels everywhere on the subway. He plays viola in five chamber music groups. He took his first lessons in Vienna when he was eight and recently was startled to realize that he's been playing for more than 80 years. "I'm an amateur," he says. He's an amateur in the truest sense of the word: one who plays for the love of it. And he finds particular pleasure playing with people he knows well.

But players move away or die, so Alt works hard to find new members and keep the groups going. At one point, he spoke to a professional cellist who was moving into his building. He told me it took a lot of courage to ask her to sit in because he'd never played with a professional before. But she enjoyed it, and invited a violinist from the Metropolitan Opera Orchestra to join them. Professional musicians help draw other good players into a group.

A newcomer to New York who wants to find other musicians can join Amateur Chamber Music Players. Members register their qualifications and rate themselves. It's a way to match musicians with jobs or amateur groups. Alt himself is not a member; "Maybe I'm prejudiced," he says about his preference for meeting people personally. But he acknowledged that one of his cellists got a call from a man in Tennessee who was coming to New York for a month and wanted to play in a group. They arranged for the visitor to join them and it worked well. Now, the Tennessean plays with them whenever he comes to New York.

I talked to Franz Alt in his apartment overlooking the Hudson River. It's within walking distance from my apartment but on a cliff high above it. I envied him his well-kept Art Deco lobby and view of the George Washington Bridge.

Alt is a lively, graceful man who was eager to tell me about his life. He was trained as a mathematician in Vienna, but, knowing that Jews had no chance to enter the Austrian academic world, he and his first wife emigrated to New York City in 1938. He served in the American army in World War II and, after the war, went to work for the U.S. Bureau of Standards in Washington, D.C. He had expected to stay at the Bureau until he retired, but he wasn't happy about working for the government during the Vietnam War. And his wife really missed New York City. So when he was offered a position at the American Institute of Physics here he accepted it, and they moved back. He was 57. Sadly, Mrs. Alt died of cancer only two years later.

During his first year of retirement, Alt learned to repair automobiles, cook, and use a sewing machine. But after about three years all that began to feel like a waste of time, so he volunteered for Clergy and Laity Concerned, an organization formed to oppose the Vietnam War. By then, the war was over but the group continued, working against nuclear proliferation and for human rights and economic justice. When Alt came to their office for the first time, the bookkeeper had just left. Alt learned bookkeeping that afternoon and stayed on to handle all the group's finances until Clergy and Laity Concerned moved its headquarters to Atlanta 15 years later.

"For the first time in my life, I felt I was doing something useful for society," Alt says. When he worked for the Bureau of Standards and for the Institute of Physics, his main purpose was to support his family, not contribute to society.

At New York Ramblers, a club for serious hikers, Franz Alt met Annice, who became his second wife. The Alts used to hike 15 miles every Sunday, but now they only go about half that distance—and more slowly.

"I was wondering which would go first, music or hiking," Alt says. "It seems that music is lasting longer." But he has to practice more now than he used to because his eyesight is poor. He can't sight-read the music quickly enough, so he has to go over it in advance. With his vision dimming and the muscles in his arms not as strong as they once were, he feels that eventually he'll have to give up the viola.

"I always feel I'm accomplishing something there [in the music groups]. In Vienna, there's a long traditional of amateurs playing classical music, and I feel I'm carrying that forward. But," he says, "the real thing in retirement for me was Clergy and Laity Concerned."

Karen McAuley

Many people worry about giving up the camaraderie of work for a lonely retirement. But not Karen McAuley. She had been working at home as a freelance textbook writer, speaking to her editors mostly by e-mail and fax. Isolated for years, she looked forward to a sociable retirement.

When the publishing house that employed her was bought by a large conglomerate and ensuing upheavals robbed her of job satisfaction, McAuley stopped accepting writing assignments. Since her husband, Jim Klausen, was retiring from the school where he taught science, she decided to retire too. But she was barely 50 and really wanted to keep on working. For quite a while she flailed about, feeling dislocated and without a sense of purpose.

McAuley thought seriously about becoming a psychologist. But she'd known, before she married, that her husband hated winter and wanted to spend about half of each year in California near his son and grandchildren. She didn't see how she could earn a graduate degree and establish herself in a new profession splitting her time between two coasts. Talking with friends helped her work through the trade-offs she had to make.

What she hadn't factored in was the joy of going back and forth between New York City and the little town in southern California. McAuley was surprised to discover that the built-in change heightens her enjoyment of both settings.

McAuley and her husband spend two three-month blocks a year in California, shifting the dates each year to alternate holidays between the East and the West. In California, they live in a small house with a garden. She teaches high school pottery four hours a week, tends the garden, bikes everywhere, and takes yoga three times a week. They both screen films for the local film festival, and she writes publicity material for the festival too. She's found it can be gratifying to work on shorter-term projects without pay.

Back in New York, McAuley finds her energy level going up. She's ready to use the city. She and Klausen live in a classic Upper West Side apartment—walls of bookcases, a crystal chandelier hanging over a lace-covered dining table, glass-fronted wooden cupboards in the kitchen. We settled down to talk in a comfortable den, large enough for a computer, bookshelves, file cabinets, and a couple of chairs.

McAuley has been a potter for 25 years but intently, she says, only after she retired. "That's what retirement is, the intensive course." She had tried jewelry-making, but the torches and saws used in metalwork seemed hostile to her. She prefers the direct tactile quality of clay. Working with clay, McAuley feels alive, mesmerized, at one with her medium.

When she told me that she made little clay houses, I pictured slightly lopsided, childlike constructions. Not so. McAuley's houses have balconies, gabled roofs, arched doors and windows, chimneys, with details she sometimes copies from buildings in her neighborhood. Roofs lift off, and so does each story, to reveal spaces for storing pills, jewelry or other small objects. When the houses are assembled the parts fit perfectly, making the joints invisible. McAuley has also made lacy bowls for herself and her sisters by impressing one of their mother's handkerchiefs into thin slabs of wet clay which she then folds to form the bowl. A remembrance of their mother.

McAuley is fairly improvisational in her potting, following leads that come up and doing what feels right at the time. She likes to make gifts: little hors d'oeuvre trays to accompany hand-carved picks that she and Klausen brought home from a trip to Africa, decorative soap dishes, little nested cabbage bowls. She likes to live with a new work for a while, enjoy it, and then give it away or allow an interested friend to buy it. She saves one or two representative pieces of each stage so she has a tangible history of her work. She sometimes thinks she ought to at least pay for her workshops and classes by selling her pottery, but so far she hasn't pursued that possibility.

Having her own studio has never appealed to McAuley. She wants to work with others and see their work. And she needs a place with a lot of open studio time. When I talked with her, she was working at Supermud Pottery Studio and at Teacher's College Community Workshop, both close to her home.

How can a new potter choose a studio? Visit, McAuley says. Find out if they're interested in teaching people, both formally in classes and informally during open studio hours. Does it feel congenial? How flexible is the fee structure? What happens when you need to change your schedule? What is expected of you? (At Community Workshop the potters help run the studio.) And is the studio convenient? McAuley likes using one in her own neighborhood, close to her hairdresser, dry cleaner, and grocer.

When she's not potting McAuley sometimes edits books and manuscripts. In California, she edited *The New Yoga for People over 50*, sparring frequently with the author who ended up praising her in the published book. She also gets involved in neighborhood activities. "Last night Halloween was so much fun. We had the annual kids party in the lobby. They all paraded around in their costumes. We set up a photo-op place in a corner, with skeletons and cobwebs for background.

"I think the most important thing is to feel connected. . . . You need a sense of purpose. It's good for your immune system. The day I lose my sense of purpose, of connection, is the day I'll get sick."

Yvette Pollack

Yvette Pollack was terrified of retirement. It seemed to her that half the retirees she knew had heart attacks or cancer or even died less than a year after they stopped working. When she asked an older friend about life after retirement, the friend came back with the discouraging response that tasks she used to finish in a few minutes now stretch out to take a long time. But the special education program where Pollack worked was going to be closed down in six months, and the other positions offered didn't appeal to her. So she used the those six months to get ready for something else.

While she was looking around, she went to a storytelling workshop. After the program she talked with the leader, Arthur Strimling. He told her about Roots&Branches, the intergenerational theater program he directs for the Jewish Association for Services for the Aged, and invited her to their spring benefit. Pollack went and was so impressed she sent Strimling a fan letter, her first since 1938 when she wrote to Orson Welles praising *War of the Worlds*.

At Roots&Branches, about 10 older people work with roughly the same number of young drama students from New York University's Tisch School of Arts. In the fall of 2000 the group ranged in age from 19 to 94, with most participants under 25 or over 60. Starting in September and continuing through the school year, they write and produce a play based on the life histories of the people in the group. In weekly workshops they tell their stories, work out dramatic exercises, and improvise. Under Strimling's guidance themes begin to emerge, and by December they have a rough script. The members of the company wrestle with the script and revise it, sometimes rewriting whole sections. By February they have a play and are in rehearsal. Roots& Branches performs at senior centers in Manhattan, Brooklyn, and Westchester, and ends the year with a gala benefit performance.

R&B plays aren't sentimental or nostalgic. Strimling says audiences tend to have low expectations for the elderly, but that most people who come are surprised to find the plays entertaining and provocative.

One production dealt with a grandparent who had just discovered his grandson had AIDS. Another retold the story of Romeo and Juliet with three pairs of actors: one version featured an old couple; the second had an older Romeo with a young Juliet; and the third, a young Romeo in love with an older Juliet. The play was set on a cruise ship where the upper deck served as Juliet's balcony. As the group was developing the story, they argued about the death scene. The resolution: Molly Seif, the 85-year-old Juliet, dies in the arms of her 20-something lover. Then, as she lies on the stage floor, the other cast members step back, and out of their stage roles. One senior says: "We can't have a death here. There're too many old people around. It'll upset them." The young ones speak up in favor of including the death and the cast argues, much as they did in the preparatory workshop, until Molly sits up. "I had to wait till I was 85 to get to play Juliet. THIS IS MY DEATH SCENE AND I LOVE IT." Then she lies down and dies—again.

You don't need to act to join Roots&Branches. Strimling is emphatic. R&B needs people to work in the office, to raise money, write the newsletter, help with sets and costumes—all the support functions that make any venture go.

Yvette Pollack started by helping in the office, working after school a couple of days a week. She wanted to know the people, the work and the general setup before her regular job ended. Even knowing exactly how to get to JASA from her apartment helped smooth the transition. At first she stuffed envelopes, answered phones, and tried to master basic computer skills. And for about a year she edited the newsletter. Eventually, her success at fundraising earned her a seat on the R&B board.

About two years ago Pollack asked Arthur Strimling if she could sit in on the workshops. Then one day, in classic theater tradition, a principal actress was sick and Strimling asked Pollack to substitute. That performance hooked Pollack.

"Where's my part?" she demanded when they cast the next year's play. Since then she's always had a part. Last year's play, *Subway Series*, wasn't about baseball but about helping young and old understand each other. The setting was the subway, with the train making historical stops instead of geographical. So young and old began telling their stories.

Pollack related how she married at 17 because there was a war on. The young drama students working on *Subway Series* and intent on their careers could scarcely believe the 1940s zeitgeist that pushed women to marry at 17.

For Pollack, working in theater assuages the loneliness of having her daughters far away on the West Coast. Arthur Strimling sees theater as a way of building community, of bringing the generations together. The age spread of the R&B group is vital to Pollack. "The thought of living only with other retired people—I'd find that deadly." Her experiences with R&B bring her closer to her grandson, who is involved in college theater. They talk a lot about acting and go to each other's performances.

Is Pollack nervous on stage? "Oh, sure. But I'm in good company. Laurence Olivier was nervous before performances." Nervousness indicates commitment, she explained. If she didn't care so much, she wouldn't be nervous. She says she'll keep on acting as long as her body cooperates. She's had three operations on same hip. "It's screwed up my whole body." During the first year she acted with a cane until a friend admonished her, "For Christ's sake, you're an actress! Act as if you don't limp!" She learned how, but it only works on stage. In real life, Pollack still limps.

Part Three: The Opportunities

Here is a sampling of places where people of all ages can listen to, study, play, or sing their favorite kind of music. Places where you can act or dance, paint or sculpt, see new or classic plays. The Web sites mentioned lead to much more. Many publications list the exhibits at the major museums and the performances at Lincoln Center and Carnegie Hall, so we concentrate on the less well-known but often very exciting work and venues that may be harder to find.

Once you step into the New York art and music world, you'll find it's infinite. Bulletin boards at the studios are covered with announcements of concerts and dance performances, ads for classes and schools, invitations to join a group. Wherever you study or practice, your fellow students will tell you about other teachers, other programs, other schools.

Opportunities to Engage in Many Forms of the Arts

92nd Street Y
1395 Lexington Avenue
New York, New York 10128
(212) 415-5500
www.92ndsty.org

A multi-faceted cultural center, the 92nd Street Y offers concerts, lectures, private and ensemble instrument lessons, voice lessons, and choral groups; art appreciation and art studio courses; pottery, jewelry-making, metalwork, and other crafts; ballet, jazz, swing, and many other dance classes.

Check chapter 9, "Education," for additional Y programs.

Bronx House
990 Pelham Parkway South
Bronx, New York 10461
(718) 792-1800

The Bronx House Music School offers private and group lessons on a wide range of instruments for serious and casual students of all ages. The school is fully equipped with pianos and other instruments, as well as state-of-the-art computers, practice rooms, and an auditorium for recitals.

Bronx House also offers arts and crafts, fine arts, and chorus for seniors, as well as physical fitness and educational programs.

Club freeTime
20 Waterside Plaza, Suite 6F
New York, New York 10010
(212) 545-8900
www.clubfreetime.com

A monthly newspaper listing, by date, of a marvelous array of free films, concerts, dance and drama performances, poetry readings, lectures, seminars, and hikes. Subscribers (called "club members") can also obtain reduced-price tickets for a number of events. $24.95 for a year's subscription.

Cooper Union
The Cooper Union for the Advancement of Science and Art
Cooper Square
New York, New York 10003
(212) 353-4000
www.cooper.edu

Cooper Union offers continuing education programs in the book
arts, drawing and painting, modern dance, photography, quilting,
and sculpture. The college mounts exhibits of special interest to
New Yorkers and sponsors Graphicooper, a special free lecture series on design.

Elaine Kaufman Cultural Center
129 West 67th Street
New York, New York 10023
(212) 501-3330
www.ekcc.org

Elaine Kaufman Cultural Center includes Merkin Concert Hall and
Lucy Moses School for Music and Dance.

Merkin Concert Hall presents ensembles playing classical, jazz,
and contemporary music, sometimes with discussions and commen-
tary by the artists and composers. Tickets run $10–$25, with sav-
ings to series subscribers.

The Lucy Moses School offers private lessons, ensemble lessons,
and workshops for adult beginners and for experienced musicians
in voice, instruments, and theory. Also classes in theater, dance and
exercise, and in figure drawing, painting, and watercolor.

Fiorello H. LaGuardia Community College
31-10 Thomson Avenue, Room M-141
Long Island City, New York 11101
www.lagcc.cuny.edu

The continuing education department of LaGuardia Community College offers art and craft workshops, choral singing, introduction to music theory, ballroom and Latin dancing (cha-cha, rhumba, salsa, merengue), and many other courses in the arts.

Greenwich House
46 Barrow Street
New York, New York 10014
(212) 242-4770
www.gharts.org
gharts@gharts.org

A multi-faceted institution at several locations in Greenwich Village, Greenwich House programs include Greenwich House Arts, Greenwich House Music School, and Greenwich House Pottery. Greenwich House Arts offers education and professional presentations in music, theater, visual arts, the spoken word, and dance. Greenwich House Pottery and Greenwich House Music School also offer rich educational programs.

National Guild of Community Schools of the Arts
Post Office Box 8018
Englewood, New Jersey 07631
(201) 871-3337
www.nationalguild.org

The Web site of the National Guild of Community Schools of the Arts lists 21 non-degree-granting schools of music, dance, theater, and visual arts in New York City. The site gives basic information about the classes offered and provides links to the Web sites of the individual schools. Member schools must support the guild's principles of artistic excellence and open access and go through a process of certification.

Snug Harbor Cultural Center
1000 Richmond Terrace
Staten Island, New York 10301
(718) 448-2500
www.snug-harbor.org

The Snug Harbor Cultural Center has 29 buildings on 86 acres of land devoted to the visual and performing arts, including two art galleries, a children's museum, and classroom buildings.

Opportunities to Engage in the Visual Arts and Crafts

Art Students League of New York
215 West 57th Street
New York, New York 10019
(212) 247-4510

The list of past and present students and instructors at the Art Students League reads like a *Who's Who in American Art*. Under the League's flexible open enrollment system, students may register in any class, with any instructor (class size permitting), with no entrance requirements. The league offers five-day-a-week, three-day-a-week, and once-a-week classes in drawing, painting, watercolor, sculpture, color theory, design, and composition. See their catalog for details.

Craft Students League
YWCA-NYC
610 Lexington Avenue at 53rd Street
New York, New York 10022
(212) 755-4500

A co-ed organization, YWCA-NYC offers classes at all levels in book arts, ceramics, fiber, jewelry, metalsmithing, and other crafts. Also drawing, painting, and mixed media.

The Crafts Students League maintains one of the only open woodworking studios in Manhattan.

Crosby Painting Studio
Spring Studio for Drawing
Minerva Durham
64 Spring Street
New York, New York 10012
(212) 226-7240

Minerva Durham offers year-round 3- to 4½-hour open studio sessions with a live model seven days a week. Come when you wish and pay only for the sessions you attend. Some participants have a background in art; others don't.

The fee for the drawing studio is $10 a session, or 10 sessions for $80; for the painting studio, $15 a session, or 10 sessions for $120.

Ms. Durham starts each session with a five-minute lecture; upon request, you can have additional instruction for no extra charge.

New York Art World
www.nyaw.com

This beautiful Web site features paintings to buy organized by artist and theme, a magazine with art reviews, explanations of various art terms and a calendar of exhibitions and events in New York–area museums and galleries.

Pottery

Some of the people and places that offer bench space and classes:

Chambers Pottery
153 Chambers Street
New York, New York 10007
Call Amanda Matthews
(212) 619-7302

A fully equipped, air-conditioned studio with 13 wheels and two large kilns, Chambers Pottery offers day and evening classes at all levels. Special intensive workshops with nationally recognized ceramic artists focus on particular themes. Class tuition includes some free studio time; interested potters can also arrange for additional studio time.

Clayworks on Columbia
195 Columbia Street
Brooklyn, New York 11231
Deborah McDermott
(718) 694-9540

A fully equipped studio with four kilns and nine wheels, Clayworks on Columbia offers classes, open studio time, and long-term rentals. Mixed classes are small enough that the instructor can give appropriate direction to each person.

Pottery by Susan
8808 Rockaway Beach Boulevard
Rockaway Beach, New York 11693
(718) 634-4565

A fully equipped studio with gas and electric kilns and space available for rent to experienced potters. No classes.

Supermud Pottery Studio
2744 Broadway, Second Level
New York, New York 10025
(212) 865-9190

Supermud Pottery offers instruction in handbuilding and on the wheel, and special workshops on raku and wood-firing. Class tuition includes materials and practice time. Experienced potters may rent additional studio time and kiln space.

Also see above:
92nd Street Y
Craft Students League
Greenwich House

Quilting

New York City has at least three quilting guilds:

Empire Quilters
Park West Finance Station
Post Office Box 200673
New York, New York 10025
(212) 662-7771

Empire Quilters holds monthly meetings and biennial exhibits of members' work. Meetings usually feature a workshop and presentation by a well-known quilter, an opportunity for members to show their own work, and breakout groups devoted to specific techniques. All quilters are welcome.

Dues are $30 a year, $25 for seniors. Non-members may attend for a $5 guest fee. Meetings take place at 1 P.M., the second Saturday of every month from September to June at Fashion Institute of Technology, Dubinsky Building, 27th Street and Eighth Avenue, New York City, Sixth Floor.

Quilters' Guild of Brooklyn
Post Office Box 180414, Kensington Station
Brooklyn, New York 11218

Quilters of Color Network of New York
300 West 110th Street, Apartment 9F
New York, New York 10026-4050
(212) 932-9226
quiltersofcolor@hotmail.com

Meets the fourth Saturday of every month.

Quilt Links
www.quiltlinks.com

This commercial site offers non-commercial information for quilters, including a calendar of quilt shows and exhibitions; a list of quilting guilds with addresses and phone numbers, sorted by state; and lists of stores where quilters can purchase fabrics and supplies.

Opportunities to See and Engage in the Performing Arts

Acoustic Live in New York City
51 McDougal Street, PMB 254
New York, New York 10012
www.acousticlive.com

A newsletter listing acoustic performances in all five boroughs. Subscription is $20; copies are available free at some cafés, and listings are posted on the Web.

Amateur Chamber Music Players, Inc.
1123 Broadway, Room 304
New York, New York 10010
(212) 645-7424
www.acmp.net

Amateur Chamber Music Players offers a self-grading guide which enables members to find other musicians and groups playing at appropriate levels. Local musicians and musicians planning to visit New York City often contact the organization to find other musicians with whom to play.

ACMP suggests an annual contribution of $20 to cover printing, postage, and other expenses.

Battery Dance Company
380 Broadway, Fifth Floor
New York, New York 10013
(212) 219-3910
www.batterydanceco.com

Established in 1976 to be a cultural anchor for dance in downtown New York City, Battery Dance presents original choreography in free outdoor performances at the Annual Downtown Dance Festival at Battery Park, and at ticketed performances at John Jay Theater and Florence Gould Hall in Manhattan. The company also performs and gives master classes in various U.S. cities and at dance festivals abroad.

Broadway Dance Center
221 West 57th Street, Fifth Floor
New York, New York 10019
(212) 582-9304
www.bwydance.com

Classes in jazz, ballet, tap, and modern dance. Also flamenco, belly dancing, hip-hop, African, and Latin; yoga, stretch, aerobics, tumbling.

Brooklyn Conservatory of Music
58 Seventh Avenue
Brooklyn, New York 11217
(718) 622-3300
and
42-76 Main Street
Flushing, New York 11355
(718) 461-8910
www.brooklynconservatory.com

Adults can take private lessons in voice and in most orchestral and jazz instruments, and may select from a full range of group classes in subjects such as music theory, sight singing, and performance. Adult students may also sing in the conservatory's adult chorus, which performs frequently throughout the year.

Dances Patrelle
Post Office Box 6802
New York, New York 10128
(212) 722-7933
www.dancespatrelle.org

Another of New York City's many small dance companies, Dances Patrelle offers programs that feature original choreography by Francis Patrelle as well as the work of other choreographers. Performances take place at the Theater of the Riverside Church and other Manhattan venues. A highlight of the year is the annual *Yorkville Nutcracker.*

Greenwich House Music School
46 Barrow Street
New York, New York 10014
(212) 242-4770

Since 1905, Greenwich House Music School has offered private lessons, group classes, ensembles, and regular student and faculty recitals for students from 2 to 82. Programs for adults include classical chamber music, theory, piano performance workshop, jazz vocal workshop, flute performance workshop, and others.

HB Playwrights Foundation and Theatre
124 Bank Street
New York, New York 10014

The HB was founded to be a theater where playwrights, actors, directors, and designers could work free of commercial pressures. Many important figures in New York City theater have trained here, and productions are consistently interesting. Admission to performances is usually free, but reservations are required.

Juilliard School of Music
60 Lincoln Center Plaza
New York, New York 10023
(212) 799-5000

One of the most highly regarded music schools in the United States, Julliard draws and trains the musical stars of tomorrow. The school offers free concerts continually. To get a calendar, mail your request, with a self-addressed stamped envelope, to the *Juilliard Concert Office* at the address above. Tickets are usually available about two weeks before the performance.

Miller Theatre
Columbia University School of the Arts
2960 Broadway (at 116th Street)
Mail Code 1801
New York, New York 10027
(212) 854-7799
www.millertheatre.com

Miller Theatre's offerings range from the gogmagogs—"seven outstanding young string players that combine virtuosic string playing with dynamic physical movement and inventive theatre"—to three concerts presenting the complete works of Tudor master Robert Parsons (c. 1530–1572). Much of Parsons's music has not been heard for centuries. As part of the project, the scores will be available free over the Web.

Programs at Miller Theatre are often accompanied by lectures and pre-concert discussions. Some programs are free; single admission tickets generally run between $10 and $25; subscriptions often yield a discount.

New Choreographers on Point
355 East 72nd Street #3G
New York, New York 10021
(212) 861-9619

At NCOP's annual Ballet Builders program, New Yorkers can see dances of new choreographers from all over the country. (Read more about this group in the profile of Ruth Chester, the co-founder, in chapter 8, "Volunteering.")

New York Choral Society
Summer Sings
CAMI Hall
165 West 57th Street
New York, New York 10019
(212) 247-3878
www.nychoral.org

The New York Choral Society runs 14 open singing sessions every summer, led by local conductors and music directors. You show up at the door; NYCS provides scores, refreshments, air-conditioning, and accompanist. Come once or as often as you like. Nine dollars per session; $40 for 5 tickets; $65 for 10.

New York South Folk Dance
www.folkdancing.org

This Web site lists opportunities to take part in American, English, and Scottish country dancing, Balkan dance, Israeli folk dancing, Western square dancing, and many other forms of folk dance. (I found the Web site somewhat difficult to use, but if you select New York South from the "Folk Dance Directory" menu on the left side of the page and scroll down, you'll find Brooklyn, Manhattan, Queens, and Staten Island; nothing for the Bronx. Click to learn about the groups near you: the kind of dancing they do, when and where they meet, and whom to contact.)

New York Swing Dance Society
Savoy Sunday at Irving Plaza
17 Irving Place at 15th Street
(212) 696-9737

Dance to live swing bands every Sunday from 8 P.M. to midnight. Free lessons from 7 to 8 P.M. the first Sunday of every month. General admission $13. Senior citizens $5. New York Swing Dance Society members $9. Membership $35 per year.

New York University Tisch School of the Arts
Graduate Acting Program
721 Broadway
New York, New York 10003
(212) 998-1820
www.nyu.edu/tisch

The Tisch School presents the plays of some of the country's best-known playwrights. For example: in one recent month the school presented *The Hostage* by Brendan Behan and *Seven Guitars* by August Wilson. Tickets for productions featuring third-year acting students are five dollars for seniors; productions by second-year students are free. Call to get on their mailing list, or check the Web site for a calendar of Tisch school exhibitions and programs in dance and music, as well as drama.

Off Broadway Online
www.offbroadwayonline.com

A Web site providing information about more than 150 different off-Broadway theaters in New York. You can search for a play you'd like by neighborhood and by more than 20 different performance categories. When you enter your category and location preferences, you see what plays are currently in production. Off Broadway Online links to other sites where you can read reviews, learn about plays on Broadway and nationwide, and sign up for individual theater mailing lists.

Off Wall Street Jam
47 Murray Street
New York, New York 10007
(212) 233-4380
www.owsj.com

Off Wall Street Jam is a membership organization through which recreational musicians can meet, get into bands, and perform in many showcases. The group sponsors daily events on a drop-in basis, open jams by genre (blues, rock, jazz), workshops, and seminars. For your special project, OWSJ will provide the other musicians, the space to meet and rehearse, and all of the instruments required for both practice sessions and live performances. Dues are $270.62 for the first year; $162.38 per year renewal.

Roots&Branches
Jewish Association for Services for the Aged (JASA)
132 West 31st Street
New York, New York 10001
(212) 273-5200

An intergenerational theater program that writes and produces original plays using senior actors and actors from the New York University Tisch Graduate Acting Program. Roots&Branches offers seniors opportunities to write, act, and work behind the scenes. Call Arthur Strimling at JASA for details.

Theater Development Fund (TDF)
1501 Broadway, 21st Floor
New York, New York 10036
(212) 221-0013
www.tdf.org

TDF is best-known for its TKTS booths in Times Square, where reduced-price tickets for Broadway shows can be bought on the day of the performance. TDF also runs a membership program that allows retirees to buy theater tickets at reduced prices. The biggest hits are seldom available at the reduced rates, but members say they have seen many new and interesting performances through TDF. In 2001 tickets ran $24 for a musical, $20 for a play. Call or check the Web site for membership information.

TDF also operates a voucher program. Members can buy four vouchers for $28 and use them to see off-off-Broadway plays, experimental theater, and other out-of-the-way productions. The office reminds us that voucher performances may be held in inconvenient locations or at sites with difficult access. Broadway shows are not offered through the voucher program.

Members learn about available performances through the TDF newsletter, the Web site, or by dialing 212-768-1818.

Vocal Area Network
www.van.org

This excellent Web site lists choral groups in the New York area. It tells the size of each group, the kind of music sung, admission requirements and audition schedules, location, meetings and performance schedules, and much more.

CHAPTER **EIGHT**

Volunteering

Part One: The Scene

"New York City runs on volunteers," Nancy Kigner says. A retired school teacher from Smithtown, Kigner takes the Long Island Rail Road into Manhattan to work at Lincoln Center and at the Jewish Board of Family and Children's Services. She's looking for an apartment in the city so she can live closer to what really interests her.

New York City is the largest not-for-profit center in the world. Because New York is the center of finance, the large foundations that sponsor not-for-profit organizations are here. And, because the large foundations are here, most national nonprofits have their headquarters here as well. This nexus of Wall Street, charitable foundations, and not-for-profit organizations makes New York particularly fertile for volunteer opportunities.

Major cultural institutions, important health and social service organizations, and a multitude of small theater and dance, community, religious, and environmental groups struggle or flourish in New York, with volunteers often shifting the balance from struggle to flourish. In this arena, retirees can choose almost any field, at almost any level, according to their own talents and interests.

Retired New Yorkers are tapping into volunteer opportunities so they can enlarge their own lives while helping others. Some retirees use the skills they've honed over decades. Others plunge or tiptoe into brand-new challenges. Some like to work on a regular schedule. Others hate routine and prefer project-based efforts. Some seek artistic, intellectual, or athletic development; others search for new friends. Volunteers can come to know all kinds of people they've never met before by working together toward a shared goal. Often, they gain a new sense of purpose from serving so generously.

Sam Pryor, a retired senior partner from one of New York City's major law firms, serves as a commissioner of the Palisades Park Commission, as chairman of the Westchester Land Trust, and as a board member of the National Forest Foundation and the Appalachian Mountain Club. "Working for these organizations is fun," says Pryor. "I travel up and down the Hudson River talking with local mayors and government officials about restoring their waterfronts, and I call on legislators in Albany and Washington to convince them of my views."

Pryor's legal expertise equips him for lobbying. He knows how to develop an argument, draft legislation, and testify in detail about issues. "It's not a big jump from practicing law." But Pryor *was* surprised to find his new work in retirement more creative than his law practice had been. "As a lawyer, you're working for your client," he explains. "Now I help make policy. No one ever asked me to make policy before; I just followed orders. I like this. That's why I keep going."

Retirees aren't the only volunteers. Young people starting their careers in New York work to clean up the Hudson River. Baby boomers with children tutor in elementary schools and raise funds or pull weeds to restore playgrounds and parks. Corporations encourage their employees to contribute to community life. So retirees volunteering at Beth Israel Hospital or Carnegie Hall meet coworkers of all ages. When Nancy Kigner was teaching school, she met only other teachers. Now she meets social workers at Family and Children's Services and retired dancers, symphony players, and editors at Lincoln Center.

Volunteering for a Large Organization

Volunteering at the American Museum of Natural History, the Museum of Modern Art, New York Philharmonic Orchestra, or Mount Sinai Hospital brings you into a world-class institution that expects high performance. Typically these institutions employ professional directors of volunteer service.

Jane Lattes, former director of volunteer services at the American Museum of Natural History, was delighted with the talented volunteers there. About half work with the public—covering the information desks, teaching schoolchildren, leading tours. A regular, mandatory training program keeps them abreast of new exhibits.

Other volunteers work behind the scenes: on *Natural History* magazine or in accounting or development, but most often in the science departments. The museum's 32 million specimens and artifacts are used by scholars worldwide. Individual scientists train volunteers to clean, repair, and catalog specimens. Some projects call for writing tiny numbers in pen and ink on fossil bones. Volunteers who want scientific work but lack the skill or desire to handle specimens can help with data entry or cataloging. Over time, as the scientist comes to appreciate the volunteer's capabilities, the job may develop into a high-level collaboration.

Most jobs require a résumé and two interviews. The museum needs specific skills, like the ability to work with young children or fluency in a foreign language. When Lattes considered an applicant, she looked at the volunteer's available time, the background to match a job that was open, and the willingness to promise half a day a week for a year. Tour guides have to commit for three years because the museum's investment in training is so high.

Like Jane Lattes, the director of volunteers at New York

City Ballet, Joan Quatrano, stresses the importance of the work and the seriousness of the commitment to the organization. Volunteering for City Ballet, she says, is as serious as a well-paid job—but with far fewer hours.

New York City Ballet has 350 to 400 volunteers ranging in age from 17 to 90. Most have full-time jobs. Quatrano knows them all and what each one does. They participate because they love ballet, and they love City Ballet in particular. Many have rich backgrounds in ballet. Quatrano doesn't evaluate people in terms of age; she thinks about their skills and personalities. Sometimes she screens for physical ability. Gift shop staff, for example, must stand for a long time on marble floors.

Quatrano's 15 committees include newsletter, seminars, and multi-cultural audience development. At the beginning of each season she circulates a schedule of needs, and volunteers sign up for the duties and times they prefer. Each activity has its own requirements and a different schedule. Some committees operate year-round, some only during the performance season or on holidays.

I first became acquainted with the volunteer program at City Ballet when I came to watch a rehearsal. A volunteer rehearsal guide told our group about the music, the choreography, the dancers, and the stories of the ballets we were to see rehearsed that afternoon.

Docents (teachers or lecturers) write and give pre-performance talks. After a 10-week preparatory course, two hours a week, they have to demonstrate that they can put a talk together. Docents and rehearsal guides do their own research, so

Quatrano needs people on her roster with a basic knowledge of ballet and reference books at home. Rehearsal guides don't know until the morning of that day which ballets will be rehearsed. They get a call in the morning and have to prepare their talk by afternoon.

Not all volunteer jobs at City Ballet require that level of expertise. For example, Rose Building reception committee members help staff and dancers and screen visitors to Rose Building studios. Ticket donations people receive donations of tickets over the telephone and sell the donated tickets in the lobby before performances.

Except for one ticket to the opening gala performance and a rare box-office donation, volunteers do not receive tickets or other tangible rewards. They do get acceptance as a member of the New York City Ballet community, in which their work is valued and appreciated. They work near the rehearsal halls and watch the dancers come and go. One volunteer was thrilled to ride in the tiny staff elevator with Peter Martins (ballet master in chief), Darci Kistler (principal ballerina), and their two large dogs. Once a year volunteers are invited to a party on the promenade. Dancers come. Peter Martins comes. And, once a year, the names of all the volunteers are listed in the Stagebill program.

Twelve years ago, New York City Ballet did an audience survey. The plan called for one thousand 45-minute telephone interviews. Although professional interviewers would have raised the cost unacceptably, the questionnaire developers thought volunteers could never do the job. Quatrano thought they could. They did. Quatrano says this job put volunteer services on the map.

Most people volunteer for an organization whose purposes they support. So if you care a lot about ballet or teaching kids to read, about planting community gardens or housing the homeless—how do you approach the organization of your choice and work out a plan of action?

Verdalee Tombelaine, longtime volunteer at the Metropolitan Museum of Art and the New York Horticultural Society, and former co-chair of Volunteer Program Administrators (an umbrella organization of directors of volunteer programs from New York City cultural institutions) talks about choosing a place to volunteer. Join the organization, says Tombelaine. Participate in activities open to the public. Hospitals often have health outreach programs, especially for older people. If you're new in town, helping out at a park clean-up or church supper is a good place to begin. By taking part, you come to know the institution, the work done there, and the kind of people who do it.

When you find an organization you like, call the office. Tell them you're interested in volunteering and ask about their program. Ask for an appointment or an application. The application usually asks when you would be available and how much time you are prepared to commit, as well as your skills and experience. It's not a good idea, Tombelaine emphasizes, to say you're available for any job at any time. The director may conclude you're unfocused or depressed and won't do much of anything. Be flexible, but say what you can do, what you want to do, and how much time you're willing to work. "Work" is the operative word for volunteers.

Treat your interview like a job interview. Prepare for it. Look up the organization on the Web. Read any available printed material. Check out its mission statement and be sure you support it. Know the kind of job you want and how it serves the purposes of the organization. Be ready to talk about your own qualifications and how you can contribute.

And, while you're there, look around. Get a sense of the place to see if you can identify with the people who are there. Do you like the way they're dressed? Maybe you'd fit in with people who wear jeans and sit on the floor. Maybe you'd feel more comfortable in a group where men wear ties and women, stockings and pearls. More important than style: do people treat each other with respect?

Find out the days and times you are to come in and how long you're expected to work. To whom will you report? Where will you work? On a card table in the controller's office? With other volunteers around a big table? On your feet in an exhibit hall? Get a precise description of the job. If you're working at the opera gift shop, will you arrange the merchandise display? Handle cash and credit cards? Tally the items sold and inventory those remaining in stock? Clear answers to these questions will tell you that your interviewer has thought through your job and will use your time effectively.

Your first job may be routine, Tombelaine says, but once you're in an organization, you learn what else might be available. If you wish, you can ask for a transfer. Imagination and flexibility on the part of both the volunteer and the staff can lead to creative partnerships: a doctor working at the information desk at the Metropolitan Museum of Art helped develop a program to X-ray mummies in the museum's Egyptian collection.

James Klausen, a former high school science teacher, wasn't doing much in retirement. His wife told him he was too young to spend his time sitting around waiting for the mail. Once he hooked up with the American Museum of Natural History, that problem was over. Klausen didn't want to teach any more, so being a docent or tour guide was out. But he was thrilled to work for the paleontologists, making casts so the museum can share fossils with other museums. The machine he used to put a clay matrix into the fossils by centrifugal force didn't work well. "Are you willing to invest $75 in parts so I can fix this?" he asked. Yes, they said. And he did.

Some retired professional and business people are frustrated by volunteer work. They find themselves operating at a slower pace or on a lower level than they're used to; they see opportunities for change and lack the authority to implement those changes. On the other hand, volunteer directors say that some volunteers who held high-level positions in the for-profit world come in with a patronizing attitude toward nonprofit organizations. It is important, these directors say, to approach volunteer work with a collegial attitude—and to remember that the paid staff of a nonprofit organization pitches in on routine tasks when needed. They and the volunteers are members of the same team.

Dottie Brier, who leads the Red Cross disaster mental health program in New York says that, any time a new group of volunteers starts, there's an initial phase in which the really good volunteers stand out and eventually get recognized and promoted. So patience may go a long way. Other dissatisfied volunteers have found it useful to speak with the director of volunteer services to try to work out a more suitable assignment. Or, if the first organization for which you volunteer isn't satisfying, you may be better off somewhere else. When you can pinpoint the reasons for your dissatisfaction, you'll know what to look for the second time around.

Volunteering for a Small Organization

Personalities differ. Not everyone prefers a major organization with a structured volunteer program. Some people like smaller groups. Robert Dorf explains why.

"It's true that big organizations with paid volunteer directors have a lot to offer," says Dorf, "but from the point of view of the volunteer, you might as well be working for IBM."

Dorf, managing director of Dances Patrelle, tells me that volunteers for small groups are closer to the artists and can have a more of an impact on the organization. Dances Patrelle, a small company with nine core dancers, can't afford a paid director of volunteers. What Dorf would like is a volunteer director of volunteers!

Small groups like Dances Patrelle need the same skills New York City Ballet and the Metropolitan Opera need to survive and be stable. Dorf could use a retired marketer to create a professional marketing plan that Dorf could present to his board.

"A retired graphic designer did our logo and our *Nutcracker* publicity. I'd like to talk with an advertising person about where we're placing our ads, whom we want to attract, what kinds of ads would be most effective. I could use a computing expert to manage my mailing list, an accountant to set up a better accounting system, an attorney who knows theater law and nonprofit law." Dances Patrelle has a part-time costume designer. Dorf could use a volunteer wardrobe mistress during performance season to mend and alter costumes and take care of costume emergencies.

New volunteers should think about their own transferable skills: nonprofits need management theory, cash flow, and other business skills from the profit world. Dorf believes the not-for-profit sector is moving toward a more professional mode of operation. He expects to see increasing opportunities for retired professionals to work at a high level of expertise for small groups like Dances Patrelle.

Holly Butler writes grant proposals for the Actors Company Theatre (TACT), one of New York's small, nonprofit repertory groups. She started by volunteering to do whatever office work they needed—mail, computing, writing. When the director saw that she could write well he sent her to a one-day course at the New School in writing grant proposals. Her proposals garnered grant money, and Butler ended up serving on the board. Even so, every summer she still works with the entire company to get out the mailings for the new season.

"A lot of people think they're above all that," Butler says. "But it's what this theater's about. Everybody working together. After the shows, actors mingle with the audience; on performance nights, actors not performing will usher."

Butler thinks anyone with the requisite skills could do what she has done but points out that you have to put yourself forward. You have to tell people you want to work and tell them what you do best.

On her final day of teaching school, Grace Polk swallowed the last bite of her retirement party cake and rode the subway directly to the WNYC radio station where she began taking phone pledges for their fund drive. Wanting to be certain of 40 hours of volunteer activity a week before she left teaching, Polk had gone to RSVP (Retired and Senior Volunteer Program) to learn what opportunities were available and sign up for one that suited her.

Creating Your Own Volunteer Opportunities

Some retirees eschew organizations altogether and create their own programs or find people who need the kind of help they can provide. Some retirees create new organizations to take care of problems they see in front of them. When Jack and Jeanlee Poggi retired and moved from Long Island to Washington Heights in Manhattan, Jeanlee met with five other people who were starting a garden group to clean up the barren, trash-filled parks in the neighborhood. The group of six has grown to more than one hundred, the restored parks have won prizes, and the West 181st Street Beautification Project has branched out to offer art, music, and a youth leadership program to the immigrant children who live nearby. The aim is to give these children the kinds of enrichment middle-class parents regularly give their children.

Now more than one hundred children volunteer in the parks and some earn money working there. After September 11, Poggi led an effort to help the neighborhood children deal with the feelings and fears evoked by the attack. Under her direction, the children organized the September 11 Unity Project to earn money for relief and to encourage the diverse ethnic groups in the neighborhood to live together peacefully. They selected a photograph of a mural they'd painted in the park the summer before and made posters and postcards to distribute and display in nearby shop windows. The mural shows a street scene with a Sikh man, a Latino family, an African-American child, a Muslim woman, and a white woman pushing a baby carriage—all at ease in the neighborhood.

Poggi, a college writing teacher and learning disability specialist had never worked in groups or taken political action. She now meets regularly with city council members and other politicians to elicit support for the West 181st Street Beautification Project. As her organization grew, she learned to handle fundraising and incorporation, to lobby for support. She's surprised to be able to do these things. The group is egalitarian, without officers, but, because most members have full-

time jobs, Poggi works about 30 hours a week and calls herself a "volunteer CEO." In October 2001, Jeanlee Poggi was
one of 29 nominees for a Brooke Russell Astor Award recog-
nizing "unsung heroes who have substantially contributed to
improving the quality of life in New York City."[10] A month
later she was named Partner of the Month by New York City
Parks Department and Partnership for Parks.

---

10 New York Public Library press release, October 24, 2001.

Part Two: The People

Creating Your Own Volunteer Program

Jeanne Turner

"After 30 years in social work, I'd had enough. I was ready for a new life in show business."

We're in Jeanne Turner's warm, colorful apartment in an historic district in Harlem. Caribbean carvings and pottery cover the tables and sit in front of the books on the shelves that line her walls. An attractive woman in her 70s wearing flowing red pants and a white smock top, Turner smiles easily. Her relaxed manner belies the dynamo she is. Jeanne Turner was once introduced on *The Cosby Show* as the "Queen of Harlem." As we talked, I came to see why.

Turner grew up in Barbados, moved to New York City after college in Kansas, earned her Master of Social Work in her 30s, and worked at several hospitals, mostly in the Bronx.

How did she get started in show business? In the early 1980s her younger son was playing in a neighborhood band. The boys practiced in her apartment and hoped to get a record contract. Turner told them they'd better learn something about the music business. Then she saw an ad for a seminar, The Business of Show Business, right in Harlem and advised the boys to go. Being teenagers, they didn't. But she did.

At the seminar she met Johnny Johnson, a ballad singer, who asked her advice about a young singer, new to the city, who needed help. As homesick as she was talented, the young woman was phoning her mother every day to talk for hours. Turner took her on—and became a manager.

She took singers on gigs, promoted their records, counseled and advised them. "Young people in singing, dancing, modeling, they all need help," Turner says. "They're very talented but they're often overwhelmed when they come to New York. I use the same skills I used with patients at the hospital."

Later, Johnson introduced Turner to the "Judy Garland of Japan"—Mariko Miyagi, a singer, dancer, and actress who had come to Harlem to make a film with Harlem children dancing and singing. But Miyagi knew practically nothing about Harlem, and what she did know was sorely out of date. Turner offered to pull together current material for her and, as the two women talked, they grew close.

When it was time for the children to go Japan with Miyagi for the filming, Turner arranged for their passports and immunizations, their permission to leave school, and a teacher to accompany them. Turner went along, overseeing the children during travel and filming. Mariko Miyagi invited Turner and all the children to private homes, shrines, and tea ceremonies—giving them an inside exposure to Japan that tourists seldom get.

Jeanne Turner has taken on a second post-retirement career. She's promoting Bessie Nickens, a 93-year-old self-taught black artist who, after running a dry-cleaning shop in Los Angeles for years, moved to New York to live with her daughter (a friend of Turner's) and began to paint every day.

An editor for Rizzoli Books saw Nickens's work and later

created *Walking the Log*, a book of stories illustrated with Nickens's paintings. Rizzoli hired a publicist but only for six months. Then Turner took over. She arranged shows and found buyers for Nickens's work. She persuaded the Smithsonian to feature Nickens's paintings in their exhibit at the 1996 Olympic Games in Atlanta.

Turner works for Miyagi, for Nickens, and for the young singers and dancers without pay. She feels amply rewarded by meeting so many interesting people, by going to Japan, to the Olympics, and to other places, and by her relationships with her clients. But she did invest her own money in an edition of 50 prints of Nickens's oil painting *Mama Quilting*, and she takes a commission on the prints she sells.

Turner has always talked to people; wherever she is, she gets involved. When her building went bankrupt in 1979, she organized the tenants and led the effort to buy it. She went to seminars on building management, was elected the building's first president, and has served on its board ever since.

It was only after she retired that Turner discovered that she is an idea person. That she can think of solutions to problems and put together complex programs to achieve a desired purpose. It seems that only after she was freed from meeting a job description did her talents fully emerge.

Ruth Chester

Dancers wearing heavy socks over their toe shoes warm up on stage while the audience gathers for Ballet Builders 2000.

Ruth Chester stands in the lobby of Florence Gould Hall, leaning forward slightly to welcome each guest personally. Chester is graceful in a black pantsuit; her dark hair falls in a perfect pageboy. With her warm smile and animated voice she projects the promise of the evening: experimental dances expertly performed.

"If you had told me 15 years ago what I'd be doing today, I'd have said it was a fantasy."

In 1989 Chester was ready for a career change. She left her Madison Avenue job and enrolled in a grant-writing course. Over coffee on the first day of class she met Mike Kraus, a choreographer also taking the course. He told her about the shortage of places in the city where ballet choreographers could show new work. Ballet dancers need special floors for their toe work, so ballet companies can't easily share studio space with jazz and modern dance groups.

When the course instructor asked the students to write a proposal for a grant, Chester wrote one asking for funds to show new ballets. From that chance meeting over coffee and that classroom exercise more than 10 years ago, New Choreographers on Point was born. Ruth Chester and Mike Kraus have been partners ever since. Chester is the managing director, Kraus, the artistic director. In their annual spring program, New Choreographers on Point gives emerging ballet choreographers an opportunity to present their work.

After the course was over, Chester shopped her proposal around and received small grants from a variety of sources. She and Kraus worked in a non-air-conditioned church basement in the East Village—a world away from corporate Madison Avenue. A dog named Lucy sat on Chester's lap while she worked.

How did Chester learn what she needed to know? Mainly by asking questions . . . listening carefully . . . and thinking hard. In that first year she and Kraus talked with dancers, arts managers, fundraisers—with everyone they could. New York is full of people experienced in all phases of arts presentation and management, and she found the experts generous with their knowledge. After each meeting, Chester and Kraus asked themselves, "Is that a good thing to do? Or is it not?"

Chester says asking for money was the hardest task of all—especially asking friends. Large foundations seldom back small groups, so Chester had no choice but to start by approaching people she already knew. She found she could ask for money and still remain friends with the people she solicited—whether they gave or not. Many gave; some did not. She also discovered that her donors weren't necessarily interested in dance; some contribute because they like to see people doing what they want to do. "When I told people I'd gone to school with years ago what I was doing, some of them just said, 'Wow!' And they'd write a check." When strangers began to send in checks, Chester was thrilled. She realized that word of her enterprise was getting around. Today New Choreographers gets private contributions, money from the city, and grants from Harkness Foundation for Dance.

Work for the group's April Ballet Builders program begins with auditions in October. Choreographers try out for slots in the Ballet Builders program and are judged by a panel of ballet and dance professionals. Chester learned how to put together professional auditions with the help of a former head of the dance department at the Juilliard School. By January, Chester is printing flyers, raising funds, and reminding fans to save the date. New Choreographers on Point also runs summer workshops where choreographers show works-in-progress and get feedback from one another. At the end of the workshop they put on an informal show and get audience feedback too.

At 64, Ruth Chester exudes confidence and verve and feels deep satisfaction from contributing to the development of ballet. She doesn't take a salary. "They couldn't pay me what I'm worth," she says.

"We make our own mistakes. My partner and I know when we do something wrong. I learned a lot about me. When you do something different from what you've done before, you learn about yourself. It's a lot of work—almost a full-time job. It's not like going somewhere for an afternoon and then going home. I think about this all the time."

Volunteering for a Large Organization

Hiroshi Inui

Hiroshi Inui is retired president and chief executive officer of Kubota Corporation, one of Japan's largest manufacturers of industrial machinery. He now works as a volunteer for New York City Ballet. Inui and his wife came to New York for

Kubota in 1983. Heading the company from its New York office, Inui worked here until he retired 10 years later. The Inuis enjoyed the cultural life of New York City so much they decided to stay.

Inui's thick gray hair and square face give him a sturdy look. When I met him, he was casually elegant in tailored slacks and a velour shirt with thin, subtle stripes. He speaks English well but with a faint hesitation.

After retirement he didn't want to do anything related to his business. But "you have to do something. You cannot just sit and watch TV." He used the first year or so of his retirement to "organize things"; then he learned that New York City Ballet was looking for Japanese volunteers. Inui, who has paid attention to ballet ever since he saw *The Red Shoes* as a boy, applied and was accepted. A few years later he and his wife moved to the West Side so he could walk to Lincoln Center.

Every Wednesday Inui works in the ballet office, stuffing envelopes, making coffee, whatever is needed. On performance nights he works in the information booths on the promenade, answering questions and talking with audience members, sometimes in Japanese, sometimes in English. Other nights, he sets out cookies and wine and talks with the patrons in the Green Room, a salon where donors mingle during intermissions. He speaks fondly of the people there, especially the children.

During performance season Inui works in the information booth twice a month and in the Green Room twice a month.

He enjoys the variety of people he meets in this theater. He and his wife want to stay in New York indefinitely: "As far as my health would permit me."

How does he feel about his shift from running a major corporation to stuffing envelopes and pouring wine—surely not work done by chief executive officers in Japan? "When I was in the company, everyone helped me. If I wrote a letter, others mailed it. If I wanted tea, others brought it. Now I do all those things for others. It's very comfortable. If you just stay home, it's lonely and boring."

In Japan, he says, people are more separated by age. "In New York, many people of all ages are enjoying to see the ballet—opera too. Young people here will talk with elderly people very frankly, but not in Japan. They just answer 'yes' or 'no.' Even on the street here, people enter into conversation. If I see someone who hurt himself, I can say, 'How did you hurt yourself?' They might answer, 'I fell while skiing.' Then I can say, 'Where do you ski?' and a conversation develops."

He believes that Americans lead more interesting lives in retirement than Japanese. In Japan retired men are more likely to stay home and watch TV. People here "know how to live after retirement. You have to do something to feed your curiosity. Fortunately in New York you have many opportunities. I really feel that in New York everyone is having the same opportunity.

"When I worked for my business everything was about business. Now I learn about artistic things." About the orchestra, for example. Inui noticed that the conductor often watches the dancers, and he wants to know more about that. What is the conductor looking for? So Inui watches, reads, and learns more.

Dottie Brier

Dottie Brier was relaxing at a spa in the Berkshires when she heard that that the World Trade Center had been destroyed. As volunteer chair of New York Red Cross Disaster Mental Health Services, she called Red Cross immediately. Then Brier learned that her own young cousin Lisa had been on hijacked Flight 11 out of Boston.

When Brier retired from hospital social work, she chose disaster relief partly as a way to escape the constraints of managed care for fresh career challenges. The Red Cross sent her to Florida after hurricane Andrew, to Oklahoma City after the bombing of the federal building there, and to Iowa and Missouri when the Mississippi River flooded. She served at the World Trade Center after the first terrorist bomb hit. Now, with the pain of her cousin's death still raw, Brier tackled her longest, most complex assignment ever.

Before September 11, Red Cross had about 170 mental health volunteers in New York. After the attack, more than two thousand volunteers from all over the country showed up at Red Cross headquarters. Brier says just about everyone she had met at the earlier disasters came to New York to help. So did many unqualified people. Brier had the thankless job of screening the two thousand volunteers and turning away those not licensed in mental health or social work. There was lots of confusion and lots of pressure at headquarters, she said, and, as she interviewed, evaluated, and rejected or assigned the volunteers, she constantly had to solve problems, mediate conflicts, and soothe ruffled tempers.

Many of the volunteers who did have their professional licenses had not worked for Red Cross before, so Brier organized and taught a short Red Cross training course to qualify more than six hundred new mental health volunteers. Over the next few months, Brier trained and supervised hundreds of caseworkers who provided mental health services to the thousands whose lives had been shattered so suddenly. Red Cross case workers talked to the families of those who had been killed or injured. They talked to children who had to leave their schools; to people who had to evacuate damaged homes; to people traumatized by seeing men and women falling from the Trade Center windows; to many who lost their coworkers, their jobs, and their businesses. Disaster counseling is extremely demanding, and mental health workers burn out quickly. Brier visited the mental health sites regularly to answer questions, and to counsel and support the caseworkers on the front lines.

The year before, Dottie Brier went to New Mexico after the wildfires had swept across that state. On her first day she joined a nurse and a caseworker to make up an outreach team. The three women put on white and tan Red Cross vests with "Disaster Services" lettered across the back and set off in a car to look for people who had fled their homes. They drove from town to town asking fire marshals and chiefs of police to help them locate evacuees. They scoured burnt sections of the county, leaving notes on fire-damaged buildings to let people know they were available. They checked churches, hospitals, and mental health centers for people needing help. The case-worker arranged for money to tide fire victims over and the nurse saw to it that they had medical care and medications. Brier talked with people to evaluate their mental and emo-tional health. She met a couple in their 60s whose home had burned down. They had lost their clothing, their furniture, their photos, and all the mementos of their life together when their home was destroyed. A six-year-old boy told her how he and his family "got in the car when we saw the big fires com-ing," but he was afraid that his pet horse had been caught in the flames. When the boy found out his horse was safe, he was okay.

Back in Santa Fe three days later, Brier visited the Red Cross Family Service Centers (where clients go for financial and medical help) to see how the centers were doing and if they needed mental health services also. Then, at Los Alamos, she worked with other mental health workers and with Red Cross staff to integrate family services with mental health services and to make sure the staff was deployed well.

Between disasters Brier's work with the Red Cross is a little calmer. She helps develop their disaster mental health pro-gram, organizes their database, and handles day-to-day ad-ministrative chores, doing much of the work on her home computer. She teaches a two-day disaster mental health course to groups all over the country. Brier points out that while volunteers for Red Cross mental health work must be professionally licensed, many other Red Cross volunteer jobs do not require licensure: work with computers, management, and office work—some of it quite sophisticated.

Dottie Brier was 61 when she retired from her longtime position as assistant director of social work at Lenox Hill Hospital in Manhattan. While she still wanted to spend some time in her profession, she also wanted a fresh challenge. After a year as a guide at the Central Park Zoo, she sent her résumé to the American Museum of Natural History. "A museum keeps changing its exhibits, but the zoo doesn't change much," she said. She welcomed the in-depth training at the museum. "Learning to be a guide at the American Museum of Natural History is almost like getting a masters' degree in natural history. Free."

The classes and the exams were demanding. And knowing the material is not enough, Brier says. You need to talk easily to the many different people who visit the museum. Social work helped her, but Brier feels that any intelligent, friendly person who is willing to learn can pass the guide course.

I join her tour of the museum's new Rose Center for Earth and Space. About 15 minutes before the tour begins, we go to the main rotunda of the museum so she can drum up business. Brier is wearing a big blue tour guide badge on a neck ribbon and carrying an orange pennant on a long rod (so she can be spotted in a crowd), She walks up to people in the ticket line, inviting them to join her tour. They ask questions. Some join, some prefer to see another hall or walk around on their own. Our group includes a family from Honolulu and a widow from New Jersey coming to New York alone for the first time.

Brier leads us into the Rose Center. Standing with her back to the large central globe so the group can look at it, and projecting her voice against the cacophony of the crowd, she talks about the relative sizes of the solar system, the galaxies, and the observable universe. She takes us into the Big Bang show and along the Cosmic Walk.

Brier gives one or two tours a week, each one an hour or a little longer. She spends the same amount of time preparing, especially when a new hall or exhibit opens. Her talks vary according to the displays and the questions the visitors ask, and she changes them to keep herself fresh. Sometimes the museum asks her to lead special tours for distinguished guests. She spends another day or two a week on Red Cross work and is careful to save time to work out at her local Y, eat lunch with friends, go to the theater and the ballet, and travel. But when the Red Cross sends her to a disaster, everything else is set aside.

Brier recommends volunteering at places with developed volunteer programs and defined jobs. "The people there will know how to use your time and skills effectively. If an organization has a paid director of volunteers, you know it's committed to volunteers and will value your work."

Volunteer work spins off rewards that Brier had not anticipated: She can treat her out-of-town guests to a personal, insider's tour of the museum—an experience they couldn't buy that costs her nothing. She enjoys inexpensive lunches in the employee cafeteria, insider tours at other New York City museums, free admission and gift shop discounts at museums all over the world, and reduced rates on the museum's Discovery Tours abroad. She's made new friends and gone to parties the museum gives for its volunteers.

When Brier's aunt asked her to visit Ground Zero to "say goodbye to Lisa," Brier chose to go on Yom Kippur, the most solemn Jewish holiday of the year and the one where Jews traditionally visit cemeteries and commemorate the dead. Brier says that when she came to where she could see the smoldering site, she heard the Star Spangled Banner in her head. No band was playing and Brier herself had never sung the anthem much. Yet she heard it in that place, that day.

Volunteering for Political Causes, and Community and Religious Groups

Jack Taylor

Jack Taylor, member of Community Board #6 and president of the Drive to Protect the Ladies' Mile District, has devoted 15 years to preserving the city's architectural heritage. Because of his efforts, the New York City Landmarks Preservations Commission has designated the Ladies' Mile Historic District (the blocks surrounding Fifth Avenue from 15th to 24th Street, where so many magnificent department stores were built) and, recently, the East 17th Street/Irving Place Historic District. Taylor retired from his position as managing editor of *Family Circle* magazine in the mid-'80s and now works occasionally as a freelance editor.

We eat breakfast at a comfortable Greek coffeehouse where the waiters know how Taylor likes his omelet. In a soft plaid shirt and tan sweater Taylor looks fit and easygoing, but as we talked I could tell that he works every minute taking care of New York City.

Shortly after he left *Family Circle*, Taylor was drawn into a developing crisis about saving Luchow's Restaurant. His parents had taken him to Luchow's for holidays and celebrations when he was a boy; he remembers heavy German food, wonderful ambiance, an oompah band, a festive atmosphere, and distinctive architecture. The struggle to save Luchow's (they lost) introduced Taylor to the preservation movement.

"People go to Europe to see old buildings," Taylor says, "but they don't recognize the value of saving the old buildings here." Europeans are fascinated by New York City. They're overwhelmed by the juxtaposition of so many different building types from different periods and by the fact that fine structures like the department stores on Ladies' Mile were houses of commerce, not churches or palaces.

Taylor explained that the first step in any preservation process in New York City begins with the Community Board, a group of 50 members, half appointed by the borough president and half by the city council. While the boards don't have legislative power, city agencies pay attention to their recommendations. The whole board meets monthly, but the bulk of the work is done by 12 committees.

"Nothing gets done without a fight. . . . New Yorkers feel they have to fight, or at least express their opinions, about everything." Taylor sees plenty of jockeying, behind-the-scenes maneuvering, and sometimes misleading or incomplete presentations by groups seeking approval.

Most community board members are middle-aged and over; on Taylor's board, the oldest is 85. Taylor is 74. There's a sprinkling of younger people, but the time commitment makes it difficult, especially for those with families. Taylor thinks you have to be retired or single to serve.

Jack Taylor was born in Greenwich Village, and for 42 years he's lived in his present building, 10 blocks uptown from where he was born. He started as a proofreader at *Family Circle* magazine and worked his way up to managing editor at a time when *Family Circle* was the fifth-largest circulation magazine in the world. In name *Family Circle* was a monthly, but with 28 different editions and about half the editorial and advertising material different in each edition, it felt like publishing 28 magazines every month. When *Family Circle* was sold, then re-sold, Taylor decided to leave. He's been able to get freelance assignments from the contacts he made over the years.

Taylor's biggest freelance job, and the one he's most proud of, was editing *Recollections of a Life*, the memoirs of Alger Hiss. Hiss lived in the same building as Taylor, and when he was writing these memoirs he was old and almost blind. Taylor would read a section of the work aloud, and Hiss would make corrections which Taylor noted. Then he would dash to his own apartment, type it up and race back to read Hiss the revision.

Taylor is trying to get out of New York, he says. "The pace is killing. Seattle and San Francisco seem like the only civilized cities left." Most of his friends have moved away or died. Why does he stay? His rent-stabilized apartment keeps him here, he tells me. After the attack on the World Trade Center, he repeated the idea: "I'm rent-stabilized. You can bet I'm not leaving New York—much as I might like to." His friends still here tell him, "You'll never leave because you'd be bored to death anywhere else."

I tell him Jane Lattes says some people have a great first year of retirement, loafing, traveling. Then it palls. Taylor laughs. He's never had a first year of retirement. He's been working all the time and never takes more than two weeks vacation a year.

This morning Taylor's phone began ringing at 7 A.M. with so many calls about tonight's community board meeting, he claims he hadn't had time to shave before our appointment. He's fighting a new disco on Park Avenue South. The zoning there allows a disco, but Taylor feels it's a residential neighborhood and the noise, public drunkenness, and traffic a disco brings are not appropriate.

How did Jack Taylor learn what he needed to know for Landmark and Community Board work? Nothing he ever studied related to it. He professes not to have any particular background, but he speaks knowledgeably about the interactions among the mayor, borough presidents, City Council, and

the now-defunct Board of Estimate with regard to landmarking issues. And he is equally at home talking about architecture, urban law, and the history and political workings of
New York. Like someone who rose from proofreader to managing editor, he learned by doing.

Jane Creel

Jane Creel, a lifelong advocate for political causes and
women's issues, traveled to the Soviet Union with the American Women for International Understanding almost immediately after President Nixon had his "kitchen sink" debate with
Premier Khrushchev. After she retired, Creel volunteered to
work at the United Nations; now she's a vice-president of the
Women's City Club of New York, an organization that studies
and then takes positions on civic issues.

"In New York City," Creel says, "I feel I'm on the cutting
edge. The country's changing and I want to be a part of the
change as it occurs." A white Anglo-Saxon Protestant, Creel
expects to be in the minority eventually. It doesn't threaten
her; she believes the changes are enriching the country.

At 76 Creel is delighted not to hear the alarm ring every
morning. Nonetheless, by 7:15, in leotards and without
makeup, she's out the door for exercise. Home by 8:30, she
eats breakfast, and three or four days each week she's at the
Women's City Club by 10. Generally, she works there until 4.

In college, Creel majored in home economics; during World
War II she joined the Red Cross and served overseas in China

and the South Pacific. After the war home economists were in demand because factories that had been turning out weapons retooled to make appliances, and new fabrics came on the market. People needed to know how to use the new appliances and care for the new fabrics. Creel went to work for Detergents, Inc., in San Francisco, putting on fashion shows at Macy's that featured the new permanent-press dresses and showed how to wash the dresses in the new automatic washers. In 1957 Lever Brothers brought Creel to New York City, where she eventually became Lever's liaison with consumer activists. She retired in 1989.

Although Lever Brothers had a comprehensive program for people nearing retirement, Creel worried about leaving the company where she had worked for more than 30 years. With no routine and no clear idea of what she wanted to do, she found the first months difficult. The United Nations rescued her.

Jane Creel is a tall, slender, aristocratic woman, fine-boned with delicate features, and short, strawberry-blond hair. She wore tailored slacks and a tailored silk blouse. One wall of her apartment matched her coral raincoat, and a coral and white tapestry hung on a white wall nearby. No black, even after 40 years in New York City.

Creel has always been active in civic and social action groups, especially in women's issues. She wrote brochures for the National Council on Women's Health and served on their board. A pioneering organization in this field, the council worked to get a better dialogue between women and their physicians and to draw attention to women's health issues. NCWH helped spark the remarkable growth in public awareness of women's health that has taken place since.

Through Lever Brothers and through her social action work, Creel knew Esther Peterson, the consumer adviser to Presidents Johnson and Carter. At Peterson's 80th birthday party, Creel told the older woman she planned to retire soon and wasn't sure what she would be doing. Peterson invited her to work for the International Organization of Consumer Unions (now called Consumer International) at the United Nations, the same organization she had worked *with* when she was liaison for consumer affairs at Lever Brothers. Creel wasn't paid, but she had good travel perks and found the work rewarding. Eventually, the management of Consumer International moved to Europe. Her job was gone but "the UN was a wonderful bridge! You need a bridge."

Jane Creel got involved in Women's City Club when she went to Albany on a pro-choice lobbying trip and met a few members of the club on the train back to New York. "By the time we got to Grand Central, I was a member." Founded by suffragists, WCC celebrated its 85th year in 2000 with the program series "Visions for the Future of New York City." Eleanor Roosevelt started her public career at Women's City Club, and many other important women have belonged. Civic committees study topics like infrastructure, housing, education; after a proposal to the board, WCC takes a position.

After she retired, Creel took up birding, taking her binoculars to Central Park. She belongs to a book club that meets monthly, and she sees a lot of offbeat theater she says she couldn't take a chance on when she was working. After a long day on the job she was always too tired to put in the energy that experimental theater requires.

"The nicest night of the whole week is Sunday night. In college on Sunday nights, I always thought, 'I didn't get my paper written.' When I was working Sunday night came and I hadn't gotten my apartment cleaned . . . my ironing done . . . my dry cleaning picked up. Now Sunday night is free."

Louise Jonsson

Louise Jonsson volunteers at the mid-19th-century Church of the Mediator, on 231st Street in the Bronx. Tall, slender, with a high forehead, medium length gray hair, and an assured manner, Jonsson is businesslike but friendly and quietly assured. We talked in a good-sized church office that might once have been a library. Dark carved bookcases held old books on church law and church history. Light filtered in through leaded windows, and iron candelabra graced the carved mantel. The steel desks and copy machines jarred.

At the church, Jonsson coordinates the Northwest Bronx Food and Hunger project: Other churches, temples, and some charitable organizations donate food which is packed into cartons at the Mediator and distributed to people who need it.

Jonsson began her volunteer work at the Cathedral of St. John the Divine in Manhattan while she was still working. When she started, the cathedral, the largest Gothic cathedral in the world, had no formal tours or educational programs. Jonsson worked with the bishop to develop the current public education tours. Now she shows the church and its artwork to visitors two Sundays a month, and works there Thursday afternoons as well. Over the years, Jonsson has been a trustee of the Cathedral and board secretary of the Episcopal Church-women of the Diocese of New York. She's also vice chair of the group of seven Episcopal churches in the Northwest Bronx.

Before she retired, Jonsson worked for the executive secretary of Local 1199, National Hospital and Health Care Employees, (now called 1199 SEIU). She handled public relations, education of new members, and the nitty-gritty of making sure that everything in contract negotiations was done according to the law.

Louise Jonsson says she's always been religious, and because of her religion she tries to "treat others better than I am treated." For example, in the hospital where she once worked, she made sure that people who were entitled to benefits were paid from the benefit funds—something that hadn't always happened before. When staff members decided they needed a union, Jonsson helped get it going. In 1972, she accepted an offer to work directly for 1199.

In April 1991, after not taking a vacation in eight years, Jonsson traveled to San Diego. "Isn't this great," she thought. A few months later, Jonsson spent two weeks visiting a retired friend in Indiana. She came home thinking, "I don't want to go back to work." She retired March 1, 1992, at the age of 67.

Retirement work came naturally. Jonsson never wanted to sit at home "twiddling my thumbs." She has fun too. Subways, city buses, and express buses all run regularly from her neighborhood in the Bronx to other parts of the city, so she can go where she likes, when she likes. Every Monday she attends lectures on art appreciation, opera, and other topics with her union's retired members group. She's traveled to Rome many times and to Sweden, where her father's relatives live.

Jonsson has lived in her apartment (built in 1929) for 30 years. She pays less than six hundred dollars a month for rent but says that when someone moves out of the building, the landlord guts that apartment, remodels it, and charges more than one thousand dollars.

"The thought of going back to a full-time job appalls me. I get sick to my stomach." She says she's very gregarious but has to have time alone, and she no longer wants to be committed to a routine. If something comes up, she wants to be able to re-schedule. Usually she can. "I've had a marvelous life. I've enjoyed every minute."

Dick Leonard and Bernie Landou

Bernie Landou has always liked to cook. So one Christmas his partner, Dick Leonard, gave him a nine-month course at the French Culinary Institute in Soho. "It was boot camp," Landou says. "You work just like you do in a professional school—on your feet every Saturday from nine to four."

Learning to cook professionally and building up stamina have both paid off. Now, besides cooking their own dinners, Landou volunteers in the kitchen of God's Love, We Deliver, an organization that provides free hot meals for people with AIDS. God's Love, We Deliver is like the army: Landou may open 10 cases of tuna, trim roast beef, or peel potatoes for three hours in his weekly stint. He also teaches cooking to inmates at Rikers Island in a program designed to help them find employment after release.

Leonard and Landou both volunteer in ways that draw on their career expertise. Leonard, a former dean at Queensboro Community College who supervised the college's departments of health, administration, and counseling, worked for 10 years as a team leader in Gay Men's Health Crisis and is now helping SAGE (Senior Action in a Gay Environment) reorganize to accommodate rapid growth. Landou, who had his own public relations firm, writes brochures and publicity material for the Macular Foundation. They also usher at City Center and at off-Broadway theaters and so see new plays free.

Both men feel you have to start planning retirement early. You have to plan more than your finances; you have to plan your life. "If you just have a job, watch TV, and sleep you'll have a hard time without the job." They've always volunteered, always been active in theater. They even volunteer on their weekends upstate where they have a country house. Both men work in the gift shop at Tanglewood and serve on the board of the Richmond Performance Series, a chamber orchestra with members from the Boston Symphony Orchestra. Landou succeeded in getting underwriting spots for the group on PBS.

Volunteering for Healthcare

Ruth Koenigsberg

Ruth Koenigsberg volunteers for both the New York Philharmonic and Lighthouse International (Hope When Vision Fails). She finds very different kinds of satisfaction working for these two different organizations.

"At the Philharmonic I meet friends; at the Lighthouse I'm really helping people." Koenigsberg, a small, intense woman with dark eyes and hair, works in the Lighthouse Store, selling specially designed products to the visually impaired. You learn how to work with blind people, Koenigsberg says, when to help and when not to. And how to help. You learn how to offer your elbow to a blind person. And what to do when you get to a door. She finds it very interesting.

At the Philharmonic, gift shops operate during intermission. "We have to wait on a lot of people quickly, and there's no chance for conversation with customers. At the Lighthouse, everyone who comes in has a story. You become aware of their needs, and you really feel important." She works at the store at least three hours a week; longer during Christmas season. When they need her she stays to work in the office after her three hours are up. "I feel I get more than I give."

A widow, Koenigsberg still lives in the Flushing home where she and her husband brought up their children. When she's not at the Lighthouse or Lincoln Center, she likes to travel, read, or play golf with friends on public greens on Long Island. Usually she travels by bus and subway to Manhattan. It takes about an hour. She'll use the subway until 9 P.M., so if she comes into the city at night, she drives, parks at 57th Street and 9th Avenue where it's cheaper, then takes a bus. "I'll never leave the city. There's so much to do here. You can have an inexpensive day or an expensive day."

Judy Loza

Almost the first thing you notice about Judy Loza is her comforting, melodic voice—warm and soft, but strong. Ironically, Loza has devoted much of her career to working with the deaf. She's fluent in sign language.

Loza got hooked on sign language when she first saw groups of students signing at New York University where she was studying for her master's degree. Because voice modulation is not available to them, she says, deaf people use facial expression and body language more vividly than hearing people do. Signers have individual styles, just as hearing speakers do. Deaf friends tell Loza she has a "soft-spoken" signing style.

"When I found myself turning 60, I thought, 'Oh, this is the year!'" Loza told me. She made plans to retire. Her job had become increasingly stressful. A vocational rehabilitation counselor with a caseload of more than 250 disabled workers, she was spending most of her time on paperwork instead of the personal counseling she preferred. In 1998, several months before she left her job, Loza began hospice training. From the programs available in New York, she chose the Beth Israel Hospital's Jacob Perlow Hospice because it has a deafness unit.

When Judy Loza's first husband died of stomach cancer in 1981, there were no hospices to help either of them deal with the blow. Afterwards Loza became interested in issues of death and dying and began assisting at Friends in Deed, an organization that provides services for people with AIDS and terminal illnesses.

Her supervisor at Perlow, Marion Edmonds, former director of volunteer services there, finds that while the death of a loved one often motivates people to volunteer for hospice work, the newly bereaved are seldom ready. Most people need at least a year to work through their own grief before they can begin to support others. Edmonds is wary of people with romanticized ideas of death, often derived from reading. The best volunteers, she's found, are the ones who come because they want to be of service.

Hospice is not a place, Edmonds pointed out. It's a program of outpatient services for people who have less than six months to live, who want to remain at home, and who ask for help to make the end of life more satisfying. (Perlow, however, does have an inpatient unit where hospice patients may come in a medical emergency, when pain is out of control, or to give the caregiver a needed rest.) The hospice patient is not just the dying person; it's the whole family. Hospice volunteers don't come in with a pre-conceived action plan. They take their cues from the patient and the family.

The hospice team—social worker, nurse, doctor, volunteer, and occasionally other specialists—functions as a team of equals, not a hierarchy with the doctor at the top. Edmonds sees hospice volunteers as modern versions of the neighbors who brought over casseroles when a family was too overburdened to cook.

When she takes on a new family, Loza talks with them to see how she can help. Her counseling experience has given her the background to draw people out and provide the kind of help they want. Volunteers with no social service background, Edmonds said, learn to recognize what patients need. In meeting those needs they gain confidence.

While many hospice volunteers elect inpatient care, Loza prefers home care; she's not comfortable with the hands-on bathing and dressing done by inpatient volunteers. She leads a drop-in bereavement support group and calls family members from time to time for a year after the death. And every Wednesday she helps with data entry and other clerical tasks in the hospice office. Altogether she works about eight hours a week for the hospice program.

Loza enjoys her patients. Her first one had a pet chicken who walked around the apartment like a dog or a cat. Another had been Miss Vienna of 1912—a very pretty lady still, who thanked her effusively at the end of each visit. Two of her patients were deaf and she signed with them. Mainly they wanted to socialize. Loza spends two to four hours a week with a family from the time the patient enters the program until death. She may attend the funeral. Even with the intimacy of the care both parties know that when the patient dies the relationship is over. She takes her next assignment.

Often the most important thing volunteers can do is sit and talk. Patients may not want to talk about dying or their illness. Some prefer to talk about sports, or play Scrabble. One hospice worker, whose patient had been a Knicks fan all his life, arranged for tickets and a car service so that she and the patient could attend a game together. Sometimes Loza runs errands or picks up prescriptions; she may organize bills or read aloud. She has not been asked to cook or do housework.

Hospice workers also help the caregivers. Loza's visits to one elderly woman gave the patient's daughter a night out every Thursday; another volunteer took the 92-year-old wife of a dying man to weekly classes at the Art Students League. Loza finds that because people know she is a volunteer, they appreciate her efforts and treat her nicely. "We get closer to the people than anybody," Loza says. Patients often want to protect their families, and therefore confide in the volunteers.

Hospice volunteers receive rigorous training. The program at Jacob Perlow begins with 20 hours of classroom work spread over 10 weeks, plus required reading. Trainees attend a team meeting and a volunteer support group meeting. Depending on their preference for home care or inpatient work, they may attend an inpatient unit orientation and follow an experienced volunteer on the inpatient unit, or go on field visits with outpatient team members. Altogether a new volunteer commits to four hours a week for six months.

At end of the training period, volunteers take an oral, open-book exam to be sure they know the basics of hospice care. Most pass the exam. Its main purpose is to encourage people to take the program seriously and to work hard. Some drop out during the training program. But even those who don't finish understand death and dying better than they did before. Some call later to say, "I never would have been able to handle my mother's death if I hadn't been in the program."

Judy Loza and her present husband lived in Sweden for a time. When they returned to the States in 1989 he didn't want to come back to New York so they moved to Florida. Sweden was nice, Judy Loza says, but Florida was not! "It was all so perfect. I just was so out of place there. I couldn't relate to the plants."

"My last trip, I drove from Florida to New York and I felt, 'My god, I'm coming home.'" The Lozas moved back to New York. They live near the South Street Seaport, and, until the attack on the World Trade Center, Judy Loza walked around the tip of Lower Manhattan every morning. Now she's lost heart for that walk, but she still practices yoga, meets friends for lunch, attends lectures, and visits the Metropolitan Museum of Art. (Her cousin gave her a museum membership as a retirement gift.) "After you've worked for so many years, it's nice to do things at a slower pace."

A retired friend warned Loza that after a year or so "You'll feel like you aren't doing anything with your life." Judy Loza believes this will not happen to her because hospice work gives her a sense of purpose.

How does she feel about working with the dying? "I'm not fearful," she says. Her wonderful voice tells you she means it.

Using Your Business Experience and Skill

Martin Lehman

A visitor needs about 10 seconds to understand why Martin Lehman is marketing chairman of New York SCORE. Lehman's lively sense of humor and ability to engage others make him a natural for the job. One of the requirements of the marketing chair, he says, is to have fun. "I'm only getting transportation money, three dollars a day. So I have to have fun." Reminded that with his senior's reduced fare MetroCard he only spends $1.50, he threatened to end the interview then and there!

The Service Corps of Retired Executives recruits experienced business executives to counsel new entrepreneurs. Sponsored by the U.S. Government Small Business Administration and funded by Congress, SCORE offers seminars and workshops as well as individual counseling all over the country. In New York City, SCORE is expanding its program with offices in Harlem, Brooklyn, and the Bronx and special programs at the Science, Industry, and Business Library at Fifth Avenue and 34th Street. They've begun offering counseling over the Internet.

The 35 men and three women in the New York office come from all the major New York industries. When they were younger, they manufactured clothing and furniture, ran hotels, designed ads, and sold real estate. They were computer operators, marketing directors and certified public accountants. Now, with years of successful business experience behind them, these men and women are teaching young people how to apply for loans, how to hire staff, how to write marketing plans and figure out the capital they'll need to launch their businesses.

Traffic is brisk in the reception area of the SCORE offices on the 31st floor of 26 Federal Plaza, in Lower Manhattan. Applicants scarcely have time to pick up the leaflets on display and fill out the form handed to them by the white-haired woman at the reception desk before the counselors walk out of their offices, ready to see them. Lehman's somewhat cluttered business cubicle seems more typical of a working middle manager than a retired executive. His desk—actually a counter against the carpeted partition—holds a computer, a printer, books, and racks of papers. A bulletin board covered with memos and pictures of his grandchildren hangs above it. Other counselors stop by to ask for Lehman's advice.

Brought up and educated in New York, Lehman interrupted his studies at City College to serve in the Army during World War II. After discharge, he graduated from New York University, courtesy of the GI Bill. He worked his way up from shipping clerk in a retail store to assistant buyer then opened his own store selling women's clothing. He expanded to six stores but closed them after difficulties with a partner. Not wanting to sit around, he went to the Mayor's office Volunteer Action Center for help and was referred to SCORE.

New SCORE volunteers go through 90 days of training. First, they sit in on interviews and listen to senior counselors work with applicants. After about nine weeks, the counselor and the trainee switch chairs; the trainee conducts the interview with the senior person sitting in. The trainee and the counselor always talk over the interview afterwards. Some prospective counselors quit during training period and a few fail to meet standards so are not accepted. SCORE counselors are a pretty stable group; only about 10 percent leave each year and some have worked there 25 years.

People coming to SCORE for help may say, "I want to go into business. What business should I pick?" They may want to know how to do something specific—set up a bookkeeping system or develop an inventory-management database; or they may be in business already and having trouble. The SCORE counselor has to listen and help. Reference materials are available and counselors call on one another for help in their respective specialties.

Lehman works at SCORE three days a week from 10 until 2. All counselors work on a regular schedule and are expected to be at their posts at the appointed times. Lehman usually arrives a little early and stays a little late. He does his own copying, and, when the receptionist is not there, he answers his own phone. "We're not executives any more.

"Part of the package is the comradeship. We eat lunch together downstairs in the cafeteria; there's lots of banter, lots of humor, and a few ground rules: we don't talk about our health, our wealth, or our grandchildren." Lehman finds his friends at SCORE intellectually curious and eager to stay current with developments in technology, law, and business. At this writing, 90 percent of SCORE volunteers were using computers.

Lehman's biggest reward comes from his success stories. He appeared on CBS recently with a client who wanted to open a restaurant. The restaurant is thriving now. Lehman and his wife eat there often, and he gets much satisfaction knowing he helped the owner get started.

Recently Lehman ran into an old friend he hadn't seen in many years. Speaking of his life, the friend said, "I live in Florida. In the lap of luxury. Waiting to die."

Marty Lehman waits for nothing. Six years ago he and his wife bought an apartment on the Upper East Side. They're delighted to have Barnes and Noble, HMV Records, and a clutch of restaurants outside their door. They take the subway everywhere. Lehman arranges radio and TV interviews to promote SCORE. He appears on talk shows and makes speeches—things he never did when he was running his retail shops.

"Maybe it extends our lives," he says.

Part Three: The Opportunities

Here are some of the places in New York that welcome volunteers, and several volunteer resource organizations and Web sites where you can find a range of opportunities. People interested in helping victims of the September 11 attack can contact almost any group listed here; most have developed special programs to help. And just about every hospital in the city needs volunteers; call the hospital of your choice and ask for the volunteer office.

Of the smaller arts organizations, this list includes only a few. Most small theater, dance, and music groups need volunteer help but don't have established programs, formal application processes, or directors of volunteers on staff. If you're interested, call the office or, better, go to a performance on a day when a reception or "meet the performers" talk is scheduled. Introduce yourself to the manager or director of the company. Explain that you'd like to volunteer and be ready to give a brief summary of your interests and skills. Ask how and when you can talk further. To get a more detailed idea of what small companies need, read about Dances Patrelle.

Directors of volunteer services speak emphatically: They count on volunteers for important work. They want serious applicants, not dilettantes. Expect to show up ready to work at the appointed hour. It's not paid, and it's not full-time, but it *is* a real job.

Volunteer Resource and Referral Centers

Action without Borders
79 Fifth Avenue, 17th Floor
New York, New York 10003
(212) 843-3973
www.idealist.org

A resource for volunteering, with links to over 24,000 organizations seeking practical solutions for social and environmental problems in 153 countries, the Web site provides both domestic and overseas volunteer opportunities. Action without Borders has no government, political, or religious affiliation.

Catholic Charities
1011 First Avenue
New York, New York 10022
(212) 371-1000
www.ny-archdiocese.org/charities

The Archdiocese of New York assists more than one hunded different agencies in reaching out to needy people of all faiths, colors, and ethnic backgrounds in all five boroughs and the counties surrounding the city. Services include feeding the hungry, helping immigrants and refugees, developing communities and neighborhoods, counseling individuals and families, tutoring, and many other forms of help.

Catholic Charities publishes *Love in Action*, a helpful booklet that organizes volunteer opportunities by neighborhood and describes the kind of help needed at each center (food service, tutoring, clerical, and so forth). The booklet also gives the date and time each service is needed and indicates where schedules can be flexible.

A second set of tables presents the information by type of service and tells where that service is needed.

The booklet includes a long list of "Unusual Volunteer Opportunities." Aerobics instructors are wanted, along with sports timers and scorekeepers, people who can sew, basketball coaches, and someone who can give religious instruction in American Sign Language.

Federation of Protestant Welfare Agencies
281 Park Avenue South
New York, New York 10010
(212) 777-4800 x 332.
www.fpwa.org/getinvolved

FPWA's alliance of more than 250 social service agencies and some 100 church-run programs in all five boroughs gives volunteers wide choices in both type and location of service. Retirees with "strong leadership skills, financial resources, business contacts and good judgment" can join FPWA's board placement program, where they will receive training and eventual placement on the board of a non-profit agency. Volunteers interested in more traditional "hands-on" service can work with the hungry, the homeless, immigrants, people with HIV/AIDS, the elderly, children, and youth. Opportunities mentioned in the catalog include painting murals on the wall of a daycare center, fixing Sunday breakfast for the homeless, and teaching salsa to older dancers.

Volunteers are interviewed, trained, and matched with an agency and program according to their skills, interests, and schedule/location preferences.

Mayor's Office, Volunteer Action Center
49–51 Chambers Street, Suite 1231
New York, New York 10007
(212) 788-7550
www.ci.nyc.ny.us/volunteer

Persons interested in volunteering in public and nonprofit agencies throughout the city can contact the Volunteer Action Center, one of the largest volunteer referral centers in the country. The center also pilots innovative volunteer programs to meet community needs.

New York Cares
116 East 16th Street
New York, New York 10003
(212) 228-5000
www.nycares.org

Most New Yorkers recognize New York Cares from the familiar picture of the Statue of Liberty huddled and shivering from the cold. But the annual December coat drive is only one of many charitable services organized by New York Cares. The group runs more than three hundred hands-on service projects a month, mobilizing volunteers to serve on flexibly scheduled, team-based projects in partnership with schools, social service agencies, and environmental groups.

Volunteers for New York Cares tutor children, feed the hungry, assist people living with HIV/AIDS, revitalize gardens, take homeless children on cultural and recreational outings, visit the elderly, and much more.

After an initial meeting you receive monthly listings of places to volunteer. You can work regularly with the same group or try different activities. New York Cares is especially good for volunteers who want a flexible schedule.

RSVP
Retired and Senior Volunteer Program
Central Office:
105 East 22nd Street, Suite 401
New York, New York 10010
(212) 674-RSVP (7787)
www.cssny.org/rsvp/front.html

If you want to volunteer and aren't sure which would be the best place for you, start with RSVP, the largest senior volunteer program in the United States. The central office will help you directly or refer you to an area office in your borough.

Public agencies and nonprofit organizations register with RSVP and provide information about the kind of help they need. Prospective volunteers meet with RSVP staff to find the organization and position that best suits their interests and skills. Assignments range from mentoring a troubled teenager to serving meals in a soup kitchen, to providing management assistance to a nonprofit agency, to conducting museum tours. At this writing, the RSVP Web site seeks volunteers to lead tours and interpret exhibits at Brooklyn Wildlife Center; usher at Queens Theater in the Park; arrange dry flowers at Queens Botanical Gardens; speak Italian at New Vanderbilt Rehabilitation and Care Center, Staten Island; conduct Prejudice Reduction Program workshops for young children; assist teachers at Head Start Centers in language development activities for three- and four-year-olds; and many more!

RSVP provides accident and liability insurance coverage, partial transportation reimbursement for volunteers, membership in a national network, and training for specialized projects.

UJA-Federation of New York
Volunteer and Leadership Development Division
130 East 59th Street
New York, New York 10022
(212) 836-1733
www.ujafedny.org

The United Jewish Appeal Federation of New York, the largest local philanthropic organization in the world, runs a leadership training program as well as a wide-ranging Hands On volunteer program that directly serves people of all religious and ethnic groups. A volunteer in the Hands On program may speak English with a new immigrant, tutor a child, help a teen learn to take tests, accompany victims of domestic violence to court, make hot soup for people with AIDS, assist in a holiday craft workshop, or take the fixings for a Hanukkah celebration to a homebound elderly person.

Leadership training may involve positions on committees or boards, depending upon an individual's skills and interests. Prospective volunteers are placed in the Hands On and leadership training programs after a private consultation with a member of the volunteer and leadership development division.

Organizations Welcoming Volunteer Assistance

American Museum of Natural History
Central Park West at 79th Street
New York, New York 10024
(212) 769-5566
www.amnh.org

About half the volunteers at the American Museum of Natural History work directly with the public, staffing information desks, teaching schoolchildren, conducting museum tours, and acting as explainers in the exhibit halls. Volunteers who prefer to work behind the scenes help produce *Natural History* magazine and assist in constructing new exhibits. They provide clerical and computer support services, work with the scientific collections and in the library, and carry out many other administrative and scientific assignments.

A volunteer is expected to commit from half a day to several days a week for at least a year. Positions that require extended training may require a longer commitment.

In return, volunteers get free admission to other museums in New York City, and to museums in many foreign countries; reduced rates on AMNH tours; the chance to participate in special tours run just for AMNH volunteers.

American Red Cross in Greater New York
150 Amsterdam Avenue
New York, New York 10023
1-877-REDCROSS
www.nyredcross.org

American Red Cross is dedicated to helping people avoid, prepare for, and cope with emergencies. Volunteers provide the bulk of the services needed to help people in emergencies. They provide half the nation's blood supply, teach first-aid and CPR courses, deliver emergency messages to members of the military, organize programs for the elderly, and fill other important needs.

Red Cross volunteers work in the field, serve on boards of directors, serve as managers and advisors, and provide behind-the-scenes support. The Red Cross offers many courses to train volunteers for Red Cross work, and to help people handle emergencies whenever they occur.

Association of the Bar of the City of New York
Community Outreach Law Program
42 West 44th Street
New York, New York 10036
Call Carol Bockner
(212) 382-4714
www.abcny.org/citybar_outreach.html

Retired attorneys and paralegals who want to provide legal services to nonprofit organizations can find challenging volunteer positions through the Community Outreach Law Program of the City Bar Association. This award-winning pro bono program provides training, placements, and case supervision to nearly one thousand volunteers representing indigent clients in a variety of different public service projects.

Pro Bono Opportunities: A Guide for Lawyers in New York City gives detailed information on over 80 organizations citywide seeking volunteer lawyers and paralegals. The guide is now available online at *www.abcny.org/probonop.htm*.

Battery Dance
380 Broadway, Fifth Floor
New York, New York 10013
(212) 219-3910
www.batterydanceco.com
E-mail Ronald Knoth, Managing Director
Knoth@bway.net or *rkju@aol.com*

For more than 25 years, Battery Dance has been bringing original choreography and music to audiences in Lower Manhattan. The company sponsors a free outdoor Downtown Dance Festival every summer, it brings dance technique classes and choreography workshops to the city's high schools, and it makes its studios available at low cost to other dance and theater companies.

Battery Dance welcomes volunteers, particularly for the Downtown Dance Festival, where they greet the audience and distribute playbills. Festival volunteers can also work out of their own homes, contacting schools, summer camps, and other programs to get the word out about the festival and/or the company's ongoing arts-in-education programs.

Battery Dance also relies on volunteers to help with bookkeeping, answering phones, and booking dance studios. But Jonathan Hollander, director of the company, reminds prospective volunteers that for these administrative jobs they must be able to walk up to the company's fifth-floor offices.

Big Apple Greeter (BAG)
One Centre Street, Suite 2035
New York, New York 10007
(212) 669-2364
www.bigapplegreeter.org

Big Apple Greeters have shown New York City to more than 30,000 visitors from every state and 75 countries. Volunteers accompany small groups of two to six visitors on two- to four-hour journeys in any of the five boroughs. These "Greeters" focus on their own favorite neighborhoods and show visitors little things they'd often miss: New York bagels, flea markets, street fairs, and festivals. Volunteers can introduce out-of-towners to the subway system and to their favorite neighborhood restaurants.

BAG volunteers are New Yorkers of all ages, from all boroughs and all walks of life, selected for their enthusiasm and knowledge of New York City. They are interviewed and screened, and required to attend one or more orientation sessions. Acceptance as a volunteer is not automatic.

People who prefer a behind-the-scenes role can work at BAG headquarters. Time commitments requested of office volunteers vary by position.

Brooklyn Museum of Art
Belle Tanenhaus, Volunteer Coordinator
200 Eastern Parkway
Brooklyn, New York 11238
 (718) 638-5000 x 347
www.brooklynart.org

Volunteers work in just about every department of the Brooklyn Museum of Art: curatorial, finance, public information and press relations, directors office, and others. Assignments depend on the museum's need, on the volunteer's skills and experience, and on the willingness to commit to a regular schedule. Persons with a background in art may work in the curatorial department; those skilled in writing or marketing may work in the press office; and people with administrative experience assist in the director's office. Higher-level assignments usually require higher-level commitments.

Tasks range from routine clerical (photocopying, stuffing envelopes) to professional. For example, a retired senior vice president from a New York City bank works essentially as a volunteer consultant to the museum's finance office. All volunteers become part of a team and even people with high-level assignments pitch in to help with routine tasks when needed.

Volunteers need to belong to the museum. (Individual memberships start at $50; $35 for persons 65 or older. Family/dual memberships start at $75; $60 for persons 65 or older.)

Submit a letter of interest and résumé to Belle Tanenhaus and call her to arrange a meeting. She stays abreast of department needs and will try to place you suitably. She may also arrange for a prospective volunteer to speak with the appropriate department head before settling on a definite assignment.

Carnegie Hall
Sean Morrow
Associate, Planning and Projects
881 Seventh Avenue
New York, New York 10019-3210
(212) 903-9614
www.carnegiehall.org

Volunteers at Carnegie Hall can lead tours, support the full-time office staff, or serve in the Carnegie Hall Shop.

Docents, who give hourlong tours emphasizing Carnegie Hall's rich history and architecture, receive eight training sessions, then follow and observe at least three tours. They should be able to do a lot of walking, and absorb and retell facts and anecdotes, and they are expected to commit one full day a week for a season.

Office volunteers handle tasks ranging from computing to calligraphy in all of Carnegie Hall's departments. They may work a regular time and day each week, or they may sign up for a specific project.

Volunteer shop salespeople, who are expected to work one day or evening shift per week, need an interest in retail and a cheerful, helpful attitude.

Dances Patrelle
Robert Dorf, Managing Director
Post Office Box 6802
New York, New York 10128
(212) 722-7933
www.dancespatrelle.org

Robert Dorf says that Dances Patrelle, a small company that presents the dramatic ballets of Francis Patrelle, needs the same skills large companies need. Dorf could use a retired marketer to draw up a marketing plan, an advertising person to plan the ad campaign, a computing expert to manage the mailing list, an accountant to set up a better accounting system, an attorney who knows theater law, a wardrobe mistress, and a volunteer director of volunteers.

The Horticultural Society of New York
128 West 58th Street
New York, New York 10019
(212) 757-0915 x 210
www.hsny.org

The Horticultural Society of New York is dedicated to improving the quality of life in New York through horticulture. Volunteers work at the Horticultural Center or in one of HSNY's many community outreach projects.

At the center, volunteers with a knowledge of indoor gardening sell books, garden tools, seasonal bulbs, and plants. They work in the largest circulating horticultural library in the tri-state area and assist in HSNY's adult education program, which offers courses, lectures, workshops, and tours on horticultural topics.

The society's community outreach programs are *GreenBranches*, *Apple Seed*, and *GreenHouse*.

GreenBranches: HSNY works with community volunteers and the public library system to design and install gardens at selected branch libraries. So far, HSNY has planted 11 gardens in Queens, Manhattan, and the Bronx.

Apple Seed: This environmental science and horticultural program has provided hands-on activities and exploratory plant studies for more than six thousand at-risk inner-city elementary school students, strengthening their critical thinking skills, and math and science literacy.

GreenHouse: This project at Rikers Island prison teaches inmates the fundamental skills of horticulture and landscape design to help them become self-supporting after release.

Verdalee Tombelaine, former HSNY Volunteer Director, points out that the GreenHouse program calls for seasoned volunteers who know how to deal with an inmate population. She cautions against a romanticized view of prison work.

Tombelaine also notes that while HSNY needs and welcomes volunteers, opportunities vary seasonally and also depend on available funding.

Jacob Perlow Hospice
Beth Israel Medical Center
First Avenue at 16th Street
New York, New York 10001
(212) 420-2844

Hospice is a program of outpatient services for people who have less than six months to live, who wish to remain at home, and who ask for help to make the last period of life more satisfying.

Volunteers work with the hospice team—social worker, nurse, doctor, and occasionally other specialists—to provide integrated care. But they also use their own judgment to determine how best to provide meaningful help. Patients may want the volunteer to talk, or play cards or board games. Volunteers may also pick up prescriptions, make out checks, take the patient on outings. Their presence may give the regular caregiver a chance to go out.

The hospice training program at Jacob Perlow includes 20 hours of classroom work spread over a two-month period, required reading, and attendance at various meetings and orientation sessions. Altogether a new volunteer commits to four hours a week for six months.

At end of the training period, volunteers take an oral, open-book exam to be sure they know the basics of hospice care. Most volunteers pass the exam.

League of Women Voters of the City of New York
45 East 33rd Street, Room 331
New York, New York 10016
(212) 725-3541
www.lwvnyc.org

The League of Women Voters of the City of New York is a nonpartisan political organization. It sponsors candidate debates, and publishes informational material about candidates for office and about issues appearing on the ballot. While the league never endorses candidates for office, it does take a stand on issues coming before the electorate. Members decide which issues to study and, after a thorough investigation, determine by consensus what stand the league will take.

Membership, which is open to men and women, provides an opportunity to be actively involved in local, state, and national issues. $50 single membership; $65 for two at the same address.

Learning Leaders
New York City School Volunteer Program
352 Park Avenue South
New York, New York 10010
(212) 213-3370
www.learningleaders.org

In Learning Leaders' core instructional program, volunteers work with individual students or small groups in all grades in reading, math, English as a second language, and other subjects. In the upper grades, they also help prepare students for critical examinations and assist with college planning.

Most volunteers are not professional teachers. Learning Leaders will help you select an appropriate program and will train you.

In addition to the core program, Learning Leaders operates a number of special projects:

Art Works: Introduces third-grade children to the permanent collections of the Metropolitan Museum of Art. Volunteers provide advance and follow-up classroom activities for each museum trip.

Literary Leader: Volunteers and students (third- to sixth-graders who are considered to be at risk) read contemporary stories and the classic Junior Great Books in order to help the children develop their abilities in reading, thinking, listening, and self-expression.

College Planning: Volunteers help students with the application and financial aid processes, essays, and decision-making.

Understanding Nations: Uses an interactive program to teach fifth-graders about other countries and cultures, and the goals of the United Nations. The program includes a class trip to the United Nations.

Learning Leaders sponsors a number of other programs, many of them focused on helping children read well. Commitment requirements differ depending on the program.

Lighthouse International
111 East 59th Street
New York, New York 10022
(212) 821-9200
www.lighthouse.org
Volunteers@lighthouse.org

Lighthouse International is a leading worldwide resource on vision impairment and rehabilitation. Through its pioneering work, Lighthouse enables blind or partially sighted people of all ages to lead independent, productive lives.

Volunteers are carefully screened and trained to work with people who have visual impairments. Volunteers can choose from among a number of programs: reading services, youth programs, therapeutic employment program, orientation and tour guides, tutors, store and clerical help. Schedules are flexible.

Museum of Modern Art
11 West 53rd Street
New York, New York 10019
(212) 708-9639
www.moma.org

Volunteers at the Museum of Modern Art welcome visitors, provide information, and assist with school and public programs and with disabled visitors.

Applicants need a background in art, art history, or education. They need to be at ease greeting and speaking with the public. Conversational skill in a foreign language or sign language is helpful. Reliability is crucial.

National Executive Service Corps
120 Wall Street, 16th Floor
New York, New York 10005
(212) 269-1234
www.help4nonprofits.org

The National Executive Service Corps provides business planning and management consultation to the nonprofit sector. NESC consultants are retired men and women who have held responsible positions in business, the professions, and nonprofit enterprises. The mission is to strengthen the management capabilities of nonprofit organizations in strategic and marketing planning, fundraising, operations, and so forth.

NESC staff interview prospective volunteers to determine the best placement for each person, then put together teams providing the necessary skills for each project. Consultants work at the client's site, at home, and sometimes at NESC headquarters. Some assignments are small; others are very large. An operations study for one of the city's major museums occupied four consultants for about one hundred hours each over five months.

Asked to compare NESC to SCORE (see below), the NESC representative said NESC serves nonprofit agencies while SCORE clients are entrepreneurs in profit-making businesses. NESC volunteers are often retired corporative executives; assignments are for longer, more abstract projects. SCORE volunteers are more likely to come from retail business; their clients are generally small business owners who need help to get started, or with specific problems that arise. SCORE volunteers may work with a client over time, but for ongoing business, not a specific project.

New York City Ballet
Joan Quatrano, Director of Volunteers
New York State Theater
Columbus Avenue at 62nd Street
New York, New York 10023
(212) 870-5666
www.nycballet.com

Even people who don't dance can be part of New York City Ballet. Volunteers can sign up for one or more of 15 committees that give docent presentations, staff the information booths at performances, or work on special event planning, gift shop sales, translation, survey interviews, ticket donations, and more.

Ballet fans from 16 to 90 volunteer at NYCB. Some work year-round, some only during performance season, some only for *Nutcracker* or for festivals. Joan Quatrano welcomes committed volunteers who understand that the assignments require serious work.

To schedule an interview, call Ms. Quatrano or fill out the on-line volunteer application form. If you live too far from Lincoln Center to come in regularly, you may still be able to handle assignments that can be done at a distance—writing, translation, editing, computing.

Partnership for Parks
(212) 360-1357
Or call outreach coordinators:
Bronx (718) 430-4641
Brooklyn (718) 965-8992
Manhattan (212) 408-0214
Queens (718) 520-5913
Staten Island (718) 815-7194
www.itsmypark.org

A joint initiative of City Parks Foundation and City of New York Parks and Recreation, Partnership for Parks supports neighborhood park groups and encourages community involvement in developing, restoring, and preserving community parks.

Typical activities include political and educational efforts to increase public and private funding for parks; writing text for historical park signs; Halloween parties in parks; workshops on organizing activities designed to drive out crime and make parks safer.

In the fall of 2001, Partnership for Parks, together with other park conservancy and support groups, organized the Daffodil Project, planting one million daffodil bulbs to commemorate those who died in the attack on the World Trade Center.

SAGE
Senior Action in a Gay Environment
305 Seventh Avenue, 16th Floor
New York, New York 10001
(212) 741-2247
www.sageusa.org

SAGE is the nation's oldest and largest social service and advocacy organization dedicated to LGBT (lesbian, gay, bisexual, transgender) senior citizens. The New York chapter serves LGBT seniors in all five boroughs.

Volunteers are involved in every aspect of SAGE's work: Friendly Visitors, Lend-A-Handers, facilitators for weekly classes and rap groups, counselors, and workshop leaders. They plan social events and city walks, run the Theater Desk, teach language and writing classes, and bring videos of opera performances to SAGE's weekly "Mornings at the Opera."

Advocacy and outreach volunteers address ageism in the wider culture as well as in the LGBT community, and bring senior LGBT issues to the attention of lawmakers, community groups, and the staff of assisted living institutions.

SAGE volunteers plan conferences, write the newsletter, create and maintain the Web page, assist in fundraising events, and help with reception, clerical and computing tasks.

Potential volunteers must complete an application form and attend an orientation; training is required for some volunteer responsibilities.

SCORE
Service Corps of Retired Executives
New York SCORE, covering Manhattan, Brooklyn,
and the Bronx
26 Federal Plaza, Room 3100
New York, New York 10278
(212) 264-4507
Queens County SCORE:
(718) 263-8961
Staten Island SCORE:
(718) 727-1221
www.score.org

SCORE's mission is to aid in the formation, growth, and success of small business. Men and women, mostly retired, advise entrepreneurs seeking help in setting up and running their own businesses. SCORE business counselors see firsthand how their counsel benefits their clients.

New York SCORE has offices in Manhattan, Brooklyn, and the Bronx. New SCORE volunteers are interviewed and receive 90 days of training. Once trained, counselors work on shifts one or more days a week and are expected to be at the office at the appointed hour.

South Street Seaport Museum
207 Front Street
New York, New York 10038
Call Richard Dorfman, Volunteer Office
(212) 748-8727
www.southstseaport.com

The South Street Seaport Museum engages volunteers to work directly on the museum's fleet of 19th-century sailing ships. At the time of this writing volunteers were needed to help with winter maintenance and spring fit-out of the coastal schooner *Pioneer*; to work on the restoration of the iron-hulled *Wavertree* and other ships; and to become the nucleus of a boat-shop crew. Volunteers who are interested in learning square-rig sail handling can train to work as crew for summer and fall sailings.

Volunteers also lead tours, assist education staff with workshops for museum audiences, and work with Elderhostel groups. Docents participate in a free four-week course in the spring, which includes training in teaching methods and in New York City and maritime history.

While many volunteer positions at South Street Seaport require a commitment of a day a week, everyone is invited to join Spring Launchings, the annual volunteer workday on the ships and piers.

The idea comes from an East Coast tradition by which an entire community turns out to ready ships for the working season. At Spring Launchings, volunteers turn out for one day to sweep and swab decks, clean exhibit areas, chip and sand, polish brass—and much more—to help ready the piers and the fleet of historic ships for the summer season.

TACT
The Actors Company Theatre
Scott Alan Evans, Co-Artistic and Executive Director
161 Sixth Avenue, 14th Floor
New York, New York 10013
(212) 645-8228

TACT's mission is "to present neglected or rarely produced plays of literary merit, with a focus on creating theatre from its essence . . . the text and the actor's ability to bring it to life." The actors give concert performances of these plays in extremely limited runs (three performances of each production).

The group needs volunteers to usher and to work in concessions, box office, and other jobs. Evans suggests getting acquainted and then telling TACT what you wish to do.

UJA/MAP
United Jewish Appeal Management Assistance Program
130 East 59th Street
New York, New York 10022
(212) 980-1000
www.ujafedny.org

Qualified volunteers use their professional skills as pro bono consultants in time-limited, project specific assignments for hospitals, synagogues, camps, schools, community centers, and other organizations that are members of the UJA Federation. MAP volunteers assist clients with advertising, facilities management, marketing, organizational management, personnel and human resources management, photography, systems technologies—all the skills required to manage a financially sound operation.

Women's City Club of New York
33 West 60th Street, Fifth Floor
New York, New York 10023
(212) 353-8070
www.wccny.org

The Women's City Club of New York is a nonpartisan, nonprofit organization fostering responsible citizen participation in shaping public policy decisions in New York City.

WCC identifies, studies, and analyzes public policy issues, and works to affect public policy. Members choose to work on one or more areas of interest: education, environment, mass transportation, children's issues, and others.

Women's City Club published the city's first voter's manual and the first comprehensive report on the city's need for better public housing; critiqued the city's system of local school boards; successfully advocated for an overhaul of the city's juvenile justice system; and produced a report which led to a revision of the building codes.

WCC organized the city's first conference on the status of women; issued the first directory of housing resources for homeless women; and produced a video promoting HIV-AIDS awareness among adolescents which was adopted by the Board of Education and distributed to high schools.

Regular membership is one hundred dollars per year.

CHAPTER NINE

Continuing Your Education

Part One: The Scene

Holly Butler figured a college town would be a good place for a retired widow to live. After an exploratory drive through elm-shaded villages in New England and across the Hudson River to Saratoga Springs, Butler landed in New York. Suddenly she realized that, although she had visited good schools on beautiful campuses, New York City is the ultimate college town.

New York has Columbia, New York University, and the New School; New York has Fordham and Hunter, City University, Pace University, and Cooper Union; Brooklyn College and Pratt Institute. New York has the School of Visual Arts, Fashion Institute of Technology, Juilliard School of Music, and the American Musical and Dramatic Academy. New York has the SUNY Maritime College, Medgar Evers College, Polytechnic and St. John's Universities, and the College of Staten Island. New York has LaGuardia Community College, Bronx Community College, and Lehman College; Yeshiva University, Jewish Theological Seminary, and Union Theological Seminary; John Jay College of Criminal Justice. New York has medical schools, law schools, business schools, and cooking schools. In New York, an inquiring retiree can study just about any topic to any depth, from a Saturday seminar in sushi to a Ph.D. in public policy. The New School offers the Philosophy of Science and Introduction to Cheese.

New York is a city of readers. Visitors often comment on the people reading while they wait to cross the street. It's a sign of the intellectual curiosity that helps give New York its cultural edge. And it's a little-appreciated side effect of public transportation: people read while they ride, and, if they're engrossed, they keep on reading after they're off the train.

Retired New Yorkers have moved far beyond the knowledge and ideas of their youth. They're learning new skills, taking up new fields of interest. They're getting acquainted with history and literature they'd known little about, and public policy issues they'd never fully understood.

Dorothy Nicolosi and her sister, Alfreda Mautner, grew up in an Italian family but hadn't learned to speak the language. They wanted to connect to their heritage, so after they retired they enrolled at Parliamo Italiano, the Italian language school on East 65th Street. Now they are fluent. In class they discuss

Italian literature *in Italian*—a real challenge, Nicolosi says. She spent five weeks at the University of Urbino in Italy, studying Italian and the history of Italian renaissance art. She says going to Parliamo Italiano helps you understand your own language better and gives you a real understanding of another language, culture, and history.

Many retirees want to go to school. Some never had a chance at college when they were young. Some weren't interested. Some barreled through college to a career, ignoring everything outside their major. But, during the years they've been working and rearing children, most people have developed new interests—interests that may engage different parts of the brain or body. Nurses take up French; accountants find themselves wanting to cook. If you learn by reading, it's easy to read a book on a new topic. But learning to use a computer, or play the flute, or identify trees in winter is a different challenge. Since we no longer have to master the new skill to earn a paycheck or care for our children and since, by this time in life, the need to prove ourselves to others may be less pressing than it once was, we're freer now to concentrate on learning for the joy of it.

Most colleges and universities in New York have special programs for seniors, and some welcome us in their regular classes as well. Columbia University runs a Lifelong Learners Program through which seniors can audit undergraduate courses; Holly Butler and her friend Nancy Tomasello audited "Jazz." Their tuition in Lifelong Learners gave them the use of the Columbia Music Library but not the password to the course's Web site, so they couldn't listen to the assigned selections on their home computers. Instead, they arrived at the library an hour before class, presented their IDs, got earphones, logged on, and listened to their assignment then and there.

Paul McNeil, associate dean of continuing education at Columbia, explained to me that the university chose to bring seniors into classrooms with undergraduates in order to give the older students a rich intellectual experience. Columbia didn't want a senior ghetto or a social service agency, so there aren't any programs on health problems or retirement issues. But the university does arrange a special lecture series for Lifelong Learners: on Fridays some of Columbia's most eminent faculty members speak and lead discussions on topics in their own fields.

McNeil said that seniors often add valuable insights to these discussions. He told me about the time a history professor lectured on Stalin. All the while the professor was speaking, a woman in the audience was practically jumping up and down, bursting to talk. When he finished and invited questions from the floor, she stood up first.

"You got it all wrong," she said. "I screwed Stalin for a year and I know!"

Then she filled in a host of details about that period in Soviet history. Later, McNeil asked the professor if he thought this woman was "for real." "Yes." Her details dovetailed accurately with the known facts.

The Institute for Retired Professionals began at the New School in 1962 and has served as a model for programs for older learners at almost three hundred colleges and universi-

ties around the country. In many places it's called the Institute
for Learning in Retirement, but, whatever the name, it operates on the same principle: retired people take responsibility
for their own learning. They study and they teach, developing
their own courses under the guidance of a curriculum committee made up of members of IRP. Most classes operate as
study groups or seminars. In time, members are expected to
develop and coordinate (teach) their own courses.

Despite the name of the program, members need not be
"professionals." Any retired or semi-retired person who
wants to participate actively in a serious, cooperative learning
and teaching effort is encouraged to apply.

Steve August, who has both taken and coordinated courses
at IRP, says the people there are "unbelievably interesting,"
and everyone benefits from the contributions of the other
members. When a class studying greek drama read *Oedipus
Rex*, a psychiatrist in the group spoke in depth about the
Oedipus complex and how it affects personal development
and family life.

Most continuing education programs also offer opportunities for cultural and social experiences. People enrolled in
LOOP, Lehman Options for Older People at Lehman College
in the Bronx, can use the college library and athletic facilities.
They are invited to Lehman concerts, plays, athletic events,
lectures, and gallery exhibits. They can join reduced-price excursions to Broadway plays and Lincoln Center concerts. And
they have their own campus center where they can hang out
with friends.

Some retirees go back to school for degrees. Every commencement, City University of New York pays special attention to graduating students who first started college more than 40 years before. If you're wondering about handling college work after a lapse of many years, you can start slowly. Twenty-five years after she received her bachelor's degree, Blossom Carron wanted to go to graduate school. But first she enrolled in a single summer school course at Columbia to be sure she could handle the work. When she found she could, she entered a master's program and eventually received her doctorate in education. Several of the colleges in the City University system allow older students to take up to two courses without matriculating. If you earn a B+ or better, you can then matriculate.

Not everyone wants formal academic work. Many who want to learn and teach in a more casual milieu look into the Learning Annex—a popular venue for one- or two-session programs in many topics, with an emphasis on self-help.

In addition, specialized schools, not directed toward a degree and generally easier to get into than a college or university, offer language studies, computing, art—just about everything. Libraries, museums, historic sites, and religious and neighborhood institutions, offer lectures, readings, and classes. And special-interest clubs welcome photographers or stamp collectors.

If you want learn to make French pastry, train a dog, or use a spreadsheet, there's a school or course for it. If you want to learn more about the Civil War or the Big Bang, you can find lectures on those topics. Stargazers can join the Amateur Astronomers Association. Cafés sponsor poetry readings and the Japan Society has run "Tokyo Style"—a symposium on the lifestyle, urban design, architecture, and fashion of Tokyo.

The Municipal Art Society schedules architectural walking tours of the city's landmarks and the Architectural League of New York sponsors exhibits and lectures by well-known practitioners. The Brooklyn Botanic Garden offers programs as demanding as study for certification in horticulture, and as relaxing as an evening garden walk. Apartment dwellers learn how to grow herbs on a deck rail and vegetables in containers.

All over New York City, people form book groups or join small discussion circles focused on particular themes or viewpoints. Margaret Pazos belongs to the Committees of Correspondence—a group of 8 to 10 people who read and discuss books and articles on social concerns and leftist philosophy. (Committees of Correspondence, a nationwide organization, is named after the original Committees of Correspondence organized by Samuel Adams to build support for the American cause before the outbreak of the Revolution.) I belong to a book group started by my friend Sharon Walsh. We meet in one another's apartments one evening a month, order up supper and talk about our book. We're serious about our reading, and we have fun too.

While most of the people profiled here are studying because they want to enrich their lives, some have parlayed their retirement education into a new career. They are amazed by what they have been able to learn.

Part Two: The People

Larry Witchel

"Looks like I'll make my career as a professor at Bronx Community College." Larry Witchel laughs when he hears himself say it. He's pushing 70 and he's already had a full career in publishing.

We're in a back room of the Upper West Side brownstone where Witchel lives with his wife, Dinah. Framed sheet music pages, and some illuminated manuscript pages he made himself, hang on the walls.

Witchel, a solidly built man, looks as though he could be a steelworker. His hair is only partly gray but his bushy mustache is white. He's wearing slacks, a sport shirt, and a loose brown leather jacket.

How did he start a new career at an age when most people are winding down? When he was growing up in Brooklyn, he was expected to go to college but, after a few courses at City College and ballet classes at Juilliard, he dropped out.

In his late 50s Witchel began to think seriously about going back to school. His kids were at Stanford and he envied their education. He'd been talking it over with a minister friend, who invited him to dinner along with a dean at New York Theological Seminary. During the dinner, the two theologians urged Witchel to consider enrolling at the seminary.

"Seminary? Are you crazy? I'm not Christian. I'm Jewish. And I'm not even religious!"

But the men continued to talk. Witchel wanted to study religious philosophy, and the seminary was eager to have him. He could go to school at night and keep on working. And it would cost only $125 a credit—whereas New York University, for example, was charging $500.

Witchel enrolled. Though the program was difficult, he completed 90 credits in two and one-half years while working at his job, which involved considerable travel. Sometimes he had a limo waiting to take him from class to a plane. He did his homework in hotels and airport lounges.

Witchel became deeply involved with the seminary. The scholars were superb, he liked studying the Bible, and he made good friends. Praying and singing hymns together several times a day forges strong bonds, he says. The focus was on God and you, the individual, and Witchel found it extremely moving to be immersed in a world where students and professors are concerned with people's souls. Christianity has a poetic dimension, he feels. If you are going to study it, you have to see it almost poetically.

But Witchel didn't convert. He remains Jewish. The seminary decided he couldn't graduate unless he "became a halfway decent Jew," so they arranged for special training with a rabbi. In 1993, when he received a master's degree in theology, they told him he was the only Jew who ever made it through New York Theological Seminary.

By that time, Witchel had retired from publishing. His company had moved to Washington and he'd been given his parachute. "Not golden, but it was there."

He applied to several graduate schools but figured that, at

his age, he couldn't spend one hundred thousand dollars to get his doctorate at a private university. He'd never earn it back. So he began to investigate graduate programs at the publicly supported City University of New York. CUNY offered nothing in religion; the closest was history. Like the brash New York businessman he was, Witchel called the head of the history department: "Hello, I'm Larry Witchel. I'm 60 and I want a doctorate."

CUNY accepted him for fall 1993; he joined the history department as an early modernist. When we spoke he'd finished all his course requirements, passed his orals, and begun work on his dissertation (*Conscience and Principle in Seventeenth-Century England*). He'll have to defend it. "Then you can call me Doctor!"

Graduate school was even more difficult than the seminary. Witchel tells me that many older people who try for advanced degrees drop out. Course work is harder than they expect and it takes more time. You need a support system, people to encourage you. Young students have their parents and teachers. He knows he couldn't have done it if he were single; he couldn't have done it without Dinah.

The culture of graduate school required a major change in personality. Witchel had been an aggressive sales type, accustomed to being in charge. Now he had to learn to be deferential. In his first year, Witchel often said things that were not acceptable in the academic world. His business humor fell flat. He'd left a world where the mark of success is money and moved into a world where the mark of success is knowledge.

The cultural shift was as great, he feels, as the shift in moving from the Dominican Republic to Harlem.

Now, nearly 70, Witchel is an adjunct professor of history at Bronx Community College, where he teaches two undergraduate classes a semester. Once he has his doctorate (he's aiming for the end of 2002), he'll have the first faculty line that becomes available for associate professor.

"Is teaching hard?"

"Ohhhh!" He groans. He'd had no training as a teacher—no experience with students, no standards for what constitutes a failure or what constitutes a B+. And he was terrified of his students. He asked a colleague for help.

"Kill 'em!" she said.

He gained confidence when he realized his students have a lot on their minds and just want to get the work done. They know they have to join the white-collar world, and they're "fighting for every inch of time" to do it. They've made a choice to learn; other things that are happening to them are not their choice. Today, for example, he saw that one of his students was tired. He found out that the young man works until one in the morning, then rises early to attend Witchel's 8 A.M. history class. Another student lives in a two-room apartment with her whole family; each of her three brothers plays his own radio—loudly. She can't study at the library because she works during library hours. Gradually he's developed sympathy for his students and the obstacles they face. And his students know it. Now, when he tells them to take their earphones off in class, they do.

Witchel hasn't figured out what would constitute "moving ahead" for himself at BCC. Although some professors have spectacular careers writing books and consulting, he knows too many who repeat the same lectures year in and year out. "I love what I do, but thank God I didn't start it when I was 25." He feels you can aim for much more in the business world, that academia's not a place for raw ambition.

What's his daily schedule? "I insured my job by teaching at 8 A.M.!" He gets up at 6, takes a thermos of coffee, and drives to the Bronx, where he stays until 10 or 11. Then back to Manhattan to work on his dissertation until dinner. He and Dinah go out with friends. They go to movies. They take trips. "We do the things that old folks do."

Witchel has no problem with the word "old." "Calling us senior citizens makes me want to retch."

Jane Randall and Norma Globerman

Jane Randall and Norma Globerman both learned to use the computer after they retired from their jobs. They started cold and learned at home without a corporate information services staff to rescue them when they were stuck. Their interest in the computer, their purpose in using it, and their feelings about it, differ considerably.

Jane Randall had been using a computer for only three months when I met her. She wasn't too crazy about it, but she needed one. Partly because the IBM Selectric typewriter she'd used for her public relations work had died, but mainly to manage her book collection. Randall collects American first editions, and she was looking for a way to keep track of titles, authors, publication dates, values, condition of books, pricing, and other data. When she joined the Grolier Club of New York, an organization for book collectors, she learned that many of the members use their computers to keep these records and also to buy and sell online.

Before she bought her system, Randall took computing courses at Marymount College, but, since she had nothing to practice on, the courses proved useless. After she got her own Dell computer, she went to computers dot mom for lessons. Their classes, one session per topic, are very small—not more than four people, sometimes only one or two.

Randall and I talked in her Upper East Side apartment. With abstract woodcuts on the wall, wicker furniture, and a cream-and-brown décor, her home office felt like an airy sunporch. The computer sat on a large desk in the corner. Randall is a small, wiry woman with a low-pitched voice and a lot of energy. She was wearing pale gray stretch pants and a striped T-shirt. Her short hair formed a light brown halo around her face.

She'd done public relations for small businesses, but after she retired she began volunteering her public relations services to nonprofit organizations. She joined and served on various committees at the Women's National Republican Club, the Cosmopolitan Club, the New York City Wellesley Club. At the Wellesley Club she did the newsletter until they put it on the computer. (She hadn't learned to use one yet.)

Her favorite is the Grolier Club, even though, not knowing many members, she had to wait a long time for her membership application to get approved. She likes discussing books with people who are really knowledgeable. When she joined Grolier they had little in the way of public relations. Club members put a lot of work into the group's exhibits, but not enough people came to see them. Since getting more people to their exhibits also helps attract funding, Randall is doubly eager to help develop publicity.

To catalog her own book collection, she engaged a computer expert who had worked with the president of Grolier on his collection. His services cost her more than the computer did. Now that she has all the information about her books in Microsoft Word, Randall can enter new books herself when she gets them. Tabs can be a problem. She doesn't really understand them yet so she has to finesse some of her input to make it look good.

Initially Randall hated her computer because it was so frustrating, but, by the time we talked, she was using e-mail, checking it every three days or so, and she'd come to like writing press releases in Word. Since she hadn't yet learned to send e-mail attachments, she was printing the releases and faxing them.

The computer has never "grabbed her," and there are lots of things she still can't do. Randall doesn't want to become addicted to her computer or fixated on it. She has no intention of using it for stock tables. She hasn't bought or sold anything on the Internet. She does keep a list of her charitable contributions on the computer—but they're not perfectly tabbed and lined up.

~

Even before she retired Norma Globerman felt she should own a computer. However, she's too practical to buy things she can't use, and she didn't see how she would use a home computer. Then she found herself getting tired of looking up things in her old *Encyclopedia Britannica*. When she heard about Encarta, Microsoft's electronic encyclopedia, she decided it was time to go shopping.

Globerman knew so little about computers that when she went to buy one she wanted to be sure it "had Encarta in it." She didn't realize that not only could she put Encarta in almost any personal computer, but also that she would *have to* put it in. Late in 1997 she bought a Compaq. When she got it out of the box, she didn't even know how to turn it on. Within a day, she was on the Internet.

The Hunter College computer whiz she'd engaged to teach her couldn't come over when the machine was delivered, so, following the printed instructions, Globerman set it up herself. The next day her young tutor spent about three hours showing her the "absolute basics"—and signed her up on AOL. The two had another three-hour session a week later.

"It hooked me immediately."

But learning to use the computer was not trouble-free. Globerman crashed frequently; she called the help line often. Ordinary procedures were difficult and frustrating. She couldn't get rid of unwanted text for weeks because functions like "select" were so automatic for her tutor, she forgot to teach them to Globerman.

Globerman persevered—with delight as well as grit—and with continuing wonder at how she was falling for the computer. She's become something of a guru, teaching her friends. However, she notes that many of them prefer to learn from strangers; they're embarrassed when they're slow or make mistakes.

Globerman is slender, with short white hair and a clear complexion. She's quick and lively and conveys her arguments and explanations with considerable logic—personality traits that seemed exactly expressed in her trim blue pants and crisp blue-and-white striped shirt.

She paints and sculpts, and is using her computer to build her own collection of favorite paintings. She told me all the major museums have Internet sites. She downloads pictures of paintings and sculpture from the Metropolitan Museum in New York, the Hermitage in St. Petersburg, the Tate in London. And the quality is superb. When she brought up Turner's *Grand Canal* for me, Globerman's screen glowed with the Venetian scene.

Two years ago she bought an external CD writer. When she's collected a group of paintings on her hard drive, she burns them onto a compact disc and deletes them from the hard drive. Using a database program, Globerman can sort her paintings by artist, by century, and by theme, and bring up a screenful of "thumbnails" (little copies of the paintings) from which she can select the one she wants. Click and she gets a full-screen view. She also designed a slipcase for her CD with a Picasso portrait on the front. She has five hundred paintings in her collection now; since the one disc will hold five thousand, she figures she may not need another in her lifetime.

What does she do with the art? She looks at it. It's like owning art books, she explains, but with the added advantage that she can keep one up on the screen, and change it at will— essentially hanging a new masterpiece whenever she feels like it.

Globerman keeps adding to her computer repertoire. She has customized her desktop and her calendar, and she's configured her e-mail to open at maximum size. She does all of her financial planning with Quicken, and for several years now she's prepared her own taxes. She likes graphics and makes greeting cards and posters which she embellishes with her own collection of clip art and sends to friends on paper and by e-mail.

She doesn't spend all day at the computer. In fact she doesn't keep it on all the time or even turn it on when she wakes up in the morning. Generally she sits down for an hour or two in the evening. She has an active social life and goes to the ballet often. She takes photographs; she's a member of the Council of Foreign Relations and she's on various boards at Hunter College, her alma mater. She takes care of her 90-something mother, who lives with her and is becoming increasingly limited.

Until she retired 13 years ago, Globerman worked for the
United Nations Development Program, where she ended her
career as director of programs for Asia. To have control over
her own time, she took early retirement at 55. She couldn't
wait, and she wasn't worried about what she'd do. She had
many interests and knew she could use her free time well. But
she was surprised to discover that she did have an adjustment
period, a time when she was uneasy in a subtle way that she
could not quite define.

Now at 69 her two main retirement activities—computer
and ceramics—are not what she'd expected when she was
working. Music had been her principal free-time activity, and
she'd planned to saturate herself with performances once she
no longer went to work. Also, she expected to continue the
painting she'd been doing for years.

But a friend was raving about a ceramics course she was
taking, urging Globerman to try it. Globerman listed politely
but wasn't interested. Then she got the idea that she'd like to
make a ballet dancer in clay to use as a model for painting.
She asked her friend's teacher how to do it.

"I can't *tell* you how. You'd have to take a course to
learn."

"I don't want to take a course. Just tell me how to do it."

Globerman got nowhere repeating her request, so that
summer she enrolled in an eight-week ceramics course. For
about a year, she both painted and sculpted, but gradually
painting receded and ceramics took over. She was flooded
with ideas for ceramic sculpture while ideas for paintings were

drying up. Ceramics turned out to be a more natural medium for her.

Over time, the uneasiness she'd felt early in her retirement faded away. Trying to figure out what had happened, she realized that she'd been missing a sense of purpose. Interests and activities weren't enough. She needed an outlet for her creativity, an opportunity to *produce* something. Ceramics, and later the computer, took over painting and music, and filled that void she'd felt but hadn't been able to identify.

Globerman's apartment is filled with her own paintings and sculpture. Her paintings are realistic, rendered with clean lines and soft colors, but her ceramics are in every style: a fountain with rain falling on people carrying umbrellas and another with a woman pouring water from a jug; menorahs and other Judaica; fruit bowls; ballet dancers dancing, opera singers singing, an Asian woman holding a bird; and abstractions with no discernable subject. She uses subtle colorings and complex glazes. Even with paintings on every wall, ceramics on every horizontal surface, and furniture with intricate inlaid veneers, the total effect is light and airy, not heavy or cluttered.

Globerman goes to sculpture class at the nearby Y on Tuesdays and Thursdays. She likes the sociability of the studio and she's made good friends in the group.

About 15 of her friends bought computers after she did, but none of them became "computer people." Why did it click so with her?

"I like organizing things. I like solving problems. It works with my kind of intelligence."

Carmen Flores Korn

Norma Globerman told her friend Carmen Flores Korn that for retirement to be satisfying you have to have an anchor. Globerman's anchors are her art and her computer. Carmen Korn's anchor is her classes.

Korn grew up in Santiago, Chile, speaking English and Spanish. Her mother was American, her father, Chilean. She started French when she was 11 and claims to have forgotten French four times. On a trip to France Korn thought she was doing well until she went to a French movie. When she couldn't understand the actors, she decided that after she retired she'd study French again. She did, and since 1984 Korn has been going to the French Institute Alliance Française every week, having a lot of fun reading, writing, and discussing books in French.

When she was planning a trip to Italy, Korn took up Italian at Parliamo Italiano. With her fluency in Spanish and French, she moved rapidly through the elementary Italian program to Intermediate 5, where she says you can stay forever. Korn is immersed in a cycle of courses on Italian opera. The class listened to and discussed 18th-century comic opera, then Rossini, then the influence of Rossini on Verdi. Now they're moving into Verdi. The teacher, Anna Maria Levi—who is herself 76 years old and retired from a career in college teaching—weaves 19th-century history into her discussion of Verdi.

Korn, a small woman with short reddish-brown hair, was wearing a dark blue silk dress with a double-strand pearl necklace and earrings, black pumps, and sheer stockings. She and her husband, Henry, live in Tudor City, a prewar apartment complex in Manhattan's East 40s. With Czech crystal on the sideboard (Henry Korn is Czech), a South American silver cross on the wall, and books in several languages, their home reflects their international roots. And their family life. Pictures of their two sons and a granddaughter cover the tables. In the hall, a photograph of Henry Korn skiing shows the form and speed that earned him a gold medal in slalom at Jackson Hole last year.

When people asked her where she'd be going when she retired, Korn said, "Right here in Tudor City." They'll only leave if their apartment rent goes to market rate, which they wouldn't be able to afford. Her philosophy: "Enjoy it while you have it."

Korn worked at the United Nations for 28 years. An economist by training, she'd moved up over the years to take charge of technical assistance for all of Latin America. "When I retired I felt that God had been very good to me, and I had to do something to give back." She volunteered to interpret for patients at Bellevue Hospital and to work at the Metropolitan Museum of Art's international visitor's desk, where she answers questions in English, Spanish, French, and Italian.

At Bellevue she discovered she could translate quickly

enough to work as a simultaneous translator. She promptly applied to be a freelance interpreter with the United States Information Agency. Foreign professional workers in all fields come to the United States to meet their counterparts here and observe our systems, Korn explained. The State Department engages USIA to provide interpreters. After she'd passed rigorous qualifying exams, Korn took two assignments a year. Her groups were largely people in law and in fields relating to economics—banking, natural resources, trade. She traveled with them all over the country, sometimes arranging the cities they'd visit and the people they'd meet.

Her first assignment was to escort four judges who came to visit United States courts. A program was prepared in every city they visited. By arranging to take her group to Portland, Oregon, instead of the more popular San Francisco, Korn was able to get them more personal attention than they might otherwise have had. Another time, a Panamanian group of judges, public defenders, and prosecutors wanted to see a particular trial in Miami in which a Panamanian was to be tried. She spoke to the judge, who encouraged her to bring her group and told the bailiffs to reserve front-row seats for them.

Korn liked the job. Over the years she met interesting people in many fields and made new friends. She interviewed defendants who'd "say *'Gracias, Señora'* no matter how criminal they are." Her last assignment was in New York City. By the end of it, she was so exhausted she decided it was time to quit. "If you get exhausted in your own city . . ."

About three times a week she works out at the YWCA at

53rd Street and Lexington Avenue—"The best buy in New York," she says. If you sign up for a year, you can exercise, swim, use the machines, and stay for aerobics, as often as you like.

Henry Korn, retired from accounting, "still has his hand in the pie" working part-time for a few clients. The Korns take advantage of the cultural opportunities in New York City. They've subscribed to the opera and philharmonic for 20 years and the Roundabout Theater for 15 years, but they're thinking about dropping some subscriptions because they prefer to pick only the programs they want.

When she was too busy to schedule a doctor's appointment recently, Korn said to herself, "You should go down on your knees [to thank the Lord] that you have so much to do you have no time to go to the doctor."

Steve Robinson

Steve Robinson walked the 60 blocks from Penn Station to our meeting at a café on Lexington Avenue at 91st Street. He'd grown up in the neighborhood, on 99th between Park and Madison, and gone to school at 96th and Lex. Ten months before I met him, Robinson retired from Proctor and Gamble, where he'd worked in sales for 29 years.

Robinson is a tall, muscular man with short, curly gray hair. He was wearing a dark blue sweater, dark gray chinos, and a light blue shirt. He's lively and personable; he talks easily, smiles broadly, and fills his narratives with rich details about his friends and associates.

He likes to cook. Robinson and his wife, Betty Ann, go to West Point football games where he serves tailgate picnics to their family, their friends, and a few cadets they invite to join them.

The West Point tailgate culinary élite don't eat franks and beans. Right there in the parking lot they cook meals worthy of a three-star chef. Some bring candelabra and flowers, and last year one man arrived at 7:30 in the morning to roast a pig on a spit before the game. A few years ago Robinson replaced his old Coleman camp stove with a portable professional model. With that he prepared—from scratch—a lobster, shrimp, and scallop dish in a tomato cream sauce that he served over pasta to 10 people.

When Steve Robinson retired, his children knew exactly what to give him: a gift certificate to Peter Kump's Cooking School. He started with Techniques of Fine Cooking, where he found himself the only man among 12 women. He went once a week for five weeks, then signed up for five more weeks. Classes are held in a big kitchen. Students read the lesson in advance. The instructor goes over techniques and explains the reasons for various actions. Then the class breaks into teams. As they work they walk around and look at what others are doing, paying close attention to the details. Robinson was surprised by how competitive cooking students are. But competition makes it more fun for him. "You try to do your best."

Cooking, he points out, gives an immediate feeling of satisfaction. You see—and eat—the results right away. It's not like sales, in which you run an ad and wait a long time before you know how well it worked.

After Techniques of Fine Cooking I and II, Robinson took Thai cooking. He recently went to Queens to find ingredients for a Thai dinner: curry paste, fish sauce, snow peas. He thinks about colors and textures, and surrounds his heap of shredded carrots with a circle of snow peas. When he sets out the carrots, he follows his instructor's admonition not to press food down with the spoon but to pile it up light and fluffy.

Betty Ann appreciates coming home from work to find a delicious dinner ready. She's on Weight Watchers and Steve had a heart attack two and one-half years ago, but they can enjoy his cooking because he exercises strict portion control, buying the exact amount he needs and no more. If a piece of salmon weighs a few ounces over, he has the fishmonger trim it. Robinson walks five miles a day, and he's lost 40 to 50 pounds since his bypass operation. He and I agreed that eating really good food engenders a sense of satisfaction that can discourage overeating.

He wants to take up bread baking. A widow he met on his walks bakes bread. Living alone, she can't eat it all, so she takes the surplus to a homeless shelter. When Robinson thinks about making bread himself, he thinks about sourdough. One of his instructors told him that, since sourdough is made from natural yeasts in the air, not commercial yeasts, sourdough on the East Side tastes different from sourdough on the West Side. It's those subtleties in cooking that delight Robinson so.

What was it like for him to switch from sales, which uses mostly verbal, analytical, and interpersonal skills, to cooking, that's mostly physical? Well, when he first got out of high school, he worked in factories where he used his hands in industrial metalwork and other fabrications. He enjoyed it and tried to be very good at it, to the point where his boss would say, "This isn't jewelry. Just make it!" Cooking brings Robinson back to exacting hand skills. He pulled out the Peter Kump school newsletter to show me a photo of an instructor fluting pastry for a tart. He likes the precision.

The Robinsons are thinking of leaving New York, mainly because it's so expensive. They could live more cheaply out west—but he'd miss this, he says, gesturing to embrace the café where we are sitting. Las Vegas might be a good choice. He doesn't gamble, but the city has a college for football games and many interesting things to do. Robinson thinks their grandchildren would visit them in Vegas more eagerly than, say, Omaha. And from the West it would be cheaper and easier to reach Hawaii (where they often vacation), so they could stay longer. Living in Hawaii—they'd love it—is problematic because it takes too much time and money to go anywhere else. The Robinsons are making plans but have no timetable in mind. If they move to a new home, he wants a new kitchen. Betty Ann can choose the colors but *he'll* design the layout and select the equipment.

Marianne Ultmann

Marianne Ultmann lives in my building. We had said "Good morning" in the elevator but not much more. Then I saw her picture in *Reform Judaism*, in which she was profiled as one of "The Unstoppables" in the magazine's issue on old age, and I realized a great person for this book lived one floor above me. I also realized, with some chagrin, that I had not gone beyond a casual greeting because, like so many Americans, I hadn't really expected a much older person to be very interesting. Was I wrong!

Ultmann is 86. She's short and walks slowly with a cane. Her posture is erect and her demeanor quietly self-assured. A cloud of white hair surrounds a strong face. Her apartment is replete with books, plants, and her own paintings. She leads a short-story reading group that meets Friday afternoons at the Nagle Avenue Y, across the street from our building. She joined the group 10 years ago as a participant and, soon after, when the leader had to leave suddenly, Ultmann took over. She picks the stories, gets them photocopied at the Y, and distributes them a week ahead so people can read them before the meeting.

Even with her bookshelves and tables laden with collections of short stories, Ultmann says it's not always easy to find good material. Modern short stories often portray very destructive relationships, she feels. She looks for serious stories that aren't morbid or too violent, and puts in a humorous piece every so often. Over the years her group has read Willa

Cather, Somerset Maugham, Rudyard Kipling, John Updike, F. Scott Fitzgerald, Isaac Bashevis Singer, William Faulkner, Eudora Welty, and newer writers like Amy Tan. Preferring to keep the sessions "haphazard," Ultmann doesn't group them by author or time period or theme. The night before her group meets, she rereads the story to find the points to emphasize. She focuses on characters and on plot development— "if there is a plot"—and likes to present a little background about the author.

Ultmann received her doctor of philosophy in German literature from the University of Vienna. She was in the last class that graduated Jewish students and wasn't permitted to take the exam for a teacher's license. In December 1939 she left Vienna for New York City.

For the first two years Ultmann worked at whatever she could. When the United States entered the war, she took a mechanical drafting job at the General Foods factory in Hoboken. Her high school in Vienna had specialized in science and math, so now, with male engineers all drafted into the armed forces, Ultmann found herself in demand. At General Foods she made blueprints and was responsible for servicing the machinery. She loved the work but the law at that time guaranteed returning soldiers their old jobs, so when the engineer she'd replaced came back from the war, Ultmann had to leave.

For a while she had a number of different and awful jobs. But her luck changed when she received a New York State stipend to study occupational therapy. In 1956 she took a position as senior therapist at Willowbrook Hospital, Staten Island, where she stayed until she retired in 1977.

Over the years she was working, Ultmann always maintained her interests in literature and the arts, in philosophy, and in Judaism. She took poetry writing workshops and, in time, made the difficult switch from writing poetry in German to writing it in English. Years ago she studied geology and went on field trips run by the American Museum of Natural History. Later she joined discussion groups at her temple.

Ultmann has painted all her life. When she was five, her father enrolled her in a radical art school in Vienna—that is, a school without formal instruction. Ultmann found the school traumatic. The artist who ran it was excellent, but Ultmann, the youngest in a mixed class of children up to age 14, was frightened by bossy older children and insensitive teaching assistants. When she started elementary school her father felt regular school was enough for a child and took her out of painting school. Later she had seven years of art in high school, and she's studied painting in New York. You can see the results in the paintings hanging in her apartment—good composition and use of color, disciplined experimentation, variations on a theme, and, more recently, a move toward abstraction.

After she retired she studied for a while at the Art Students League, but now she does most of her painting at an adult camp in the Poconos where she goes every summer. The camp bus picks her up at the Y across the street. The sponsoring organization, Associated Camps, is affiliated with both United

Jewish Appeal and Elderhostel and offers a lively program of hikes, crafts, painting, drama, music, yoga, tennis, lectures, and Jewish studies. The brochure shows a broad green lawn with modern sculpture, and picnic tables in a grove along a lake; campers live in simple one-story accommodations. Ultmann enjoys the discussion groups held under the trees and painting in the camp studio. Back in the city, she exhibits from time to time at Arts Interaction, a neighborhood gallery, and at the branch library on 179th Street.

Ultmann belongs to nearby Temple Beth Am, where the rabbi has encouraged her to give talks. She gave several talks a few years back; one, *My Ten Commandments for the Son or Daughter I Never Had,* was a humorous version of the biblical 10 commandments. For a Yom Kippur talk on life after death, Ultmann drew on a poem by Schiller that dealt with justice, reward, and punishment.

But she hasn't given a talk since 1998. It's gotten harder for her to concentrate enough to write serious material. And she's had to cut down her temple attendance because it's gotten more difficult to get out to evening services. The study groups she likes are held in the morning, but she says she's "not a morning person." Afternoons are her best time.

So in certain ways Ultmann's life is narrowing. She no longer uses the subway, but she does travel by bus and taxi. In winter she goes to Florida with a group that picks her up at home and handles all the arrangements including a wheelchair at the airport.

Ultmann's best friend lives in upstate New York; they talk

on the phone several times a week. She also has friends on Staten Island and in Riverdale, but her friends in this building have moved away. She feels the loss of close personal contact with the temple, and the rabbi she liked so much has taken another pulpit.

Ultmann has help with cleaning and shopping, and she pays her bills electronically. How long will she be able to stay in her apartment? She's trying to decide what she'll do next. She visited an assisted living facility recently and, although it was attractive and well-run, she found it depressing. "If I were there, I'd be dead in six months." The people there are very old, and many are no longer alert. Even as she grows weaker physically, Ultmann wants to remain active intellectually—to learn Spanish, maybe, or how to use a computer. She's taken a few Spanish classes but so far has not continued.

"I'm hanging onto the short story with nails and teeth. It gets me out of the house—with people."

Steve August

At the Institute for Retired Professionals, Steve August immerses himself in his two great loves: poetry and baseball. He's *taking* a course in modern Irish poetry, and he *teaches* one on baseball.

Strangely enough, it was through baseball that he got into poetry. In college, majoring in English and playing varsity ball, he had to do much of his reading on the team bus traveling to games. Given that, his professor thought poetry would work better than fiction. It would be too hard for August keep track of a novel when he had to pick it up and put it down so many times. But he could read, annotate, and think about one poem in one trip. Following his professor's practical suggestion, August got hooked on the language and cadence of poetry.

He grew up in the Bronx and says he was a poor student in school and college. Yet August notes that he chose work that required quick learning and discovered he could do it. He spent his career writing: as a reporter covering the police beat for *New York Journal American*, on the staff of *Esquire* magazine, and in advertising.

August was working for one of New York's large advertising agencies and teaching advertising and marketing at New York University when he looked at his collection of novels about baseball and began to think about teaching a different kind of course, the Literature of Baseball. He'd use some of his favorite novels: *The Natural*, by Bernard Malamud; Philip Roth's *The Great American Novel*. And the one he likes best, *The Celebrant* by Eric Greenberg, a story of an immigrant boy who plays baseball to become an American.

But before August had a chance to teach the baseball course, he needed an operation. He was 70 and knew he'd be unable to work for a while following surgery, so he figured he might as well retire. After he recovered and was looking around for something to do, he saw an ad for the Institute for Retired Professionals at the New School. He scheduled an interview. When he told his interviewer about his idea for a course on the literature of baseball, she asked how soon he could teach it at IRP. He started the next semester.

Since then August has taught several courses at IRP: Photography as Fine Art; American Radicals; Ireland: History, Folklore, Culture. He takes courses there too, and he's enthusiastic about how much he learns from his knowledgeable, forthright students and classmates. Bringing diverse careerfuls of experience to the sessions, the other students "make you realize you don't know as much as you think you do."

At 73 August has straight white hair, and the bones of his face are strong. He's fit, weighing within five pounds of his college weight. Beside his work at IRP, he's an accomplished amateur photographer and he plays tennis. He and his wife (a teacher not yet retired) go to poetry readings and take advantage of many other cultural opportunities in the city.

Advertising gave August good training for teaching, he says. He had to make stand-up presentations; he had to be enthusiastic; he had to change his approach on the fly if he saw his audience drifting off. It was show biz. Now he uses all the techniques he learned in advertising to keep his courses lively. He doesn't write out his lectures; reading them would be dull.

IRP has a curriculum committee which oversees the entire program. People who want to teach submit proposals to the committee, and sometimes the committee suggests an idea to a coordinator. They asked August if he would teach a course on America's first ladies, and he agreed to do so. He has more plans of his own in the back of his mind: At the Strand Book Store recently, he found an *Encyclopedia of Negro Baseball* that got him to thinking about a course on the history of the Negro baseball leagues.

Each semester, IRP members are required to register and take part in at least two IRP study groups and one course at New School University. August studies photography at New School and has the use of their darkrooms. He also serves on several IRP committees: public relations, diversity, and interviewing. And he's working with a group planning the 2002 East Coast conference of Lifetime Learning groups.

The Institute for Retired Professionals at the New School has given Steve August more than intellectual stimulation. After retiring and recovering from his operation, he realized that "you can only play so much tennis, you can only work out so much." He began to worry.

His biggest challenge in retirement was replacing his routines. August says routines give you a purpose. You know that at certain times you're due at certain places, and you know what you're going to do when you get there. He feels it's easy to lose your sense of self-worth when nobody wants the experience you've acquired over so many years. The hardest thing for him was to reestablish routines and "not lose sight of the fact that I was still valuable." IRP has given August the routines he needs. He has to prepare for his classes and be there on time. And, as he sees that the class members value his knowledge and abilities, his sense of purpose and his feeling of self-worth have begun to come back.

August gets a big charge now because "I wear jeans all the

time. I don't have to wear a necktie. I don't have to wear a suit."

He has a friend who calls himself a curmudgeon. That's Steve August's ambition—to be "a well-known curmudgeon." He'd like to found a society with three or four other curmudgeons he knows.

What's he objecting to? "Everything. Particularly getting old!" It takes longer now to recover from playing tennis. And he doesn't play baseball anymore. One day, when he was in his early 40s, his wife said, "You look like the father of the other members of the team." August figured it was time to hang up his glove.

Part Three: The Opportunities

A small percentage of retirees enroll in undergraduate or graduate programs for credit or for a degree. To be accepted into a degree-granting program, a retiree has to qualify in the same way that a younger applicant does, although some of the city's colleges and universities offer credit for life experience. (This usually involves analytical or interpretive writing about one's life experience.)

Our list here presents non-degree continuing education programs, which most of the city's colleges and universities offer and most retirees elect. We also list schools that specialize in one discipline or one approach, and places where you can hear lectures or take part in half-day or one-day programs in many fields.

For more information about a program, call the individual school, get a catalog, or log on to its Web site. The schools listed below are but a fraction of the educational opportunities available in New York City. Virtually every college and university in the city offers programs for seniors or invites seniors to join ongoing courses. Most of the larger city parks, neighborhood Ys, senior centers, museums, historic sites, churches, synagogues, and mosques have adult education programs. Prices may have changed since publication.

Colleges and Universities

City University of New York (CUNY)
The Graduate Center
Continuing Education and Public Programs
365 Fifth Avenue at 34th Street
New York, New York 10016
(212) 817-8215
web.gc.cuny.edu/cepp

The CUNY Graduate Center brings together 4,000 students and 1,700 faculty scholars from all parts of the City University. Within this atmosphere of intellectual ferment, the continuing education and public programs offer workshops, courses, seminars, and cultural and artistic events that address a wide range of personal, political, and professional interests.

CUNY Graduate Center Continuing Education and Public Programs has recently allied with AARP to develop programs that encourage seniors to become involved in community efforts. The CUNY/AARP program integrates academic study with courses in skill development and leadership training, and creates bridges to community groups, thereby giving participants the wherewithal to put their academic learning to public use. Another goal of the program is to reduce the isolation of older people and build a sense of community.

Cost: CUNY course costs vary widely. Many public lectures are free.

Columbia University
Lifelong Learners Program
Information Center
303 Lewisohn
2970 Broadway, Mail Code 4110
New York, New York 10027-6902
(212) 854-9699
www.ce.columbia.edu/auditing

The Lifelong Learners Program gives seniors the opportunity to participate in the intellectual life of Columbia University as auditors of undergraduate arts and science courses, and as participants in special programs designed for seniors.

Lifelong Learners are encouraged to attend class and to keep up with the reading, but they do not take exams or receive credit. They do have reading and reserve borrowing privileges at the university's libraries. Class participation is at the discretion of the instructor. There is no minimum age for Lifelong Learners, but they must be retired.

In addition to their classes, Lifelong Learners attend weekly faculty lectures on a wide range of topics given by some of the most eminent professors in the university. At these lectures faculty speakers engage Lifelong Learners in discussions in which seniors can bring their intellectual interests, professional background, and personal experiences to bear on the topic.

Cost: In 2001, the Lifelong Learner fee was $225 per course (reduced from the regular auditing fee of $375) and included the faculty lecture series.

Cooper Union
The Cooper Union for the Advancement of Science and Art
Cooper Square
New York, New York 10003
(212) 353-4000
www.cooper.edu

Peter Cooper established Cooper Union in 1859 to educate working people in art and science. The school provides free college tuition for students in art, architecture, and engineering, and also offers a non-credit adult education program at moderate cost. Classes include CityScapes (walking tours led by architectural historians), Drawing and Painting, Spanish and Italian Language, Modern Dance, Photography.

The Great Hall at Cooper Union, which has seen the birth of many historic American social movements, continues to host speakers on contemporary social, political, and economic issues, as well as cutting-edge programs in the performing and literary arts.

Cost: Most 10-session courses are $250. Many individual lectures and concerts are free. Some carry a charge of $15 to $25.

Hebrew Union College–Jewish Institute of Religion
New York Kollel
One West Fourth Street
New York, New York 10012
(212) 674-5300
www.huc.edu/kollel

Jews of all denominations and non-Jews who want to study Jewish texts, beliefs, and practices can enroll in HUC-JIR's New York Kollel (gathering). Courses meet on Tuesday or Thursday evening once a week for 5 to 10 weeks.

The Hebrew program, for Biblical and prayerbook Hebrew, offers courses at all levels, from absolute beginners to "Scholar's Circle." Theology and Bible courses probe more deeply than most synagogue or Y courses and are open to all seriously interested in Judaism. Students range from 30 to 70 years of age.

The HUC-JIR Kollel also offers free public lectures on Biblical archeology and other topics, and a number of special activities like the traditional *Tikkun Leil Shavuot,* an "all-night Torah study for the city that never sleeps" held annually on the holiday of *Shavuot.*

Cost: Varies. Six two-hour sessions usually run $165, with a 20 percent discount for registrants age 60 or over. Public lectures and the *Tikkun Leil Shavuot* are free.

Institute for Retired Professionals
New School University
66 West 12th Street, Room 502
New York, New York 10011
(212) 229-5682
www.newschool.edu/centers/irp

This first peer learning program for retired people has served as a model for similar Institutes for Learning in Retirement at more than three hundred colleges and universities across the United States, including Harvard, Northwestern, UCLA, and Duke.

The IRP comprises study groups and workshops developed and led by the members themselves. Study groups—akin to advanced college seminars—are offered in art, drama, history, literature, and natural and social sciences; workshops are offered in ceramics, writing, exercise, language studies. Class sizes range from 10 to 35.

The only requirements for membership are serious interest and the ability to participate in college-level study. Applicants must file an application and be interviewed. Since the continuance of the program depends upon members teaching as well as learning, it is expected that members will serve as study group leaders (called "coordinators").

Cost: Membership fees in 2001 were $405 a semester. This entitles the student to register for up to four IRP study groups and one New School class, to participate in the activities of the institute, and to use facilities at New School University.

LOOP
Lehman Options for Older People
Lehman College, CUNY
Office of Continuing Education
Carman Hall, Room 129
250 Bedford Park Boulevard West
Bronx, New York 10468
(718) 960-8512

Designed for people at or near retirement age, these educational, cultural, social, and recreational programs offer intellectual stimulus in a comfortable environment. Registered members attend colloquia and enjoy other benefits: their own e-mail address; access to computer training and admission to the Information Technology Center; use of the Lehman College Library and athletic facility; free or reduced-price admission to concerts, plays, films, lectures, and excursions; and many other privileges.

Cost: $175 each for the spring and fall semesters; $100 for the summer.

Specialized Schools

DOROT University without Walls

171 West 85th Street
New York, New York 10024
(212) 769-2850
www.dorotusa.org

DOROT, which means "generations" in Hebrew, offers courses via teleconferencing. Participants need only a telephone to be connected to a group of not more than 12 people who meet in weekly conference calls to listen, discuss, and learn under the direction of a facilitator. Classes are weekly for 3–14 weeks; participants can enroll in programs in the arts, contemporary issues, Judaic studies, health, and many other topics. Newer courses include Abstraction in the 20th Century: Art and Architecture; Here's a Howdy-Do: The Operettas of Gilbert and Sullivan; In Whose Opinion, a discussion of selected columns and editorials on the *New York Times* op-ed page; Royal Arts of West Africa before Colonization; Finding a Place for Women in American Judaism. For art courses, the sponsoring museums put together packages of reproductions which are sent to participants' homes ahead of time.

DOROT courses are particularly valuable for people who find it physically difficult to travel to class, especially in bad weather.

Cost: $8 registration fee; $10 per course.

French Institute Alliance Française
22 East 60th Street
New York, New York 10022
(212) 355-6100
www.fiaf.org

FIAF offers a comprehensive selection of courses in French from elementary to advanced levels: conversation, French civilization, literature, grammar, writing techniques, and pronunciation. The school offers courses and workshops in many aspects of French culture, including film, dance, and culinary arts.

Class registrants get automatic associate membership benefits, which include full library privileges, free admission to the Ciné-Club film screenings, and lectures on French culture; member discounts to music, theater, and dance performances at Florence Gould Hall and other events.

Cost: Varies. A "regular" French language course, 90 minutes once a week for 11 weeks, is $255. More intense workshops with a smaller number of students may cost more. Members of the Institute receive discounts. Memberships begin at $75; $60 for seniors and students.

Gotham Writers' Workshop
1841 Broadway at West 60th Street, Suite 809
New York, New York 10023
(212) 974-8377
www.writingclasses.com

Ten-week, one-day, and online workshops in fiction, nonfiction, screenwriting, memoir writing, poetry, children's writing, and other forms. GWW emphasizes the craft of writing; student works are read and discussed in class, and a diploma program is available.

Classes are limited to 14 students in a 10-week classroom workshop and 18 in a 10-week online workshop.

Pick up a catalog from a street-corner box and check the Web site for a sample online class.

Cost: $395 for 10 3-hour classroom courses or a 10-week online program. Returning students pay $345. One-day intensive workshops (12 noon to 7 P.M.) cost $125 plus $20 registration fee. Various discounts are available.

The Open Center
83 Spring Street
New York, New York 10012
(212) 219-2527
www.opencenter.org

A holistic learning center offering classes, long-term training programs, conferences, lectures, performances, and weekend workshops that integrate Eastern and Western learning and worldviews. Topics include mind-body medicine techniques, social and environmental issues, classic and indigenous religions, spiritual practices, nutrition, bodywork, and movement. The Open Center presents more than six hundred programs a year, many of them taught by persons well known in their fields.

Cost: Varies. A quick perusal of their catalog turned up individual lectures for $17, one-day workshops for $110, six-session programs from $80 to $185, and many other arrangements. Members usually receive a discount.

Parliamo Italiano
Italian Language School
132 East 65th Street
New York, New York 10021
(212) 744-4793
www.parliamo.com

The largest Italian language school in New York City offers courses at all levels. Faculty are professional Italian teachers, all native speakers holding degrees from Italian universities. All are trained in the school's methods, and all use original materials developed by the founder and director.

Classes are limited to about 14 people, and conducted in Italian. Advanced students can focus on Italian literature and poetry; listen to and discuss Italian opera; or read writings of Michelangelo, Leonardo, Galileo, and other great Italian artists and thinkers.

Cost: A course of 10 1½-hour classes is $270; 20 1½-hour classes are $420; 10 2-hour classes are $320; 20 2-hour classes are $460. Twenty percent discount for seniors.

Peter Kump's Cooking School
50 West 23rd Street
New York, New York 10010
(212) 847-0770
www.newyorkculinary.com

A school for professional chefs, Peter Kump's also offers an extensive recreational cooking program. The core of the program is Techniques of Fine Cooking I–III, a series which teaches fundamental cooking techniques in hands-on classes that meet in the school's kitchens. Other technique courses include Fish and Shellfish, Italian Cooking, Asian Cooking, Pastry, Bread Baking, and Chocolate.

Peter Kump's also offers intensive courses (five sessions in one week instead of sessions once a week for five weeks), an array of one-day workshops, culinary walking tours, and other food-related programs.

Cost: Tuition and materials fee for Techniques of Fine Cooking is $515 for five five-hour sessions. Single-session workshops run from $40 to $110 depending upon length and other factors.

Spanish Classes in New York
Adrian Gonzalez Martinez
304 West 30th Street, Suite 1
New York, New York 10001
(212) 643-1525
www.spanishnewyork.com

Señor Gonzalez Martinez and others teach individuals and small groups to read, write, and speak Spanish. Schedules are flexible and designed to meet individual needs. Instruction covers beginning, intermediate, and advanced Spanish.

Señor Gonzalez, a native of Argentina, is a university graduate with specialized training in language instruction.

Cost: $66 per hour for private tutorial; $47 per hour for small group classes (two to three students).

Libraries, Houses of Worship, and Other Public and Private Organizations That Offer Lectures and Classes

Amateur Astronomers Association of New York, Inc.
1010 Park Avenue
New York, New York 10028
(212) 535-2922
(718) 390-3432 for Staten Island chapter
www.aaa.org

The association offers evening stargazing sessions in Manhattan, Brooklyn, and Staten Island; classes in basic astronomy and an advanced seminar; lectures at the American Museum of Natural History.
Dues: $20 per year.

Brooklyn Botanic Garden
1000 Washington Avenue
Brooklyn, New York 11225
(718) 623-7200
www.bbg.org

Besides being an extraordinarily beautiful place to stroll—among Japanese lagoons and cherry trees, herb gardens, rose gardens, and native woods—the Brooklyn Botanic Garden offers courses in flower arrangement and crafts, horticultural therapy, health, herbs and cooking, and garden basics. People who want to develop community gardens learn how here. And people who want to involve children in gardening can join City Kids Get Green: Adult Leaders' Workshop.

Courses of particular interest to apartment dwellers include Orchids for Beginners, Mini Deck Rail Herb Gardens, Vegetables in

Containers, and Indoor Gardening. All about Trees takes participants to Brooklyn Botanic Garden, Prospect Park, and Central Park in three sessions; Evening Garden Walks provide in-depth tours of particular areas.

Cost: Varies. Many programs run approximately $20 per class hour, with discounts to members.

Center for Christian Studies
Fifth Avenue Presbyterian Church
Seven West 55th Street
New York, New York 10019-1993

The center offers a multi-level program of study in five disciplines: Bible, theology, church history, practical theology/Christian living, and literature and the arts. Open to people of all faiths, the courses range beyond usual religious education: in Great Organs in Worship Spaces, the class listens to recordings of the great pipe organs of New York City and learns about the function of these instruments in worship. Another unusual course is a study of the American sermon and its effect on life in the United States.

Cost: The center charges a fee of $10 for members and $15 for non-members, and requests a donation. Recommended books are available at cost.

The Interfaith Center
40 East 30th Street
New York, New York 10016
(212) 685-4242
www.interfaithcenter.org

The Interfaith Center offers cultural and educational programs, and joint projects for practical action, to promote understanding and respect among the different religious communities whose members live in New York.

The center offers programs on Buddhism, Christianity, Confucianism, Hinduism, Islam, Judaism, Taoism, and other religions. Lectures, roundtables, workshops, and panel discussions provide opportunities to learn about the world's major religions and to explore contemporary issues from the perspectives of various religious traditions.

Cost: Many lectures are free. A few charge nominal amounts or request a donation. Workshops may charge fees.

Japan Society
333 East 47th Street
New York, New York 10017
(212) 832-1155
www.jpnsoc.org

Films, lectures, exhibits, and symposia on Japanese and Asian-American topics. Recent programs included "Encounters with Frank Lloyd Wright" and an accompanying exhibit, "Frank Lloyd Wright and the Art of Japan."

The Japan Society also offers classes, workshops, and immersion weekends in the Japanese language.

Cost: An 18½-hour Japanese language course is $230. Memberships start at $55. Members receive discounts for most programs and classes.

The Learning Annex
16 East 53rd Street, Fourth Floor
New York, New York 10022
(212) 371-0280
www.learningannex.com

The Learning Annex offers short, inexpensive courses on many topics, with a focus on how-to, personal improvement, and health and healing. A random scan of the catalog (found in street-corner boxes all over town) finds classes on how to: publish your own book; overcome your fear of public speaking; make a tabletop fountain garden; prevent osteoporosis; improve your sex life; earn more money; design a Web site; let go of any bad habit. The Learning Annex has an extensive computer training department with courses in Macintosh and PC, and in many popular software programs.

People interested in teaching may submit a short proposal. Phone or check the Web site for details.

Cost: Most single, three-hour sessions run between $39 and $65. Some give discounts for members and for online registration.

New York Botanical Garden
200th Street and Kazimiroff Boulevard
Bronx, New York 10458
(718) 817-8700
www.nybg.org

The New York Botanical Garden offers permanent and seasonal exhibits in the conservatory with related talks, music and dance performances, classes, and docent-led tours. You can study for a Garden Certificate or take certificate-level courses even if you're not pursuing a certificate.

Basic courses include Arranging Summer Garden Flowers, Designing with Foliage, Botany, Botanical Illustration, and Flora. The garden offers a Colorful Garden Weekend with two days of classes.

Course numbers indicate the level of required background, and program coordinators will help you figure out where you belong.

Cost: Fees vary widely and many courses carry an additional materials fee.

New York Public Library
Fifth Avenue and 42nd Street, Room M-6
New York, New York 10018-2788
(212) 930-0571
www.nypl.org

Lectures and panel discussions in the library's Celeste Bartos Forum are open to all. "In the Forum," a continuing series of lectures, interviews, and discussions, presents distinguished writers, artists, scientists, historians, scholars, and political figures in all fields.

The program for Spring 2001 included Warren Christopher and Robert B. Reich, former United States secretaries of state and labor; novelists Julian Barnes and Joyce Carol Oates; Felix Rohatyn, financier who managed the negotiations that enabled the city to pull itself out of its financial crisis in the late 1970s; Ruth Reichl, former *New York Times* restaurant critic and now editor-in-chief of *Gourmet* magazine.

Cost: Lectures $10; $7 for Library Friends and Conservators. For donors who contribute $40 or more, the library also offers special lectures, readings, trips, and luncheons with speakers.

92nd Street Y
1395 Lexington Avenue
New York, New York 10128
(212) 415-5500
www.92ndsty.org

The regular programs and the 60+ Program of the 92nd Street Y offer an unusually wide range of courses in career and finance, the humanities, Jewish education, languages, personal growth, technology, and many other topics. The Y also invites political, literary, sports, media, and scientific leaders to lecture and take part in dialogues and panel discussions.

Through the Y's 60+ Program, seniors can take courses on drama and the short story; on Hebrew, Yiddish, and Ladino folk music; on social action planning, world events, creative writing, and poetry.

Costs: Vary widely

Urban Center
457 Madison Avenue
New York, New York 10022

Located in the landmark Villard Houses, the Urban Center is home to several organizations concerned with the architecture and landscape of the city:

Architectural League of New York
(212) 753-1722
www.archleague.org

Municipal Art Society of New York
(212) 935-3960
www.mas.org

Parks Council
(212) 838-9410
www.parkscouncil.org

Urban Center Books
(212) 935-3592
www.colophon.com/urbancenterbooks

These organizations offer lectures, courses, and exhibits on architecture and design; and opportunities to become involved in current zoning, landmarking, development, and preservation issues. Some of the most popular programs are the Municipal Art Society's free tour of Grand Central Terminal on Wednesdays and their course Dutch to Disney: The Architectural History of New York (six slide lectures followed by six walking tours). The Architectural League recently sponsored Architecture and the City, a series of talks by architects with strong connections to particular cities examining the relationship of place to the activities of contemporary life.

Urban Center Books carries more than 10,000 titles relating to architecture, interior design, urban planning, landscape, and related disciplines.

Costs: Many lectures at the Architectural League are free to members, $10 to nonmembers. A few are a little more. Basic membership: $85; $125 for two.

Municipal Art Society tours generally run $12–$15. Members receive discounts on tours and also on Urban Center Books. Individual memberships in the Municipal Art Society start at $50; $25 for seniors.

Parks Council, an advocacy organization, offers memberships beginning at $35, with membership categories up to $1,000 per year.

CHAPTER **TEN**

Sports and Outdoor Activities

Part One: The Scene

Even in the dense urban environment of New York City, re-tirees have generous opportunities to enjoy the out-of-doors. We have easy access to mountains and rivers and ocean beaches. We have thousands of acres of parkland; we have hiking trails, boat docks, and marshes full of nesting birds within walking distance of a bus or subway stop.

Last Christmas my granddaughters' visit was extended by a snowfall heavy enough to close the airport. So my neighbor—and contributing author of this book—Rita Henley Jensen brought out sleds. We all crossed the street to Fort Tryon Park and joined the gang whizzing down a long, wide hill. When the sledding got too hectic, Rita took the girls on a tour around the park. At dusk, when the park lamps lighted up, it felt like a scene from Currier and Ives, or Paris.

Outdoor activity in an urban setting has a special quality. Scrambling over rocks in Central Park, with the Fifth Avenue skyline in the background, feels different from clambering near the ocean at Rockport. It used to be that, when I faced the lower Hudson from a waterside path in Battery Park City, I was pulled up tall by the twin towers of the World Trade Center behind me, strengthened in a way that never happened on a dock in Ogunquit, Maine. I miss those towers dreadfully but I'm still strengthened by the stone and concrete of New York, and I still feel that open spaces within the city have an appeal all their own. Maybe it's the anomaly that makes it more exciting, the quick switch from orderly grid to apparent wilderness. Maybe it's undisciplined nature within a disciplined urban frame. Whatever it is, urban wilderness catches my breath and touches my spirit in a way that country meadows and windswept beaches cannot duplicate.

New York is a walking city. Sign up for a local walking tour. Tours are often led by historians or writers. Learn about everyone from O. Henry to Fiorello La Guardia and get some exercise at the same time. Call the Municipal Art Society at the Urban Center for a schedule, or look at catalogs from the 92nd Street Y. (See chapter 9 for contact information.) The Municipal Art Society conducts walking tours that explore specific neighborhoods, the city's cultural and architectural landmarks, or the legacy of a particular individual (the architect Stanford White, for example). The Y's tours follow George Gershwin through Tin Pan Alley and the Great White Way. They stroll Victorian Brooklyn Heights and the Hudson River Promenade at dusk. The leader talks about Walt Whitman's writing for the *Brooklyn Eagle* and tells how the abolitionist orator Rev. Henry Beecher swayed New Yorkers against slavery—and seduced women of his congregation.

You can cross the Brooklyn Bridge on a walkway suspended among the cables, high above the cars and trucks. Brooklyn Heights on one side, Wall Street on the other, the Statue of Liberty farther out. Tugboats, barges, container ships, the Staten Island Ferry, and luncheon cruises ply the harbor below.

But walking is not just for sightseeing. In New York, walking is part of everyday life—part of food shopping; part of getting to class, getting to work. After work, hungry crowds eager for dim sum fill the sidewalks of Main Street Flushing. An hour later opera and dance aficionados walk to Lincoln Center and Brooklyn Academy of Music. There are supermarkets in New York, but city shoppers are more likely to stop at an Italian market for fresh pasta, at a greenmarket for strawberries, at a bakery for bagels—walking from one place to another. When I go to ballet class, I try to leave home early enough to walk across Central Park to the 92nd Street Y. And when I go to a movie with a friend, we walk to a café afterwards to have death-by-chocolate cake with our decaf.

New Yorkers tend to get more exercise in the course of their daily routine than is possible in many other parts of the country. A young bride in Greenwich Village told me about the first time her mother came to visit from her home in Virginia horse country. The older woman couldn't see how city people could ever get any exercise. After a day with her daughter, the mother was exhausted.

Everyone who uses the subway climbs a lot of stairs. It's good for your heart, good for your lungs, good for your legs—and more. Since I lug bags of vegetables from the Union Square greenmarket up and down subway stairs every Saturday, I'm developing strong arms too.

The New York City park system surprised me. I go to Fort Tryon Park and Central Park all the time, and I've been to other parks on occasion. But not until I started the research for this chapter did I learn just how much they offer. New York has 1,700 parks, beaches, pools, and recreation centers on more than 28,000 acres of parkland—more parkland than any other city in the country. In fact, one-quarter of the city's five boroughs is open public green space and ponds. Much has been superbly planned to offset the stone and steel, the grid and mechanics of the city. A few steps off the street and you can be in a ramble, a marsh, or a meadow. You can walk your dog, or run, or jog. You can ride your bike, or swim, or hike. In the parks, New Yorkers of all ages sunbathe and ice skate, play tennis and golf, ride horses, spot rare birds, train for the marathon, or just plain stroll.

Lovers of surf and sand enjoy the beaches at Gateway National Recreation Area, and Jones Beach and Fire Island State Parks. You can take the A train to the Far Rockaway beaches or the D train to Coney Island. Intrepid New Yorkers visit the beach in the winter to watch the ocean in different weather and experience an invigorating beach or boardwalk walk.

If you like walking, hiking, skiing, sailing, cycling, backpacking, or canoeing, and want to do it with others, you might join the Appalachian Mountain Club. Almost every weekend, summer and winter, the club schedules trips and outings for people of all ages and levels of ability. If you've never paddled a canoe or handled the lines of a sailboat, AMC offers lessons. More experienced canoeists can learn to roll a kayak in the safety of an indoor pool.

Trips are rated for difficulty, and you can talk to the leader before signing up to be sure the one you pick will be right for you. If you hesitate to go on a trip where you don't know anyone, go to one of the regular AMC orientation nights, learn about the club, and meet other members. You can also check out the New York Hiking Club, the New York Cycle Club, the New York Road Runners Club—all good opportunities to join others in a sport you enjoy. All good opportunities to make friends.

Indoor sports. The city has health clubs in spades, with weight rooms, Olympic pools, racquet courts, StairMaster, NordicTrack—equipment for any kind of exercise you want. Ys and other nonprofit organizations offer similar facilities. And City of New York/Parks and Recreation operates 35 recreation and senior centers with indoor pools, weight rooms, basketball courts, dance studios, boxing rings, art studios, game rooms, and libraries. These recreation centers also offer aerobics, Tai Chi, fencing, dancing, theater, and sculpture. Most are free or modestly priced. All are open to the general public.

Some of the city swimming pools reflect a pride in the design and construction of public facilities. The 59th Street Pool, built nearly a century ago—before "Olympic-size" defined a pool—has marble decks and heavy brass rails on the steps leading into the water. Y pools can be lovely too. The West Side Y on 63th Street has stained glass windows and tiles supposedly patterned after the mosaics of Pompeii.

How often I hear people say, "Oh, I'd love to live in New York but I'd really miss my garden." Sometimes I miss my garden too—especially in the spring, when I see flats of seedlings for sale in greenmarkets and flower marts. I want to buy them all, but I only have three window boxes! So I walk up the hill to Fort Tryon Park, where I watch the yearly progression from daffodil to tulip to peony to sunflower to chrysanthemum. I've come to appreciate the fact that they all bloom while my trowel rusts slowly under the sink. People who really want to garden can volunteer for park clean-up or planting days. They can apply for space in a community garden and grow their own tomatoes. They can join the New York Botanical Garden's Bronx Green-Up and help schoolchildren develop neighborhood gardens. Or sign up to assist the professional gardeners at Brooklyn Botanic Garden.

Exercise is no longer the exclusive province of the young. Medical experts and laypeople alike recognize that regular physical activity is key to health and well-being for all of us.

The older you get, the more important it is. In New York, no one need choose between mental stimulation and physical activity. Opportunities for both abound. The next section of this chapter introduces some New Yorkers who are making sports and outdoor activities the cornerstone of their life in retirement. The last section of the chapter presents a healthy selection of things to do and places to go.

Part Two: The People

Edwin Langsam

Some retirees say that, after 30 or 40 years on the job, they want freedom. Freedom to go to a movie or go to Alaska, to stop for a pastry or stop cooking altogether. Freedom to act on impulse, not on schedule. Others have found that an unstructured life soon begins to lose its charm.

Edwin Langsam has arranged to have both freedom and structure. On Monday and Thursday mornings he audits classes at Hunter College. On Tuesday mornings he volunteers at Lenox Hill Hospital. His afternoons, evenings, and long weekends remain open for adventure. That's when he may decide to go to a museum, an art gallery, or the theater. Or he may stay home and read a book.

In winter he skis at Hunter Mountain on Wednesdays and with the Miramar Ski Club in Vermont on weekends. In summer, Langsam and his wife go to their home in Amagansett, where he does a lot of sailing.

The beauty of scheduled mornings, Langsam says, is that they force him to get up and out. Since he often stays up late reading, the discipline imposed by early appointments nets him longer days.

For most of his career, Langsam was a corporate writer, producer, and marketer. He wrote speeches, produced films, and handled media relations and TV marketing—first on staff for corporations, then on his own. It was fun, he says, but he grew tired of using brochures and films to connect to other people, tired of using the written word to cajole and convince. He wanted to work directly with people, in relationships that didn't involve buying and selling. And he wanted more physical activity. So he gradually wound down his business, closing it completely in 1995.

Just about this time Langsam discovered he had cancer. All of a sudden he began to worry: "How long will I live?" "Will I get over it?" All of a sudden there was more he wanted to do. And he began to focus on "what I like—not what I don't like." Needing closer contact with people, he decided he would teach skiing. His cancer responded to treatment, and he's had a clean slate for the last four years. He feels very fortunate.

Now Langsam keeps physically fit skiing, hiking, sailing, and working out, and he keeps mentally fit auditing courses at Hunter College.[11] He finds that helping patients at Lenox Hill Hospital and managing Miramar Ski Club's Vermont lodge have brought him into a new world of freer relationships with people. And he gets tremendous satisfaction from teaching skiing, from seeing his students improve. Altogether, he says, "I feel more complete, less inward-looking. I look more to others."

At Lenox Hill, Langsam works on the orthopedic ward, feeding patients, taking them around in their wheelchairs, helping the nurses with a specific task or patient. When he's free, he looks around the ward for people who might need as-

---

11 For $70 a semester a senior can audit as many courses as desired.

sistance: someone having trouble eating or dialing the phone; someone in a bad mood who could use a little friendly conversation. He enjoys the work very much.

The Miramar Ski Lodge is a two-hundred-year-old former grist mill on the Mad River in Waitsfield, Vermont. Every weekend in winter, up to 50 club members take the chartered bus from New York City for two days of skiing and sociability. They keep costs low by performing the simpler housekeeping chores themselves. As volunteer operations manager for the lodge, Langsam runs the place. He hires the paid staff and sees that the pantry is stocked, the linens clean, and the firewood dry.

Major jobs are saved for summer, when the lodge is not so busy with groups. Langsam was going up the weekend after we met to oversee repairing the stove, replacing the carpets, upgrading the plumbing, and building a new firewood shelter. At Miramar, Langsam works with the other volunteers as well as with the paid staff. Dealing with volunteers is different from dealing with employees, he says. You need more finesse, more patience.

Langsam is slender and supple with silvery hair and moustache. Steve Balicer, the Miramar member who introduced me to Ed Langsam, says Langsam is the most graceful skier he's ever seen. Now over 70, Langsam doesn't ski to be outdoors or for exercise; he skis because it makes him feel free and unencumbered—like a bird. It's not the wind or the tide, as in sailing, he says. It's gravity. "At my age it's no longer speed or bashing the moguls—it's grace and style."

Almost every winter, the Miramar skiers take a longer trip. Last year they traveled to Chamonix in the French Alps, where they were led by a guide who had won a bronze medal for the French Olympic Team. Once, when most of the group couldn't understand something this guide was explaining, Langsam translated, prompting the guide to ask the translator about himself. Before Langsam could answer, another Miramar skier boasted that Langsam was a ski instructor in the States, embarrassing him by appearing to put him in the same league as an Olympic medalist. The Frenchman then invited Langsam to lead the next run and addressed him as *le professeur* for the rest of the trip. When Miramar had its end-of-the-season party with an original musical revue, they parodied the episode. And they wrote the song "Cuffs and Arches," to the tune of "Love and Marriage," because Cuffs and Arches is Langsam's teaching mantra: Skiing is all about stance, he says. To ski properly, you have to keep your weight over your arches and lean forward enough to feel your boot cuffs against your shins. To Langsam, the banter, the skit, and the song reflect the warm relationships he's developed with the other Miramar skiers.

Why is a ski lodge in the Green Mountains of Vermont called Miramar (roughly translated as "Sea View")? It turns out that in 1949 members of the Miramar Yacht club (on Sheepshead Bay, Brooklyn) formed the Miramar Ski Club. But somehow the two clubs had a falling out and didn't speak to each other for 50 years. When Langsam joined Miramar Yacht Club, no one ever mentioned Miramar Ski Club. He learned about it by chance from another skier at Hunter Mountain.

Since most of the original feuding members were dead and gone, Langsam thought it would be a good idea for the two clubs to get back together. He began to promote a reunion, with the result that, the weekend before he and I talked, the skiers spent a day on the water as guests of the sailors. They were most hospitable, Langsam says, with sailing, various events, and good food. A big success. Next winter, the ski club will invite the yacht club to the Vermont lodge.

Langsam and his wife, a psychoanalyst, moved to Long Island City in 2000 when their Manhattan landlord raised the rent beyond their limit. They live in a new high-rise development with a 180-degree view of the East River and Manhattan. It's 10 minutes to Grand Central on the subway and right across the river from the United Nations. Langsam first heard of the development from his daughter, a painter with a studio in Long Island City. A number of artists have studios in the neighborhood, and the Museum of Modern Art is opening a branch there too. It's still a good buy if you can get in, he tells me. I'm tempted to look myself.

Langsam spends about half of his time in New York City, splitting the rest between the Miramar Lodge and the house in Amagansett. He has to come back to New York City just about every week, "because I can't do without it. Ballet, theater, museum openings, galleries—the excitement. Gotta get my fix . . . gotta plug into the current."

He misses certain things from work: the excitement of seeing his story in the paper; traveling; making films, TV. Langsam was running all the time. But he points out that, during his professional career, he never let his job be his whole life. He always had many interests. Langsam thinks people who have had no life beyond work have a harder time in retirement.

Langsam expects mental and physical changes as he grows older. "And I want to put them off as long as I can." He never thinks of slowing down. Psychoanalysts can work to a very old age, and his wife says she wants to die in her chair. Langsam adds, "If my wife wants to die in her chair, I want to die in my ski boots."

Emily Goldstein

Emily Goldstein first became interested in birdwatching on a visit to the national parks of Australia. After her return she went birdwatching in Central Park and joined the Brooklyn Bird Club. Later she went on birdwatching trips to Central and South America and on her first birdwatching trip in the U.S.: to Arizona with the New York City Audubon Society. All that time, she told me, she was only a beginner, just interested in the pretty, showy birds—the parrots and toucans, the cardinals and blue jays. Since I'd never imagined anyone looking for birds other than the pretty, showy ones, I asked her what she meant.

Goldstein says she knew she was a true birdwatcher when she realized she was interested in the LBJs (little brown jobs).

There are many varieties of small brown birds like sparrows, each identified by a subtle marking: a deeper brown spot next to the beak, a stripe on the breast, a lighter wing edge. Experienced birdwatchers look for them.

At first Goldstein didn't even know how to find the bird she was looking at in her guidebook, but gradually she learned. She finds it easier to spot birds visually, harder to identify them by their song. She goes on walks with the Brooklyn Bird Club. She may go with a friend or by herself, sometimes on the spur of the moment. Even if you go alone, she says, you often meet other birders on the trail.

Goldstein is small, slender, and pixie-like, with blue eyes, short white hair and clear light skin. She used to teach high school mathematics in Brooklyn and play tennis every day after school. She continues to play almost every day. Her regular partner is a former student, 18 years younger than she, who now lives with her husband and child in Westchester. Goldstein lives in Brooklyn, so Monday she goes to Westchester, Tuesday her friend comes to Brooklyn, and Wednesday and Friday the two play in Central Park. On Saturday and Sunday, Goldstein plays doubles with a men's group in Brooklyn. She says the men she plays with are better than she, but they accept her because she always shows up.

She plays golf too, but prefers tennis because she can play tennis for an hour. Golf takes the whole day. She gave up skiing long ago, when indoor tennis became available. And it takes an hour longer to get to the ski slopes from where she lives in Brooklyn than it does from Manhattan.

Goldstein explained the system for tennis in the parks. At the beginning of the season, you buy a tennis permit for $50 ($20 if you're 62 or over) which allows you to play as often as you like. (Each borough requires its own permit). A few courts are set aside for reservation at $5; otherwise it's "catch as catch can." You can play for an hour (doubles have the courts for two hours), and if no one's waiting you can play longer. Brooklyn courts open at 8 A.M.; on weekends they're usually all taken by 7:15. In Central Park the busiest hours are weekdays 7–9 A.M. Younger people like to play before work, showering and changing in the park locker rooms. "Then the retired types come along."

Goldstein retired seven years ago. She hasn't taken up anything new in retirement; she's just doing more of the things she did before. Bridge, for instance. She always knew how to play—her parents played. But when she retired she began to play with more interest. Now she plays socially once a week, duplicate bridge once or twice. She's getting to where she'd like to play every day.

On the whole Goldstein found her transition to retirement easy. She thinks maybe that's because she's single and because she developed other interests before retirement. But she's not completely carefree. She thinks a lot about her mother, who's in a nursing home in Baltimore, where Goldstein's sister lives. Although her sister handles most of the responsibilities, Goldstein finds the situation takes a lot of her emotional energy. She doesn't miss teaching school, although she loved it when she was doing it. But that was a different phase of her life.

Now she may have something planned for every day, but she doesn't like to be committed, for instance, to showing up for a volunteer job every Thursday. She does need to be physically active, and she goes out every single day. When it's raining, and all her regular activities have been cancelled, Goldstein may spend the day reading a book, but at the very least she goes out to buy food. She doesn't eat meat, only fish. And she likes fresh fish—not day-old or frozen fish. So she has to shop every day. If she can't be physically active for three days in a row, she's unhappy.

Goldstein sees or talks to her tennis partner and a couple of other longtime friends almost every day. Her other friends are new friends—from tennis, bridge, and birdwatching. She says she's not so comfortable at parties and prefers to meet people in connection with some activity.

The desire to be active and make friends has factored into some of her major decisions. Early in her career, Goldstein won a special fellowship awarded to math and science teachers. Of the institutions she could attend, she chose Illinois Institute of Technology in Chicago because, at the time, she was folk dancing every day and wanted a city where she could find plenty of folk dancing. In Chicago she went folk dancing eight times a week—every day and twice on Sunday. And it was a good way to meet men. Goldstein loved Chicago but came back to New York. The fellowship year was the only time she's lived away from the city.

Goldstein has a car but never drives to Manhattan. She can't stand to drive in and then spend an hour looking for parking or pay $20 to a garage. The subway is terrific. And she can read on the train.

Marion Chalat

"The first year of retirement is like being a new bride."

Marion Chalat and her friends, four or five teachers who retired at the same time, say they felt like a bunch of new brides. "Parties all the time. We just loved each other." Six years later they continue to get together at least twice a year.

I found myself smiling the entire time I talked with Chalat, because her own fetching smile lights up her face continually. Looking at her reddish-brown bangs and listening to her lively musical voice, I could easily imagine the 65-year-old Chalat as a young bride.

Chalat taught biology and general science at Evander Childs High School in the Bronx. After she retired she missed her students and her subject, but she didn't miss getting up at 5:30. Yet she couldn't be as carefree as she might have wished, because the first two years of retirement were the last two years of her mother's life; Chalat was taking care of her.

When Chalat was a girl she hiked with her father. In her early married years she didn't go often, until the 1970s when she started to hike seriously again. At first she went not for the hiking itself, but to see the exotic plants that grow at the tops of mountains or in the New Jersey Pine Barrens. But she soon came to enjoy hiking for its own sake, and now she hikes several days every week. On Saturdays Chalat joins the

Appalachian Mountain Club hikes in Harriman State Park or
the New Jersey Ramapos. She tramps through Central Park
or Inwood Hill Park on Sundays, weekdays, and whenever a
heavy snowfall interrupts the bus schedule or a planned trip
is cancelled due to inclement weather but it clears up early.
She has designed her own architectural tours along the Hudson to look at the estates in Riverdale. And sometimes she
goes on longer AMC trips to the Adirondacks or the White
Mountains.

When Chalat's parked car was totaled by an SUV, she didn't
replace it. She doesn't need it. Ninety percent of the AMC
meeting spots are reachable by bus; for the others, trip leaders
arrange carpools. When she hikes alone, Chalat gets to the
trailheads by bus or subway.

In the summer of 2000 Chalat served as one of the trip
leaders at the Appalachian Mountain Club's August Camp on
Mount Rainier in Washington State. About 54 campers, plus
staff, spent two weeks at a base camp at a low elevation. Each
day the group split up, with members selecting hikes according to their interest and ability. The second week at Rainier,
Marion Chalat led 12 to 16 people on the C hikes—the most
moderate offered. She planned and announced a hike for
every day; arranged transportation, handled the sign-ups, and
selected the route and the lunch stops; and, most important,
got the group back to the campground by dinnertime. Until
that year, C hikers had taken only day trips, but Chalat
arranged an overnight excursion to the Pacific coast. They
camped on Cape Disappointment, the westernmost spot

Lewis and Clark reached on their famous journey. The overnighter involved finding a campground, arranging for tents, cooking meals . . . altogether more complicated than a day hike.

In 1990, Marion Chalat was co-chair of the AMC New York–North Jersey Chapter hiking committee. Hiking is the most popular AMC activity, and the hiking committee is the most active of all club committees. The hiking committee plans some six hundred outings a year, arranging for a proper mix of places, dates, and difficulty of hikes. They recruit competent leaders, run leader training sessions, oversee a safety committee, and publish the schedule in a booklet distributed to all AMC members three times a year. Leading hikes and working with AMC gives Chalat the satisfaction of contributing to something that has sustained and nourished her for many years.

She's hiked all over the world—India, Ireland, Scotland, the Inca Trail in Peru. In Morocco recently Chalat and her friends climbed Mount Toubkal, the highest mountain in North Africa. She enjoys meeting people in other cultures, and seeing new and different sights. Because she wants the money she spends to stay in the country she's visiting, she goes with a tour group that eats in local restaurants, sleeps in local inns, and engages local guides.

Chalat finds hiking somewhat of a meditation. "Hikers are gregarious loners," she says. Even if you're with a group, you're doing your own thing. Going up a hill, you're very focused. Physically, you may focus on your breath, your arms, your legs. You use every bit of energy you've got to pull your-self over the rocks. You can't be distracted by conversation because you need to know exactly where to put your foot on every step. But you do want to see the wildflowers, the lichen, the views. And at the same time you're focusing on your own thoughts. "I solve all my problems when I hike."

Chalat also goes cross-country skiing, snow shoeing and ice skating. Recently she's taken up belly dancing. Belly dancing? At 65? She says, "You have to accept the fact that before you start looking good, you look very bad." It takes a lot of control to isolate those muscles and it can be painful. But it's fun.

The challenge of retirement, Chalat feels, is to make life meaningful, to be interested in the world around you, but to avoid letting a volunteer job or favorite activity take over your whole life. So she goes to the opera and the theater as often as she can. She reads. And at election time she works for political candidates. But Chalat always has to do something physical. She's not as strong as she used to be. And while she intends to continue hiking for a long time, she figures swim-ming may become more important as she grows older. She and her friends joke that they'll go to a retirement home where they can hike out on the lawn.

New York Road Runners Club
Senior Fitness Walkers

On a sunny Thursday in August, when I didn't have my usual ballet class, I turned up in Central Park for the New York

Road Runners' Senior Fitness Walk. People were gathering at the Road Runners' colorful little booth near the Engineers' Gate (Fifth Avenue at 90th Street). About half the crowd were young mothers pushing babies in strollers; the other half, sitting on benches and chatting amiably, had gray hair and not quite such curvy shapes. I could tell which was the senior fitness group, and when I joined them they made me feel welcome.

Every Tuesday and Thursday at 10 A.M., NYRRC runs hour-long Senior Fitness Walks. They're free and open to everyone 60 and over. I signed in, met the club representative who had invited me, Steve Boland, and learned I had a choice of walks: a mile-and-a-half circle around the reservoir or three miles through the park. I chose the three-miler. Steve led.

"It's two minutes after 10. Why haven't we left?" The walkers were eager to get going and enjoyed teasing Steve; I soon discovered he enjoyed teasing them back. We started off and soon were walking through meadows, pine groves, and picnic areas, each more beautiful than the last. (When I got home I tried plotting our route on my map of Central Park, but I couldn't. No matter how often I walk in the park, I can never memorize the layout, and I always find places I haven't seen before.)

Jeannette Dean couldn't stop exclaiming over the lawns, footbridges, arching trees. "When I die and go to heaven, I'll tell them I've already been to Central Park." She walks in the park every day and owns just about every book that's ever been published on Central Park. Once a week she volunteers at the park's children's zoo, where she reads animal stories to visiting children.

At 84 Dean is trim and lively. Her doctor says he doesn't have to ask her if she exercises. As a young child, she didn't exercise much because she had a heart murmur, and the doctors wanted her to stay quiet. In those days a lot of children were diagnosed with heart murmurs, and they were expected to die young. When Dean started high school, her parents said, "Well, you're still alive, so you might as well exercise." They walked around the reservoir in the Bronx every day. She's still walking at least two miles a day: Tuesday and Thursday with Road Runners, the other days on her own—almost always in Central Park. Dean tells me she's named after Jeannette Rankin, the first woman elected to the United States House of Representatives. Rankin took her seat in 1917, the year Dean was born. Dean figures her parents had fairly advanced ideas about women.

We continued through part of the ramble, along the lake and over bridges, and made a pit stop at the boathouse café. I learned that Steve takes a different path every time. These walks are called "Walk and Talk," and people do. I found the pace lively enough to give me a real feeling of exercise but not so fast that it was hard to talk or keep up.

Ephraim Schaefer has been coming on these walks pretty regularly for several years now. He walks a lot in the course of his daily routine, walking instead of taking a bus when he has 10 or 15 blocks to go. He never did this when he was working. He also does the Royal Canadian Air Force exercises every day—a good program that only takes about 15 minutes and is outlined in book *Royal Canadian Air Force Exercise Plans for Physical Fitness.* (Out of print, but second-hand copies can sometimes be found.) As we went along, Schaefer talked about his plans for a trip to the Norwegian fjords this coming October. He'll be on a boat which starts above the Arctic Circle and sails down, along, and into the fjords. He's bought thermal underwear.

We passed a long line of people camped on air mattresses, blankets, and folding chairs, waiting for free tickets to *The Seagull* at the park's Delacorte Theater. Some were asleep. One man told Steve he'd gotten there at three the previous afternoon! Tickets—for that evening's performance only—would be distributed at 1 P.M. A certain number are set aside for seniors. Closer to the box office, we came upon the separate, shorter seniors line—with benches.

I walked a while with Bill Gutman. Gutman, who's 68, runs in the ultramarathon. It's 50 kilometers, or 31 miles, five miles longer than the regular marathon. He runs the regular marathon too; in 2001 he finished in 3 hours and 45 minutes.

Gutman has run all his life. But when he was working he didn't have time to train for the marathon; he started marathon training when he retired. Now he runs several times a week; he had run this morning near his apartment in Washington Heights before coming to Central Park to walk with the group. "You have to keep busy," he says. He has no special hobbies, but he does hike, usually with the Sierra Club, occasionally with the Appalachian Mountain Club.

"Look at that man with a fox on a leash," Steve said. The animal's somewhat pointy head and ears didn't look quite right to me, so I asked, "How can you tell a fox from a dog?" The others clued me in. It really was a dog.

Back at the Engineers' Gate at 11:15, I felt light on my feet. Loose-limbed and floating slightly. Mellow. I drank my bottle of water and bought an ice cream sandwich from a park vendor. Why do these walks have to be at the same time as my ballet class?

Coda: Talking with Steve a few months later, I learned that the Senior Fitness Walkers were gathering in Central Park as usual on the morning of September 11 when they learned of the attack on the World Trade Center. Steve offered to cancel. Nobody wanted to. "What are we going to do? Go home and hide in our apartments?" They walked.

Part Three: The Opportunities

Here are some of the groups you can join and places you can go for sports and outdoor activities in and around New York City. The emphasis is on participation not spectator sports. The organizations listed here welcome members of all ages and, where appropriate, rate activities by level of difficulty. Ask the leader to help you find the gentle introduction or spirited challenge that's right for you. And check Web sites, brochures, and newsletters for more details.

The costs, phone numbers, and Web addresses listed here are all subject to change. It's a good idea to verify specifics before turning up for an event or joining a group.

Opportunities for Many Kinds of Outdoor Activities

Appalachian Mountain Club
New York–North Jersey Chapter
Five Tudor City Place
New York, New York 10017
(212) 986-1430
www.amc-ny.org

With more than 16,000 members of every age, the New York–North Jersey chapter of the Appalachian Mountain Club offers more than 20 outdoor activities most weekends, many for beginners. In the course of a year they run about one thousand hikes or walks, one hundred canoe/kayak trips, and a generous number of biking, sailing, skiing, climbing, camping, shore and beach, and social events. Trips are rated by level of difficulty and many meeting places are reachable by public transportation.

New and potential members are invited to the club's monthly orientation nights and new-member parties.

Cost: Individual dues are $40; family, $65; discounts for people over 69. A four-month guest card (trial membership) costs $15.

Club freeTime
20 Waterside Plaza, Suite 6F
New York, New York 10010
(212) 545-8900
www.clubfreetime.com

In a June issue, this monthly newsletter of free or low-cost events in Manhattan listed about 40 hikes along the Hudson River and to places like the Croton Aqueduct and Shu Swamp Preserve in Locust Valley. The same issue listed nearly 60 garden, park, and city walks, and more than three dozen opportunities for indoor climbing, in-line skating, Tai Chi, yoga, and other sports, classes, and outings.

Cost: A subscription is $24.95 per year.

Elderhostel
11 Avenue de Lafayette
Boston, Massachusetts 02111-1746
(877) 426-8056
www.elderhostel.org

Out of its more than 10,000 programs given in more than one hundred countries, Elderhostel offers a number of Active Outdoor Programs for people 55 and older with varying interests and physical capabilities. Examples of programs within easy reach of New York City include Ridgetop Rambles at Frost Valley in the Catskills, a five-night autumn hiking program for experienced hikers in good physical condition; hiking for beginners, walking trips, and golf at Lake Placid; weeklong intergenerational camping programs (grandparents with grandchildren) at Great Camp Sagamore in the Adirondacks.

Cost: Five-night Active Outdoor Programs usually range from four to six hundred dollars (your grandchild's camp tuition is less).

Gateway National Recreation Area
Public Affairs Office
210 New York Avenue
Staten Island, New York 10305
(718) 354-4606
www.nps.gov/gate/index.htm

Gateway National Recreation Area, at the entrance to New York Harbor, is America's first urban national park. All but one of its units (Sandy Hook, New Jersey) lie within the New York city limits. Visitors to Gateway swim, sail, surf, and fish. The park offers bird-watching, sandy ocean beaches, and nature talks; boating, camping, cycling, fishing, and sunset walks; horseback riding, stargazing, and wildlife viewing; and a roster of artistic and musical events.

Cost: Gateway has no entrance fees. However, beach parking fees are charged at Sandy Hook and Jacob Riis Park during the summer, and certain activities require permits.

Long Island Rail Road
One-Day Getaways
(718) 217-LIRR
www.mta.ny.nyc.us

The Long Island Rail Road schedules more than 19 different trips to historic mansions, vineyards, beaches, and estates within easy reach of New York City. Paddleboat cruises through Port Jefferson Harbor and across Long Island's Great South Bay may offer lunch aboard ship; some dock at seaside villages where tour members can stroll and shop.

Cost: Tour prices range from $22 to $59; beach getaways from $8 to $18.

City of New York/Parks and Recreation

nycparks.completeinet.net

New York City has 1,700 parks, beaches, pools, and recreation centers on more than 28,000 acres of parkland. The eight largest, the "Flagship Parks," are the most precious jewels in the city's emerald necklace. Their woods, meadows, marshes, and ravines bring wild and serene landscapes into easy reach of the most congested urban neighborhoods. The smaller parks, often underutilized, also offer New Yorkers greenery and gardens, hiking and horseback riding, boathouses and baseball. Park service volunteers can take part in the gardening, landscaping, and clean-up of the parks, or assist in the organizational, political, and educational activities necessary for an effective parks program.

The resources and programs of the city parks are too extensive to detail here, but the phone numbers below can get you started. For the full array of opportunities available in the city parks, consult the above Web site, or call the outreach coordinators listed below.

NEIGHBORHOOD PARKS

Parks and Recreation Outreach Coordinators
Bronx (718) 430-4641
Brooklyn (718) 965-8992
Manhattan (212) 408-0214
Queens (718) 520-5913
Staten Island (718) 815-7194

For information on volunteer and other opportunities in the neighborhood parks, call the outreach coordinator, who will direct you to the person, group, activity, or neighborhood you want.

FLAGSHIP PARKS

The Flagship Parks generally have their own organizations or conservancies to maintain them and organize activities. We've listed phone numbers for *some* of the activities available in each of these parks. Contact the park of your choice for more information.

BRONX

Van Cortland Park
(718) 430-1890
Golf Course (718) 543-4595
Riding Stable (718) 548-4848
Tennis Permits (718) 430-1838

Pelham Bay Park
(718) 430-1890
Golf Course (718) 885-1258
Sports Permits (718) 430-1840
Tennis Permits (718) 430-1838

BROOKLYN

Prospect Park
(718) 965-8951
Outreach (718) 965-8952
Park Rangers (718) 438-0100
www.prospectpark.org

MANHATTAN

Central Park
(212) 360-3444
Bicycle rental (212) 517-3623
Boathouse (212) 517-3623

MANHATTAN (cont)

Fishing at Harlem Meer
    (212) 860-1370
Horseback Riding (212) 724-5100
Skating
    Lasker Rink (212) 534-7639
    Wollman Rink (212) 439-6900
Tai Chi (212) 348-4867
Tennis (212) 280-0201
www.centralparknyc.org

Riverside Park
(212) 408-0264
79th Street Boat Basin (public
    marina) (212) 496-2105

QUEENS

**Flushing Meadows–
  Corona Park**
(718) 760-6565
Shea Stadium (718) 699-4220
Wildlife Center (718) 271-1500
USTA National Tennis Center
    (718) 760-6200
Marina (718) 478-0480
Skating Rink (718) 271-1996

Forest Park
(718) 235-0815
Golf Course (718) 296-0999

STATEN ISLAND

Greenbelt Park
(718) 667-2165

Specialized Outdoor Opportunities

Beaches and Pools

nycparks.completeinet.net

New York City Parks and Recreation operates 14 miles of
beaches in four boroughs (none in Manhattan), as well as indoor and outdoor pools in all five boroughs. Jones Beach
State Park and Gateway National Recreation Area also offer
ocean bathing and bayside swimming.

Along with breathtaking ocean views, waves, and respite
from the summer heat, these beaches have boardwalks, food

concessions, picnic areas, bathhouses and lockers, pavilions for summer concerts, and other amenities.

Cost: City, state and national park beaches are generally free, but some charge for parking.

CITY PARK BEACHES

BRONX

Orchard Beach and Promenade
On Long Island Sound in
Pelham Bay Park.
(718) 885-2275

BROOKLYN

Brighton Beach, Coney Island, and Coney Island Boardwalk
On the Atlantic Ocean, from West
37th Street to Corbin Place.
(718) 946-1350

Manhattan Beach
On the Atlantic Ocean, Oriental
Boulevard from Ocean Avenue to
Mackenzie Street.
(718) 946-1373

QUEENS

Rockaway Beach and Boardwalk
On Atlantic Ocean, from Beach First
Street, Far Rockaway, to Beach
149th Street, Neponsit.
(718) 318-4000

STATEN ISLAND

South and Midland Beaches and Franklin D. Roosevelt Boardwalk
On Lower New York Bay, from Fort
Wadsworth to Miller Field.
Midland Beach
(718) 987-0709 (Main Office)
South Beach
(718) 816-6804 (Satellite Office)

Wolfe's Pond Beach
On Raritan Bay and Prince's Bay,
Holton to Cornelia Avenues.
(718) 984-8266

Jones Beach State Park
Long Island
(516) 785-1600
www.nysparks.com/maps (follow the links to Jones Beach)

One of the country's most famous ocean beaches, Jones Beach has six and one-half miles of sandy beach for surf bathing, a bay beach for still-water bathing, two swimming pools, a two-mile board-walk, surf fishing, a boat basin, an amphitheater with frequent concerts, and many other attractions.

Riis Park and Sandy Hook
Gateway National Recreation Area
www.nps.gov/gate/index.htm

Designated swimming beaches include
Jacob Riis Park
Rockaway, New York (718) 318-4300

Great Kills Park
Staten Island, New York (718) 987-6790

Sandy Hook, New Jersey (732) 872-5970

POOLS

New York City Parks and Recreation operates 58 indoor and 10 outdoor pools—too many to list here. For locations and information, consult *nycparks.completeinet.net* on the Web, or the blue-bordered "New York City Offices" section of the telephone directory white pages.

Birding

Habitats in the city parks, around the bays and estuaries of New York harbor, and on the Long Island and New Jersey shorelines attract native and rare birds migrating along the Atlantic flyway, breeding birds, shorebirds, and wintering waterfowl. If you want to join a birdwatching group, there are many in the city; if you prefer to tramp through the parks and marshes with a few friends (safer than alone), you can reach most trailheads and access points by public transportation.

Local sites and groups include:

Brooklyn Bird Club
www.brooklynbirdclub.org

Almost every weekend, members of all ages and skill levels take part in club birdwatching walks in Prospect Park and Jamaica Bay. Longer trips take members to the eastern end of Long Island and Cape May, New Jersey.

Cost: Dues are $20 per year; $15 for seniors.

Central Park
(212) 772-0210
www.centralparknyc.org/thingstodo.php

All of Central Park is a sanctuary for migrating and nesting birds. Almost two hundred species can be seen in a year and the Ramble (Frederick Law Olmsted's 38-acre "wild garden" in the park) is rated one of the top 15 birdwatching sites in the United States.

Call Belvedere Castle at the number above for a schedule of bird walks, and to reserve a free Discovery Kit backpack with binoculars, a guidebook, maps, and sketching materials.

Jamaica Bay Wildlife Refuge
Cross Bay Boulevard, Queens
(718) 318-4340

Each year thousands of migrating water, land, and shorebirds stop at the Jamaica Bay Wildlife Refuge; more than 325 species have been recorded over the last 25 years. The Refuge's 9,155 acres include salt marsh, upland field and woods, fresh and brackish water ponds, and an open expanse of bay and islands—all within the boundaries of New York City.

Trails are open daily from sunrise to sunset. The visitor center, featuring exhibits on the natural history of the area and a small selection of field guides and related materials for sale, is open every day from 8:30 A.M. to 5 P.M. (except Thanksgiving, Christmas, and New Year's Day).

New York City Audubon Society
71 West 23rd Street, Room 1529
New York, New York 10010-4102
(212) 691-7483
www.nycas.org

Audubon promotes conservation education and policies, brings together birders of different ages and skill levels, and offers classes in bird identification and nature photography.

Monthly membership programs (open free to the public) cover topics like the birds or butterflies of a particular region, marine life in Jamaica Bay, wildlife of the arctic tundra and more.

Cost: Dues are $20 a year; $15 for seniors.

Pelham Bay Park

With 2,700 acres, Pelham Bay is the largest of the city parks. Within its salt marshes, birders will find egrets and herons and, on the marsh's upland edges, red-winged blackbirds and marsh wren. The Lagoon, a remnant of the original Pelham Bay, and Turtle Cove, an inlet to the south, provide excellent bird shelter and feeding grounds.

Camping

Associated Camps
271 Route 46, Suite A-109
Fairfield, New Jersey 07004
www.bhvc.org

Associated Camps, partially sponsored by United Jewish Appeal, runs an adult camp situated along a lake in the Poconos. Summer camp activities include ceramics, choral singing, computer, crafts, drama, dancing, hiking, lectures and discussions on Jewish and contemporary issues, painting, pool and waterfront activities, tennis, and yoga. The camp is open to adults 55 and over; most campers are in their 70s.

Associated Camps also runs intergenerational weekends for grandparents to camp with their grandchildren, five-day Lifelong Learning and Elderhostel programs, and shorter sessions for Jewish holidays.

Cost: A two-week summer camp session is $745.

Campers' Group
David Levner
63-36 98th Place, #5J
Rego Park, (Queens) New York 11374
(718) 897-1448
www.campersgroup.org

David Levner points out that camping is a low-impact sport enjoyed by people of every age. Most members of Campers' Group are between 30 and 60, and people from 3 to 73 have gone on the trips.

Each weekend the group goes to a different rustic, secluded campsite far from crowds, trailers, and radios, but within a three-hour drive of New York City.

Campgrounds may be along beaches, glacial lakes, or waterfalls; near forests, ridges, or ravines. Some campers bring their lounge chairs and books, others their hiking boots and day packs. Trippers swim, canoe, hike, jog, play Scrabble, sing, play musical instruments, dance, and roast marshmallows around the campfire.

Trips average 10–20 people with two members coordinating, collecting fees, and arranging rides. Every active member is expected to take a turn coordinating. Members bring their own food and most equipment, but tents are available for first-timers who want to try camping before they invest.

Cost: Individual dues are $12 per year; family dues are $18. Reductions available for those electing to receive the newsletter by e-mail instead of postal mail.

Site fees are $0–$10 per night; the total for a camping weekend is seldom more than $40.

Cycling

Bicycle Touring Club of North Jersey
Post Office Box 839
Mahwah, New Jersey 07430-0839
(973) 284-0404
www.btcnj.com

BTCNJ is a nonprofit, all-volunteer bicycling club with over 1,500 members and one of the most active ride schedules in the country. The club holds several annual events and a monthly club meeting with bicycling-related programs, followed by socializing and refreshments.

Cost: Individual dues are $27; family dues are $32; discounts for multi-year payments.

New York Cycle Club
Columbus Circle Station
Post Office Box 20541
New York, New York 10023
(212) 828-5711
www.nycc.org

With 1,400 enthusiastic members, the New York Cycle Club organizes weekly rides, weekend trips, training programs, and special events for novice and experienced cyclists. Club members explore some of the most beautiful routes in the tri-state area.

Members receive a monthly bulletin (also available online), discounts at local bike shops, access to an annual training series, the semi-annual club roster, and lists of books, maps, how-tos, biker-friendly diner destinations, and other useful information about cycling in and around New York City.

Cost: Individual dues are $21; $27 for a couple residing at the same address.

Gardening

Several groups accept volunteers for community gardening projects: City of New York Parks and Recreation and Green Thumb, an organization that provides materials and technical support to create public gardens in former empty lots. You can sign up for a regular job or for a one-time assignment during Spring Green-Up (April and May) or Fall Clean-Up (October). You may be able to organize a community garden of your own.

Call Green Thumb or the parks outreach coordinator in your borough to be connected with a group, neighborhood, or park of your choice.

City of New York/Parks and Recreation
Bronx (718) 430-4641
Brooklyn (718) 965-8992
Manhattan (212) 408-0214
Queens (718) 520-5913
Staten Island (718) 815-7194

Green Thumb
49 Chambers Street, Room 1020
New York, New York 10007
(212) 788-8070

Brooklyn Botanic Garden
1000 Washington Avenue
Brooklyn, New York 11225
(718) 623-7261
www.bbg.org

Brooklyn Botanic Garden accepts volunteers with some gardening experience to work in the gardens and behind the scenes in plant propagation. Volunteers aid in pruning, planting, raking, mulching, and weeding, and are trained in their specific tasks by professional gardeners.

The greatest need is for garden guides. These volunteers assist in classroom workshops, lead schoolchildren and adult groups on walking tours, and help plan special theme tours.

Golf

New York City Parks and Recreation operates 13 golf courses, open to all. The Van Cortlandt Golf Course, opened in 1895, was the nation's first public course. The Golf Clubhouse at Van Cortlandt Park, built in 1902, is situated on a lake and contains equipment rental facilities, lockers, and a snack shop.

All Parks and Recreation golf courses have the same registration policies and fees; reserve seven days in advance.

Cost: Greens fees are $21; $9 for seniors. Reservation fee is $2

Bronx Golf Courses
Van Cortlandt (718) 543-4595
Mosholu (718) 655-9164
Pelham/Split Rock (718) 885-1258

Brooklyn Golf Courses
Dyker Beach (718) 836-9722
Marine Park (718) 338-7149

Queens Golf Courses
Forest Park (718) 296-0999
Clearview (718) 229-2570
Douglaston (718) 428-1617
Kissena (718) 939-4594

Staten Island Golf Courses
Silver Lake (718) 447-5686
LaTourette (718) 351-1889
South Shore (718) 984-0101

Hiking

New York Hiking Club
1408 East 49th Street
Brooklyn, New York 11234
(718) 258-7276
www.nynjtc.org/clubpages/nyh.html

The New York Hiking Club, a member of the New York–New Jersey Trail Conference, runs hikes every weekend in season, and other outdoor activities and social events throughout the year. All hikes are described in the club's newsletter and rated according to difficulty. Hiking groups meet at Grand Central or other terminals and travel together to the trailhead.

Cost: Dues are five dollars.

New York–New Jersey Trail Conference
156 Ramapo Valley Road
Mahwah, New Jersey 07430
(201) 512-9348
www.nynjtc.org

The New York–New Jersey Trail Conference comprises more than 85 hiking and environmental organizations dedicated to building and maintaining systems of marked hiking trails, protecting related open space, and ensuring public access to 1,300 miles of foot trails from the Delaware Water Gap north to beyond the Catskills.

Members receive a list of the more than 85 groups belonging to the conference, and many other benefits that complement those offered by the individual hiking clubs.

Cost: Individual dues are $21, senior $15; family dues are $26, senior family $20.

Running

New York Road Runners Club
Nine East 89th Street
New York, New York 10128
(212) 860-4455
www.nyrrc.org

Runners of all ages take part in New York City running events—including the marathon and the ultramarathon, an even longer run.

But people who have not been running and who may never enter a race can begin to improve their own fitness level with New York

Road Runners. Every Tuesday and Thursday morning at 10, NYRRC offers a beginning fitness program for people 60 and over. No need to sign up in advance. Just show up at the club's information booth in Central Park—Fifth Avenue at 90th Street.

Cost: Dues are $30 a year. The Tuesday and Thursday walks are free, and open to non-members.

Skiing

Miramar Ski Club
71 West 23rd Street, Box B3
New York, New York 10010-4190
www.miramar.org

Miramar is a multigenerational ski club that owns a lodge on the Mad River in Waitsfield, Vermont. Members and their guests board buses every Friday evening in the winter season for downhill skiing and snowboarding at Sugarbush, Mad River Glen, Killington, or Stowe, and cross-country at Ole's and Mt. Mansfield Touring Center. The club also runs summer trips, and the lodge is open year-round.

Miramar has about two hundred members—of all ages and ability levels. The lodge accommodates 54 people, mostly in twin-bedded rooms. Members keep costs low by helping with light housekeeping chores. On off-season work weekends they tackle the bigger jobs.

Cost: Basic annual dues are $135. New members pay an initiation fee of $250 ($125 each of the first two years).

Two-day weekend trips typically cost $140, which covers round-trip bus travel, lodging, breakfasts, dinners, and various parties. Members receive discounts on lift tickets and can use the lodge for $15 a day off-season.

Tennis

City of New York/Parks and Recreation
Permit information by telephone:
Bronx (718) 430-1830
Brooklyn (718) 965-8993
Manhattan (212) 360-8131
Queens (718) 263-4121
Staten Island (718) 390-8035

Parks and Recreation operates outdoor tennis courts in every borough and indoor courts in every borough except Staten Island.

A season permit, good on any court in the issuing borough, allows you to play as often as you want, for an hour (two hours for doubles) on a first come, first served basis. If no one is waiting at the end of the hour, you can play longer.

Cost: Permits for adults 18–61 are $50; 62 and older, $20. A single-play permit is $5. Some courts can be reserved for an additional $5.

Senior Tennis Programs
USTA National Tennis Center
Flushing Meadows–Corona Park
Flushing, New York 11368
(718) 760-6200

City Parks Foundation offers free lessons for seniors 62 and over at the USTA National Tennis Center in Queens. Lessons are Mondays 8:30–9:30 A.M., January through March. Registration is limited, and available on a first come, first serve basis. Call Burt Rosen at 718-699-4200 for more information or e-mail *parktennis@aol.com*.

Opportunities for Indoor Sports and Exercise

Chelsea Piers Sports Center
Pier 60
23rd Street and the Hudson River
New York, New York 10011
(212) 336-6100
www.chelseapiers.com

Chelsea Piers offers a special discounted off-peak membership to seniors 60 and older. This membership option gives full, unlimited access to all facilities and classes, from 6 A.M. to 4 P.M., Monday through Friday. Facilities include a six-lane pool, a quarter-mile track, and extensive cardio- and strength-training equipment. Activities include bowling, dance, golf, ice skating, sailing, and swimming. The Sports Center offers over 125 group fitness classes per week including yoga, stretch, aqua strength, and dance. No sign-up or reservations required. Just come.

Cost: Discounted off-peak membership fee is $100 initial, $65 per month.

DOROT Wellness Program for Seniors
171 West 85th Street
New York, New York 10024
(212) 769-2850
www.dorotusa.org

DOROT's Stretch and Strength Weight Training class draws upon the "Strong Women Stay Young" Program. Men coming to DOROT are more likely to join Chinese Exercise with Cheng-de Gu, Tai Chi Master. Other classes include Yoga, Movement to

Music, Brain Gym (exercises to integrate the right and left sides of the brain), and more than a dozen different Wellness Workshops.

Cost: Suggested donation of three to five dollars per lecture or class.

Recreation Centers, City of New York/Parks and Recreation (212) 360-8211

New York City Parks and Recreation operates more than 35 recreation centers and 13 senior centers in the five boroughs. Centers differ but usually have indoor pools, weight rooms, basketball courts, dance studios, boxing rings, art studios, game rooms, and libraries. Adult programs vary among the centers; typical offerings include aerobics, Tai Chi, fencing, dancing, theater, and sculpture. Most are free or modestly priced, and all are open to the general public. Call 212-360-8211 to find the recreation and senior centers in your borough.

Cost: Suggested donations of $5–$25 per year for adults 18–55; $5–10 per year for people over 55. To receive a membership card, pay by check or money order and bring two photos of yourself.

Sport and Fitness Clubs

New York City has a large number of sport and fitness clubs, cardio fitness centers, gymnasiums, martial arts centers, racquet clubs, YM- and YWCAs, and other places for indoor physical activity. Consult the Yellow Pages under Exercise and Physical Fitness Programs or Health Clubs and Gymnasiums for guidance.

CHAPTER **ELEVEN**

Freelance and Part-Time Work, and New Career Opportunities

Part One: The Scene

Some people say they never want to retire. And even people who've had it with rush-hour subway trains or bumper-to-bumper commuter traffic may want to stay connected with the work world. For one thing, there's the money. There's also the camaraderie and the desire to remain part of a fast-moving, disciplined atmosphere. To use the knowledge and skills acquired over as much as half a century. For these reasons, and surely others, many retirees want to continue working—but not necessarily full-time.

Not everyone retires willingly. Older workers are especially vulnerable in a faltering economy, a corporate merger, or downsizing. Even entrepreneurs, self-employed and presumably able to continue as long as they want, may run into hard times, faltering health, disputes with partners, or other circumstances that force them to stop before they're ready. And people may figure it makes good financial sense to take retirement when generous corporate benefits are offered, but they may still want to work outside the home.

I'm writing this chapter shortly after the attack on the World Trade Center, and following a year in which the economy gradually softened. Many knowledgeable people believe the New York City economy is inherently sound and will pick up again, offering myriad opportunities as before. But no one knows for sure. Whatever the economy, if you want to continue working for either your company or another one after you retire, try to lay the groundwork ahead of time. Take the initiative to structure a job for yourself. Don't just say, "I'd like to keep working. Is there anything I could do part-time?" You'll do better and find the work more satisfying if you can define a project or a niche that fills an unmet need. And don't wait until your retirement party to propose it. Start conversations with the people involved well in advance.

If you plan to move to New York when you retire and expect to look for work in the city, talk to everyone you know before you leave your hometown. If your company has an office in the city, ask your boss for an introduction to his or her New York counterpart. Here again, if you know your company well, you may be able to carve out a part-time job for yourself by identifying a set of responsibilities you would like to take on.

If your company does not have an office in New York, talk to your colleagues, customers, or clients before you come. Surely, someone knows someone here. You may be surprised at the names you can add to your Palm Pilot. Think about how people in allied fields of work can help you. Richard Cummings, retired from a vice-presidency in the financial department of a bank, continues to handle tax and accounting work for a few longtime clients. Cummings suggests that, if an accountant is moving to New York and looking for new clients here, he or she should connect with an attorney who can make referrals. The attorneys you know in your hometown may be able to refer you to attorneys in New York. Ask them.

Join your college alumni or alumnae association. Most have career service offices that can help you. The associations also run programs and social gatherings at which you'll meet people who know New York's movers and shakers, and have ideas that can lead you to consider new prospects.

It's a good idea to keep up your professional memberships and perhaps join some new groups. From the Association of the Bar of the City of New York to the Association of Magicians, just about every trade and profession has its own organization. Some, like Dancers over 40 and Retired Teachers Association, deal specifically with concerns in retirement, including job search. Other groups, like Single Women's Alliance Network (SWAN) and the MIT Enterprise Forum (not limited to MIT graduates) cut across professional lines to bring together people with a common life thread.

But coming back to the workplace can be discouraging. Your old buddies may be gone now, and none of the new members know a thing about the good programs you ran back in the 1980s. Wandering around a networking reception with a glass of white wine in your hand, on the outside of a dozen clusters of lively strangers—all 30 years old—would drive most of us back to the shuffleboard court. If you feel that an organization could help you, try volunteering for a committee. Most groups need volunteers desperately; you offer experience and a perspective that will add depth to their operation. Working in a definite role with other members will bring you into the fold.

Help Wanted ads can help. A few years ago I submitted a proposal in response to an ad and became an on-call freelance writer for the Metropolitan Transportation Authority. The MTA has approved me and we've agreed on an hourly rate so, when their corporate communications department is over-worked and calls me, we have the basic contract items in place. Other work relationships start more casually: I met one potential client on the chair lift at a ski resort. These writing assignments are irregular, however, and wouldn't be enough for me if I didn't have this book. The idea for *Retire in New York City* surfaced in a conversation I had driving back from a ski weekend in the Adirondacks, and I latched onto it. The moral: be ready to leap for the butterfly when it flits by.

Some of the people in this book have drawn on their work experience to do interesting part-time, paid work: Marion Chalat mentors new young teachers. Steve August, Jane Randall, and Bernie Landou write brochures and press releases for nonprofit organizations whose purposes they support. Jack Taylor edited the memoirs of Alger Hiss. Others, like Arline Rubin (profiled later in this chapter), drew on skills from another part of life. Rubin turned a hobby into a business.

It's not easy to keep up a satisfactory level of freelance work. Anyone who's earned a living freelance knows you have to market yourself all the time. And that there always seems to be too little work, or too much. A retiree who wants part-time work as one component of a life that also includes travel, sports, volunteering, and other pursuits may have to forgo the footloose fun at first and invest serious effort in getting started. Retirees with a long history of work in a particular field and close ties to people in it do best, even when they shift their own job descriptions. It helps to build relationships with people younger than yourself while you're still working. If everyone you know at the company retires when you do, you won't have any friends back in the office to call you when the director of sales goes on maternity leave and they need a replacement for three months.

Serious workers who have spent 30 or 40 years in a field have a reservoir of knowledge from which they can make a creative leap once they're free of the daily pressure to produce. Some retirees profiled in this chapter have written books, designed research projects, or developed independent consultancies in their fields. Others, after leaving longtime professional appointments, have started completely new businesses based on their hobbies or other interests. Some say they're working harder than ever before; others limit work to 10 or 20 hours a week. Their stories follow.

Part Two: The People

Claudia Zaslavsky

Claudia Zaslavsky is known as "the mother of ethnomathematics." She developed her specialty, multicultural perspectives in mathematics education, almost completely after she retired from teaching high school math. Her first book, *Africa Counts: Number and Pattern in African Culture*, was published when she was still teaching, and is in its third edition. Now, at 84, Zaslavsky has 12 published books to her credit. She lectures, consults, and runs colloquia for teachers of mathematics.

Zaslavsky lives only a few blocks from me. When she walks over to meet me she walks quickly, with zest. Her voice and face are animated; her smile is broad. And her white hair, parted on the side and combed in a pageboy, vaguely echoes the 1940s. She's self-assured but unpretentious about her accomplishments.

During the 1960s Zaslavsky taught high-school mathematics in a Westchester County district that had voted to integrate its schools by busing three years before the Supreme Court decision on school desegregation. She had black and white students from wealthy neighborhoods, and black and white students from poor neighborhoods. The school administration, wanting to bring aspects of African culture into the curriculum, engaged native Africans to teach Swahili, African literature and African history. In 1969 Zaslavsky's school offered a course in African history for its teachers, and she took it. She decided to write her term paper on African mathematics.

African mathematics? Zaslavsky soon found that virtually nothing had been written on the topic. It wasn't even listed in library catalogs. She wrote to authorities on African languages, only to discover that no one seemed to know about African math or have much regard for the mathematical ability of African people.

Zaslavsky knew that people in every culture use numbers to measure, keep records, and do business; they need mathematics for their architecture, for design forms and patterns, and for games of strategy and chance. In one of her papers she points out that the African game mancala "is considered by some game experts to be one of the best mathematical games in the world." And she discovered that, in play, African children drew a graph-like figure in the sand by easily following a set of rules to that a Hungarian anthropologist who observed them found impossible to master.

When the course at her high school was over, Zaslavsky continued her research. She wrote an article for the *Mathematics Teacher*, and gradually began to find a few people who knew something about African math. About that time, a textbook publisher invited her to write a book on African mathematics. To research it, Zaslavsky traveled to London, Kenya, and Tanzania and was helped by her son, who was teaching mathematics in a town near Nairobi. It seems they'd both gotten interested in the same remote subject at the same time—but independently.

Zaslavsky found African cultures to be sophisticated in their use of mathematics. And she was able to incorporate much of what she had learned in her Westchester classroom. She has always tried to help students see mathematics as integral to life. For example, she felt that learning to count to 10 in Yoruba would not be enough. But when she showed her American students how in some African communities people build round houses because the round shape yields the greatest enclosed floor area for the material used, her students could then calculate and think about the shapes of houses in different cultures with respect to available materials and customs.

To complete her book, Zaslavsky interviewed African graduate students in the United States about the mathematics of their own cultures. She read books by anthropologists and colonial officers (you have to understand a culture in order to govern it effectively, she says). *Africa Counts* came out in 1973. And, for Claudia Zaslavsky, a new career had begun.

In 1977, when she stopped teaching, Zaslavsky was asked to write a book for parents of young children. Since then she's published 10 more books and revised *Africa Counts*. Some of her books are for educators, some for any educated adult, and some specifically for children. I bought *Number Sense and Nonsense* and *Math Games and Activities from Around the World* for two of my grandchildren.

Zaslavsky has worked as a consultant to textbook publishers, taught at Bank Street College of Education, and conducted workshops for Brooklyn elementary schools and for other school systems. She gets paid for some workshops, but not for all. She had been in a doctoral program at Teachers College, Columbia University, but after she wrote *Africa Counts* she didn't want to do that much research again. And, since she could get published without a doctorate, she saw no reason to get one.

Living in New York gives Zaslavsky access to the libraries and universities she uses in her work. And she's developed strong relationships with teachers willing to try out her ideas in their classrooms. Educational journals welcome her articles because they are based on real classroom experience with diverse groups of children.

Zaslavsky has gone beyond Africa. In her workshops she meets teachers from all over the world who contribute ideas that enrich her books and articles. She consults for the University of Alaska on incorporating Eskimo perspectives into the K–8 mathematics and science curriculum. And she recently published *Fear of Math: How to Get Over It and Get On with Your Life*. It's the only book that probes deeply into the fear of math among minorities. To write it she sent out a questionnaire to a number of colleagues, and an instructor at Florida A&M gave it to his students. Altogether, she got about five hundred responses, rich material for the book.

Zaslavsky had no new project in mind when we talked and has no grand plan for future work. She's not attempting systematic or worldwide coverage of mathematics. She prefers to keep working and let new book ideas emerge.

Dick Andros

At 75, Dick Andros is one of the oldest male dancers teaching an open ballet class in New York City. Tall, with sparkling blue eyes, a rosy complexion, and a trim white beard, Andros walks with a dancer's turnout—and a cane. Age and arthritis force him to teach sitting down, but in his mind's eye he sees his youthful self executing the steps with vigor and élan. The contrast sometimes depresses him. But, even while seated, he never misses the angle of an ankle, and he keeps a class of regulars moving and learning—and devoted to him.

On days when he's feeling up to it, Andros demonstrates combinations at the *barre*. But usually he calls the steps from his chair at the front of the class, and his students remember the patterns. Even without demonstrating, he's able to explain how to "lift your body while your knees bend."

The crosstown bus trip from his apartment to the studio is hard for Andros, but he continues to teach five mornings a week because it gets him up and out of the house every day. And he feels his arthritis would be a lot worse if he had stopped moving when he stopped performing.

Loss of physical ability is especially devastating to dancers, Andros says. Their careers and sense of self rest on their physical capabilities. He tells me of a male dancer in his 80s who avoided an opportunity to reconnect with a woman he'd partnered 60 years before because he didn't want to see how she had aged. Andros says this is not uncommon. Elderly dancers sometimes forgo the possibility of current friendship in order to preserve the memory of youth and agility.

The lucky ones have found other things to do in retirement. One friend went into dance administration, first running and now consulting to the Merce Cunningham Studio. One is an officer for Actors' Equity Union. Another has become a sculptor. Choreography would seem a natural for retired dancers, but it's expensive. You need dancers, a studio, music. Although he has written and choreographed shows of all kinds, Andros doesn't have that kind of backing now.

Dick Andros grew up through the Depression and the dust storms of Oklahoma. When he was six years old he whirled around the living room to records played on his mother's hand-cranked phonograph. Later his aunt enrolled him and his brother in a ballroom dance class. When he was 15, he saw the Ballet Russe de Monte Carlo and applied to ballet school the next morning, only to be rejected because he weighed 225 pounds. Later he dieted down to 150.

Called to serve in the U.S. Army near the end of World War II, Andros was sent to Japan and assigned to Club Ichiban, the largest enlisted-men's club in the Pacific theater. He started out painting signs and within a year, at the age of 19, became director of the club, a four-story establishment with a theater, ballroom, bar, and 80 employees. He says now that he was not at all ready for such responsibility.

It was at Club Ichiban that his ballet career began. Andros and one of the USO entertainers performed together. They were a great success and he says his fellow soldiers were very supportive.

Andros has had a rich career: dancing, teaching, and choreographing, mostly in New York but also in Pittsburgh, London, Israel, and Scotland. He's written and produced shows all over the New York metropolitan area and worked with some of the most respected theater and dance figures of our time. He's organized and run schools of dance and taught in summer camps. Occasionally, his height (six foot one) and his hairy chest prevented him from getting roles for which he was otherwise qualified. His philosophy is succinct: "Train your mind. Rehearse a show and do a show."

In 1987 Andros bought a computer. Knowing that most of his dance students had only the sketchiest idea of ballet history, he decided to write the story of the art. He would begin with Catherine de Médicis, who started ballet as we know it in 1581, and concentrate on the innovators. He planned to self-publish the work in segments as the *Dick Andros Newsletter.* He didn't have any idea how to write this history, but after 36 issues the concept came to him. He would start all over again and write it chronological order.

He wrote another piece, "Has Ballet Become Track and Field?" arguing that, in dance, technique has pushed out art; he attached it to his newsletter. The editor of the magazine *Dance Pages* saw the piece, published it, and invited Andros to write a regular column. Andros wrote 18 "Ballet Beat" columns, before the magazine folded. Recently he became the editor of the Dancers over 40 newsletter.

For more than 12 years Andros has been researching the history of ballet at the Lincoln Center branch of the New York Public Library. He also interviews elderly dancers, spending hours talking with them to capture the details of individual dances and the stories of the performers, choreographers, and musicians who created the work. Without Andros, many of these stories would be lost. He's putting them all into a book with the working title *The Underbelly of Ballet.*

Andros likes to write but he says he doesn't have the "burning in the gut" to get published or the ambition to bring all the material together and edit it for publication. He's also writing autobiographical vignettes which he plans to collect on a CD for distribution to his friends at his funeral. (Andros has written his own funeral service, arranged with the Neptune Society for burial at sea, and prepaid everything.)

Recently he's put much of the material planned for *Underbelly*, including the history of dance with a timeline, on a Web site, *members.tripod.com/androsdance*. His underlying purpose in writing the history of dance and of his own life is to tell people who are uncertain about their capabilities that, by keeping at it, they can achieve their goals. The cover page of his book will convey his message: "You thrust your right foot forward and put weight on it, then you take your left foot and thrust it forward and put weight on it. You continue this action until you get where you want to go."

Arline Rubin

Arline Rubin makes and sells ten thousand pressed-flower cards a year in a cottage industry she developed after she retired. She lives in a modern one-bedroom apartment in Manhattan. Everything is so neat, uncrowded, and airy that I have to ask where she does her work. Right here, at a small dining table where we're sitting.

With her voluptuous figure, high coloring, and full shoulder-length white hair that still has some black in it, Rubin makes a striking appearance. Her apartment is decorated with her own crafts: A wall quilt made from upholstery scraps and samples picks up the color scheme of the room. Opposite the quilt, an award-winning macramé hangs from a driftwood branch. On the coffee table I see small boxes and rocks with paper pictures or collages glued onto them; the technique is called *découpage*. Just when I'm thinking that the wraparound windows with their wide sills would be excellent for plants (she doesn't have any) and wondering about the absence of radiators (which cook my plants every winter), Rubin tells me she's taken her radiators out. There's no heat in the living room now but there's lots of sunshine and it's warm all winter long, she says.

Rubin pulls a box of her handmade cards from a bookshelf, each card an interesting arrangement of dried leaves, grasses, blossoms, and petals pressed flat and glued onto heavy paper card stock. She gathers fallen leaves and grasses in city parks and on trips to the country. Shopping in the

Chelsea flower market, she keeps her eyes open for interesting material that has fallen to the floor, plucking it up before it's swept away. She even grows her own plants in the little plot of ground in front of her building.

At this point, Rubin opens a closet door to reveal stacks of telephone books that have flowers and leaves drying between the pages. She doesn't use a pressing frame; the books' own weight provides the necessary pressure. When the flowers have dried, Rubin simply tears the page out of the phone book and puts it, with its flower still on it, in a box or file folder. A second closet holds the flower files, boxes of card stock in assorted colors, envelopes, and supplies. She carries a small telephone book wherever she goes so she can pick up good plant material when she sees it.

Rubin spends about 10 hours a week on her business. She hires a few people to assemble cards in their homes, training them first and giving them color photocopies of samples she wants them to copy. But she gathers and prepares the plant material herself, designs the cards, and assembles many of them, wrapping each one in cellophane and boxing them for shipment. She handles the business as well as the art—selling, invoicing, and shipping. Sometimes she has to chase unpaid bills or workers who don't deliver as promised. Even though Rubin runs this business out of her one-bedroom apartment, when she's not working, her home reveals no hint of the work.

Three and a half years ago Arline Rubin retired from a long career as a professor in the department of health and nutrition sciences at Brooklyn College, where she focused on human sexuality and family issues. She has continued to teach and lecture; this year, she and a friend are jointly teaching "Being Single: Ages 45 and Older" at the 92nd Street Y.

Rubin began making pressed-flower cards about 15 years ago but has only been selling them for about five years. Originally she used them herself or brought a few, instead of wine, to dinner party hosts. She found the recipients often wanted more and offered to pay for them. When she showed her cards to the buyers in upscale gift shops, they bought them too. Gradually she developed a small business.

Her new business required skills beyond crafts. Sales, for one. Rubin calls on shops in New York and in the towns she visits on vacation. She's found that shop owners are willing to look at her cards, but since they're very busy she's had to learn to be focused and concise in her presentation. So she's developed a few short, well-rehearsed sentences, and she keeps her samples ready to show without fuss.

Rubin says she has to be able to deal with rejection. People have many reasons for not buying: the cards may not be appropriate for a particular shop; the store may have just bought a large supply of cards and have no need or money for new stock; they may lack display space.

AARP has made a video of Rubin's pressed-flower card workshop and shown it on their monthly cable program as part of a series about making money from your hobbies and talents. Rubin worries about her eyesight and her hands but says cards are fun and she'll make them as long as she can.

She belongs to a "cooperative skill bank" called Woman-share, a group of 85–100 women, ages 30–80, who barter services on a time basis—an hour for an hour, all skills count equally. When she needed to speak with a lawyer, the lawyer used her credit to get a massage from a third member.

For her contributions, Rubin has shown other women how to transfer photos onto fabric. When a member's daughter became engaged, Rubin prepared a large casserole for the engagement party. And she's given communication workshops for small groups of Womanshare members, teaching them how to listen and how to communicate their feelings.

In return, a Womanshare member drove Rubin and all her things to a crafts fair. Another member helped fit a pattern to her measurements so that now Rubin has a basic custom pattern for making clothes. She's received computer help. And an interior designer came over to help her figure out what color to paint her apartment.

One member has a vacation house, and Rubin has used her workshop credits to stay there. (For more complex services, like seminars or the use of vacation houses, the group has developed formulas to calculate hourly equivalences.)

Transition to retirement was easy for Rubin. At Brooklyn College she taught only three days a week, and her schedule gave her time to do craft work between classes. Especially on days when she had a morning lecture and an evening lecture, Rubin would quilt, sew, or make cards in her office during the intervening hours. Four years ago she took up bridge. The group meets at her house once a week, and plays bridge at the same table she uses to make her cards. Now that she's retired, she plays tennis and golf and reads novels. On weekends she goes ballroom dancing at studios around town. She's on the board of her building, and in charge of the garden in front of it and the flowers in her lobby.

Rubin doesn't mind telling people she's retired, and she doesn't hide her age. She turned 66 in 2001 but says she feels 38. She takes care of her finances, researching stocks on the Internet and trading actively. But she buys and sells through a discount broker because she's afraid she could hit the wrong key and make the wrong purchase. Not wanting to tie up her only phone line during the day, she takes her laptop to bed and works on the Net until 2 or 3 or 4 A.M. Arline Rubin enjoys her life.

Jack Talbot

Jack Talbot[12] is an architect. For years he ran his own firm, specializing in hospital and nursing home design; I worked there from 1982 to 1992. When I saw him in 2001, he looked just the same—slender as ever, no new lines in his face, no new gray in his hair. (The office bookkeeper used to swear that Talbot kept a picture in his attic that grew old while he stayed young.) He had on the kind of chinos and plaid shirt he'd always liked but seldom wore to his Midtown office. I figure he's about 76 now.

---

12 Not his real name.

When he neared retirement age, Talbot sold his firm to a large national outfit. Then, when the direction of the practice began to change under the new owners, he left, bought himself a better computer, and tried to figure out what to do next.

Talbot's main architectural interest has always been the relationship between design and function. How does the design of a hospital or nursing home affect patient care? What's the relation among facility design, staff organization, and operating costs? Finding answers to these questions drove much of his working life; now he wants to use his expertise to further the state of the art in nursing home care. Encouraged by a former client who received the Drucker Prize for organizational innovation in long-term care management, Talbot has linked up with a colleague to seek funding for a research project. They want study 24 nursing homes in the Northeast to measure the effect of what Talbot calls "broom-closet changes"—changes in architectural design and management methods that nursing homes can make easily—on quality of life, resident health, and operating costs.

Calling on various prospects and acquainting himself more fully with the field, Talbot discovered the Pioneer Network, a "culture change" organization dedicated to changing the way nursing home staff think about and deal with residents. It took him about a year to get Pioneer interested in his own ideas but now, he says, they're enthusiastic.

Talbot is excited about the possibility of improving care and reducing operating expenses at the same time. He also knows that, while some administrators are receptive and eager, many others are totally opposed to the kind of change involved. He doesn't know which way the tide will flow, but he's optimistic. Culture-change pioneers are developing chapters all over the country. The director of Pioneer Network wants to create an "epidemic of change."

Talbot works out of his home in the Bronx, communicating electronically with people everywhere. E-mail lets him live in New York City and work with people far away—the reverse of the more conventional choice to live in the Adirondacks and work for a firm in the city. The amount of time he spends promoting nursing home research varies. When he's doing a proposal, or calling on people, he works intensely. Then pressure may let up. At times, he may be working hard on an architectural project; nursing home assignments come from old colleagues and clients, residential projects from friends. Often, just when he's finishing a job and thinking nothing else will come along, something does.

Altogether, he's working longer hours, and harder, than he ever worked before. He writes a monthly nursing home performance newsletter. Writing it takes two days, printing and mailing another day.

What does he see for his future? Like most of us, he finds that the value of his retirement portfolio has shrunk and he worries about money. Feeling mismanaged by investment professionals, he now manages his money himself. Talbot and his wife are thinking of moving to Kendall, a continuing-care retirement community under development in North Tarrytown, a Hudson River community about 30 miles north of New

York City. You live independently in your own apartment, and you'll have assisted care and nursing care available when you need it. Talbot would like to travel and have more vacation, but that's not what he'd like to do all the time. It's not what defines him. "The thing that haunts me most is not having anything to do."

Talbot has a professional dream to do research in nursing home design. If he can't get his proposal accepted anywhere, he doesn't know what he'll do next. But if the research gets funded, "It'll be great fun to work on it." He retains his optimism. "The older I get, the more I feel ready to take a risk."

Eleanor Jacobs

Eleanor Jacobs could never have anticipated how her life would change in the summer of 1969. She was a full-time housewife and mother then. Her husband, Raymond, a photographer, had just finished a demanding movie job. Unhappy about life in the United States at the end of the 1960s, they had picked up their two daughters and left for Europe.

In Europe they visited every museum, every church, and every monument. Jacobs's feet were killing her. In each new city she bought new shoes, hoping to find a pair that would let her walk without wincing. Finally, on an obscure side street in Copenhagen, she found a funny-looking pair, Anne Kalsø's Minus Heels, that made her feel like she was walking barefoot on the beach. Raymond bought a pair too and, as the Jacobses traveled through Norway in unexpected comfort,

Raymond came up with an idea: he and Eleanor could become the United States distributors for Anne Kalsø's Minus Heels.

They called Kalsø, who agreed to see them once she learned that they were astrologically correct: Raymond was a Taurus and Eleanor a Leo. After several conversations, Kalsø decided to let them sell her shoes in the United States, and in September the Jacobses flew home to start work. Eleanor said they were going from show business to shoe business.

Eleanor Jacobs had worked in advertising before her children were born, and she knew that a name like Anne Kalsø's Minus Heels would never sell in the United States. But they couldn't think of a better one right off. So while the shoes were being manufactured in Denmark Eleanor and Raymond concentrated on developing their business and marketing plans, and leasing, designing, and setting up a store. These weren't "mall" shoes, so they picked an offbeat location—East 17th Street in Manhattan. By April 1970, the shoes had arrived and everything was ready to go.

The day they opened the store, the Jacobses saw scores of young people streaming by, all the same direction, wearing love beads, tie-dyed shirts, and headbands. "What's up?" they asked. "It's Earth Day, man!" The young people invited them to join the celebration in Union Square.

"Earth Day!" Eleanor and Raymond looked at each other. "That's it!" Raymond crayoned a sign and hung it in the window—EARTH SHOES. Almost immediately a crowd came in. The kids liked the shoes, but they didn't have enough "bread" to buy them. Right then Eleanor made the fastest, most important business decision of her life: "If you really want to try these shoes, you may have them. Free. Later you can pay us— or not."

Jacobs gave away dozens of pairs of shoes over the next few days. Eventually the young people all came back—with checks for their shoes and friends who bought shoes too. Her decision triggered a publicity blitz. The *Village Voice* wrote them up. Everything took off. Within six years the Jacobses had 135 stores in the United States and Europe. Eleanor Jacobs was thriving. She found she could do more than she'd ever imagined. In charge of advertising and promotion for Earth Shoes, she traveled with Anne Kalsø, giving TV, newspaper, and radio interviews.

The Jacobses had stores in college towns all over the country. But the store owners were flower children, not businesslike and with little startup capital to invest. Jacobs figured it would work out in the long run, like her original decision to give away shoes. But the bank was not so forgiving and eventually froze their account. In 1977 Earth Shoes was forced into bankruptcy. The Jacobses lost their business in the debacle.

Eleanor and Raymond collapsed too. Then, after a few months, Eleanor went to work and Raymond gradually took up photography again. "We lost a lot of money," she told her husband, "but we're still who we are. We're artists."

In 1972 Eleanor Jacobs had begun studying art history at New York University, taking as many as three courses a semester while working full-time with the shoe stores. She graduated in 1979, and in 1980 went to work, first for Sotheby's Art Auction House, then for Hirschl and Adler Galleries. At Hirschl and Adler, Jacobs assisted the primary owner of the gallery. She was essentially the general manager—a troubleshooter and crisis manager, the person who kept the place running smoothly. And she learned a great deal about art. "Working there gave me my Ph.D. in art," she says. The Jacobses moved into a house in Connecticut that Raymond's mother had owned. Raymond worked from there and Eleanor continued at H&A, commuting to Connecticut on weekends.

In June 1992 Raymond Jacobs became ill, and on St. Patrick's Day 1993 he died. By then Eleanor Jacobs was 62. Finding it harder and harder to keep up with her work and her commute, she left H&A in June 1993 and lived on a small fixed income and social security. With Raymond gone and no job, Jacobs felt as though "I'd been cast out on the open sea in a rowboat and was watching the big ship that left me sail away."

For a few months, she sat around in a state of hypnotic passivity, not even knowing what to do when she got up the in morning—the same thing that had happened when they lost Earth Shoes. She says she tends to be catatonic for a time, but then her energy kicks back in. Little by little she finds something to do every day and rebuilds the structure of her life.

Six months after Raymond died, Eleanor Jacobs began to spread the word that she would help people buy and sell art. She usually represents sellers who come to her with a piece of art. She knows where to get the work authenticated and appraised, and which collector or which gallery to approach for a particular item. Jacobs started with American painting (the strongest focus of H&A) but over time the range of pieces she handles has broadened to include rugs, an Alaskan totem pole, and works by Diego Rivera and Frieda Kahlo. Recently someone asked her to sell a piece by Tiffany. She doesn't advertise but gets new clients by word of mouth. So she didn't retire; she changed from managing an art gallery to working as an independent agent.

Today Jacobs leads two lives: one in Connecticut, the other in New York City. In Connecticut, she lives near her daughter and grandchild and sees them often. She plays tennis and visits museums. A couple of years ago, she began writing humorous essays, about Earth Shoes and other personal and life topics. The *Litchfield County Times* has published her work and paid for it. In New York she spends about three days a week contacting art galleries, visiting private sellers, and arranging sales. Also, Jacobs has all of her husband's photographs, and when we last spoke she was trying to arrange a retrospective show of his work. Her dual life suits her. She intends to keep it up indefinitely.

Roni Henning

Roni Henning lives with her two daughters and her granddaughter in a detached two-story private home in Bay Ridge, Brooklyn. Flowers bloom in the yard, pumpkins dress the front steps, and an American flag hangs from the porch roof. Three separate apartments in the building allow the family members to live privately but close to one another. Henning's own second-floor living room, with its rattan chairs, flowered slipcovers, bay window looking out on a glassed-in porch, and two large collies sleeping on the braided rug, bespeaks relaxation and comfort. The house is so quiet a visitor would never guess that three golden retrievers, three Scotties, and a cocker spaniel are living in the other rooms.

Henning runs a dog boarding business out of her home. She takes care of dogs whose owners want their animals in a home rather than a kennel when they are out of town. Usually she boards no more than four dogs at a time, but when I saw her it was only a month after the attack on the World Trade Center. Several of her regular clients had been evacuated from their apartments in Battery Park City and couldn't take their pets into their temporary quarters. Henning was keeping the dogs until their owners could move back home again.

The dog boarding business is a relatively new venture for her. Until 1995 Henning was master printer-in-residence at the New York Institute of Technology's campus in Old Westbury. She ran their screenprint workshop, taught classes in silkscreen printing, and made limited-edition prints of fine artwork.

For many years Henning and her husband lived in Battery Park City, but he died in 1992. Two years later she bought the Bay Ridge house. Her mother was developing Alzheimer's, and one daughter was a single parent. Henning figured they could all be together, help one another, and take care of mother at home.

Then Old Westbury decided to downsize its art department, eliminating just about everything except computer art. Henning was 56 and had intended to work 5, even 10 more years but, with the department pulled out from under her, she had no choice but to accept the school's retirement package. For a while she did color separations at a large print studio in Manhattan, but she soon came to feel she didn't want a regular schedule anymore.

Meanwhile, since she now had a house and yard, people Henning knew in Battery Park City kept asking if she could take care of their dogs while they traveled. About the same time, a friend who worked on Wall Street and walked dogs on her lunch hour suggested that dog boarding would be a good business.

Missing her husband, Henning wanted work that was nurturing, so she started taking in dogs. She's always liked dogs, and she knows a lot about animals and animal behavior. Even so, it took a while to work out systems that make it possible for a group of unrelated animals to live together peacefully in a strange home. Dogs are pack animals, she explains, and when they come together they set up a hierarchy. At a kennel each dog would have its own cage and outdoor running space. A kennel director doesn't have to be concerned with interactions among the dogs, with dogs that chew on furniture or jump on guests. Henning has to cope with all this—and more.

At first she let the dogs get in bed with her. "Owners

would ask me, 'Where is my dog going to sleep? He usually sleeps with me.'" Henning tried to accommodate the owners but soon found she didn't get any sleep herself. At first she let the dogs run freely through the house, but the dogs were over-stimulated and life became too chaotic. She's learned to size up dogs, separating those that play together too much and get too worked up, grouping together those that get along well. She's put gates between the rooms and developed a logistical plan for controlling the movement of dogs around the house. Now her home is quiet and peaceful.

Each dog has its own diet too. She feeds them one at a time, making up their dishes while they line up outside the swinging doors that lead to her kitchen. The dogs learn their place in line and, knowing they'll get their turn, they wait patiently.

All this works because as soon as a dog arrives at her house, Henning lets it know she's the boss. She doesn't allow the dogs to form their own hierarchy. Each dog responds to her and they're all equal. "I'm . . . the real alpha dog," she tells me.

Henning "interviews" each dog before she takes it for the first time; the interview consists of an overnight stay. The dog has to get along with all the other dogs. If it's a barker, or mean, or aggressive, she doesn't take it. And usually it has to be spayed or neutered. "People will tell you their dogs are housebroken when they're not," she confides.

When it was time to let the seven boarders and her own two dogs out to play in her backyard, Henning opened the gates and pushed the dogs toward the stairs. Instead of racing ahead, they waited for her. When she led them out they trotted quickly, then frolicked around the picnic table and among the bushes. One Scottie and one retriever played particularly with each other. They're two who are too lively to keep in the same room inside, but for short periods outdoors they can enjoy playing together. Henning's yard is not a barren run. It's pretty. Mindful of her neighbors, she's careful to control the barking.

"You have to have the right personality for this," Henning says. "You have to be easygoing; you can't care too much about your furniture. And you're constantly cleaning." While it sometimes feels like she's working 24 hours a day and she may need to get up with a dog at night, at other times Henning enjoys a real sense of freedom. She can go out, paint in her studio, or spend time with her granddaughter. "It's nice not to have a boss."

Henning worries about the effect of the September 11 attack on the future of her business. About 60 percent of her clients come from Battery Park City. Many work in financial services and used to leave their dogs with her when they traveled for business. Now their offices are scattered, some are moving away, and others fear a prolonged downturn in the economy. Ordinarily by October she'd be booked for Thanksgiving. This year she's not. Maybe people aren't planning trips. It's a luxury business, she says. Kennels are cheaper.

Roni Henning's own artwork hangs on the walls of her living room and dining room. Most of her pieces are silkscreen prints that combine a living animal with a still life, often a ceramic or pottery piece. She aims for an abstract exploration of space and paint, not a realistic rendering of an animal. A viewer sees shapes and their relationship to each other before identifying one as a rabbit, the other as a teapot.

On the ground floor of her home Henning has a print studio equipped with screening table and drying racks. She teaches there and makes her own prints, and another artist pays her for part-time use of it. She gives occasional workshops at the Hunterdon Museum in New Jersey, and she teaches two courses a year at the Lower East Side print workshop in New York. Henning says her students are "the best."

She needs more money than her pension yields. Boarding dogs, teaching art, and renting out her studio help. She's thinking of writing a book about boarding dogs in her home, illustrating it with photos she's taken of the dogs she's kept. It wouldn't be her first book. Henning wrote *Screen Printing: Water-Based Techniques* after her husband died. She'd sit on the sofa and cry for a whole day. Then she'd write for a day—and cry the next day. Gradually, writing her book helped pull her out of grief. She thinks there might be a book in this too. She'd call it *Weeping to Working*.

Henning has made more of her own personal art since she started the dog business than she did when she was teaching at Old Westbury. Then, classes, students, and running the print shop filled her day. Now, with her freer schedule, she can work seriously in her studio while the dogs stay upstairs. She also finds she's meeting a broader range of people than she

used to. At Old Westbury, she met mainly other artists. Boarding dogs, she meets people engaged in many kinds of work.

On my way out she shows me how she's stripped dark
brown paint off the doors of her old house, revealing solid
oak with beautiful carving.

Part Three: The Opportunities

By joining a business or professional organization, retired people can keep up with their fields, network with others in order to find consulting or longer-term assignments, and contribute their own expertise to the organization. This list presents a selection of such organizations as well as Web sites dedicated to finding work.

Art Teaching
New York City Public Schools
Sharon Dunn, Ph.D.
Senior Assistant for the Arts
Board of Education
110 Livingston Street Room 340
Brooklyn, New York
(718) 935-3554
www.nycenet.edu/projectarts

Retired teachers and artists can take part-time teaching and consulting positions in Project Arts, a program that brings education in art, dance, theater, and music to children in all grades of the New York City Public Schools. The Web site shows the range of work being done by the students and provides curriculum and programming material for teachers.

All teachers are hired through the central office. Retired teachers interested in working part-time with the schools should submit their résumés to the Arts Education Office with a cover letter explaining the kind of work they would like to do, desired location, and the amount of time they are available to work. E-mail *NShankm@nycboe.net*, or send postal mail to Nancy Shankman, Director of Arts Education, care of the Board of Education at the above address.

Teachers interested in working full-time should call 800-TEACHNY. Artists who are not teachers can be certified through the Arts Connection: 212-302-7433.

Association of the Bar of the City of New York
42 West 44th Street
New York, New York 10036
(212) 382-6600
www.abcny.org

The city bar association has a program of luncheons, conferences, workshops, concerts, and other professional and non-professional events at which retired attorneys can keep up their professional contacts and interests. The Association of the Bar maintains an extensive library, runs a continuing legal education program, and offers members health, life, and other kinds of insurance at reduced rates.

The Web site lists positions open and positions wanted for lawyers, paralegals, and legal secretaries. It also lists many volunteer opportunities.

Cost: New York City resident attorneys admitted to practice eight years or more pay a one-time admissions fee of $395 plus semiannual dues of $197.50. Other membership classes have different fees. A Positions Wanted notice is $25 for members, $50 for non-members.

Dancers over 40
Scarlett Antonia
Post Office Box 237098
New York, New York 10023
(800) 799-5831

Dancers over 40 has a motto: "Age as a Resource, Not a Limitation."

This organization runs a pension eligibility hotline, and panel discussions on health and housing issues. It also helps dancers continue working by finding opportunities for members to perform and choreograph.

Each year the organization puts on its own showcase program, choreographed and danced by members. Throughout the year meetings create opportunities for dancers who may have worked together in a show years ago to meet again.

Cost: $45 a year for members living in New York, New Jersey, or Connecticut.

Editorial Freelancers Association
71 West 23rd Street, Suite 1910
New York, New York 10010
(212) 929-5400
www.the-efa.org

Retirees who have worked in marketing, public relations, corporate communications, journalism, and other professions that call for writing may want to continue to work part-time as freelancers. The Editorial Freelancers Association is a national, nonprofit, professional organization of self-employed workers in the publishing and communications industries. Members are editors, writers, indexers, proofreaders, researchers, desktop publishers, translators, and others with related skills and specialties. When you attend an EFA meeting, seminar or workshop, you have a chance to meet people in all these fields, learn more about different facets of the profession, and find leads and new assignments.

Members can subscribe to JobList: clients post their jobs and the request is sent to all subscribers, usually within a few hours.

Cost: Dues in the New York Metropolitan Area are $115 a year; JobList subscription is $25 a year.

Elance
www.elance.com

This Web site for freelancers bills itself as the world's largest professional services marketplace. Work categories include: Accounting and Finance, Software and Technology, Business and Marketing Plans, Writing and Translation, Graphic Design, Tutoring, Legal Contracts, Music, and many others.

You can use Elance to sell your professional services and deliver them online. Subscribers create an online service profile (i.e. your résumé, the services you offer, and samples of your work) and can then browse the project marketplace and submit bids. Potential clients can browse samples of Elancers' work online.

If you are selected and accept a project, you deliver the work and get paid through Elance.

Cost: A basic subscription for $25 a month or $225 a year showcases your work with a profile and portfolio, and allows you to bid on projects worldwide. Elance also charges a 10 percent transaction fee on projects you accept and deliver. Other subscription packages are available.

MIT Enterprise Forum of New York City
317 Madison Avenue, Suite 1900
New York, New York 10017
(212) 681-1112
www.mitef-nyc.org

The Enterprise Forum, an activity of the MIT Alumni Association, is open to all. The forum serves the entrepreneurial community in the New York area with symposia on new industries, technologies, and business models; business plan presentations; and a monthly Business Plan Introduction, which is a short tutorial and roundtable discussion directed at the "entry-level" entrepreneur.

The executive board is composed of entrepreneurs, venture capitalists, and service providers, and the forum has committees on which a retired entrepreneur can serve doing interesting and rewarding work. Association with other members can lead to opportunities for work or investment.

Cost: One hundred dollars a year

National Association for Female Executives (NAFE)
(800) 634-NAFE
www.nafe.com

With 125,000 members nationwide, NAFE (pronounced "naffy"—rhymes with "taffy") is the largest businesswomen's association in the country. A cornucopia of services and benefits to members includes everything from discounts on designer fashions to job expos to information on pension funds. NAFE's local and regional networking groups and alliances offer opportunities to meet and talk with other working women.

Cost: $29 a year

National Conference of CPA Practitioners
342 Madison Avenue at East 43rd Street
New York, New York
(212) 599-7204
www.nccpap.org

The National Conference of CPA Practitioners represents medium-sized local and regional CPA firms and sole practitioners. Retired CPAs can keep up with changes in tax law and public accounting practice, and can also obtain the continuing professional education necessary to maintain a license.

Network of Enterprising Women
Gail Cramer
Post Office Box 663
Locust Valley, New York 11560
(516) 759-5098
www.newonline.info
sol21@msn.com

The Network of Enterprising Women welcomes men and women of all ages who have marketable skills and an upbeat attitude. Members are a diverse group of entrepreneurs, many running their own businesses, some working for corporations.

An affiliate member of the much larger National Association for Female Executives, the Network of Enterprising Women offers both the resources of a long-established national association and the intimacy and networking opportunities of a smaller local group. Meetings four times a year (usually held in the offices of Salomon Smith Barney at 767 Fifth Avenue) feature panel discussions on topics like health, finance, and communications.

Unlike other networking groups, whose members are in the

same or similar businesses, NEW attracts people from a wide variety of backgrounds. Members say the exposure to these varied skills and viewpoints stimulates creativity.

Cost: $50 per year, which includes $29 for membership in NAFE.

Places for Publishers
www.absolute-sway.com/pfp

This Web site calls itself "The Book Industry Search Engine." It lists a large number of organizations and publications of interest to publishers, writers, agents, graphic designers, indexers, and others associated with the publishing industry. Organizations listed serve particular locations (the New York–based Magazine Publishers of America, for example), trades (the Bookbinders' Guild of New York), market segments (the Multicultural Publishing and Education Council), practitioners (the Small Publishers, Artists, and Writers Network), and many others.

Seasoned Solutions
Mary Ann Brice
201 East 25th Street
New York, New York 10010
(212) 684-1488

Seasoned Solutions is a new employment agency specializing in temporary and permanent employment for people over 40. The company handles regular office work and higher-echelon positions in all five boroughs.

Society for Marketing Professional Services (SMPS)
(800) 292-7677 x 225
www.smpsny.org

SMPS provides support for those who market the services of architects, engineers, construction professionals, and others concerned with the built environment. New York City has a remarkable amount of construction going on at all times, so there are often good opportunities for retirees with relevant marketing experience. Firms with full-time marketing staff sometimes need extra help in all aspects of marketing. Smaller firms without in-house staff may engage part-time services. Interested retirees can keep up with the field and meet prospective clients at the New York chapter's educational seminars, monthly meetings, and special events. SMPS also runs a job bank through which members can learn about new positions.

Call the SMPS national office at the above number to join, or to get the name of the current New York City contact. You can also join online at *www.smps.org*.

Cost: $250 year plus $50 one-time origination fee for new members.

Womanshare
680 West End Avenue
New York, New York 10025
www.womanshare.org
Wshare@aol.com

Womanshare is a cooperative in which members exchange services, paying with "time dollars." Upon joining, each member makes a list of the skills, interests, and resources she has to share—and what she needs or wants. These lists are provided to all members in a directory of Womanshare offerings.

A member wanting a service consults the directory to find a person who offers it. The provider then earns a credit that she can spend with anyone in the group. The recipient is debited the same amount, and clears that debt when she provides a service to someone else. All work time, no matter what the exchange, is valued equally, hour for hour.

Womanshare also runs potluck suppers at members' homes and other group activities for mutual assistance or just for fun and camaraderie.

Because Womanshare has no paid office staff to answer phone calls, prospective members are encouraged to check the Web site and communicate by e-mail.

CHAPTER **TWELVE**

Conclusion: Works in Progress

"New York would be a beautiful city, if they'd ever finish it," a visitor was heard to say.

New York *is* a beautiful city. And part of its beauty comes from the fact that it is *not* finished. In the 20th century New York was called the Capital of the World, as were London in the 19th century and Paris in the 18th. But New York City has not become a theme park of the 20th century, a place where people visit to see what life used to be like—and then go home. Scaffolding and cranes may inconvenience us, and we may argue about whether New York should build a stadium on the West Side or develop a park along the bank of the East River in Brooklyn, but it's this energy driving into the future that keeps New Yorkers of every age alert, dynamic, curious, and contentious.

While building for the future, New York City reaches deep into its past. Much of our architectural heritage—Pennsylvania Station, the old Waldorf-Astoria—has been destroyed. But New Yorkers are coming to value the Old Merchant's House (1832) in Manhattan; the Edgar Allan Poe Cottage (1812) in the Bronx; the Conference House (1680) in Staten Island; and the brownstones, row houses, old forts, and old taverns that stand among the skyscrapers and recall our past to us. The juxtaposition shows us that our lives are a reciprocity of old and new.

Those of us who are retiring can look back on long, rich histories, too. But our lives are not done. We continue to be nourished by those histories and to grasp new energy from the electric air around us. We and the city reflect each other. We're both works in progress and we keep each other that way.

At first, Ragnar Naess, a potter, resisted his friend's comment that the life plan they had developed in their 20s and 30s was used up. He didn't want to face the fact that the time had come to build a new plan. Then he began find it harder to drag heavy bags of clay, to spend long hours at the wheel, to set up and take down an exhibit booth almost every month. For aesthetic as well as practical reasons, he wanted to cut back on production pottery and concentrate on sculpture. But he still needed an income. To solve the problem, Naess reorganized his finances, his studio, his whole life.

Years ago, Naess had joined a group buying hilltop acreage in California. Later he came east and bought a four-story frame row house in Brooklyn, where he now has his apartment, his studio, and a kiln in the backyard. Recently, when the California land was sold, Naess used his share of the proceeds to buy an identical house next door. Rent from the lower duplex in the house and from an apartment above his own quarters gives him the income he needs to focus on his art.

The key to that house next door is key to his new life. Naess is converting the upper duplex into a communal living space for a group of friends. Five rooms will be individual bedrooms with a common kitchen and living room. An elevator chair between floors and a wheelchair-accessible bathroom on the first floor make it readily adaptable to older people. The collective, which will comprise both houses, anticipates being able to hire help as needed. Naess has formed a limited liability corporation and will sell shares.

He is opening doors between his house and this new one, and he's connecting the backyards to make one large sunny garden. Naess has totally renovated his old studio. Suddenly the previous layout, a warren of small, poorly-lit rooms he tolerated for so long, had become impossible for him. He opened up the ground floor to make one large airy room with a window to the new garden. He installed good lighting, built convenient storage space, and designed a solid wooden table,

high enough to let him work comfortably while standing. It's
on wheels so he can push it wherever he wants. He feels altogether different working in his studio now.

On a visit to Mexico, Naess had bought four ceremonial
masks. "Each mask represented a piece of myself. I called
them my committee." He'd hung them in his old studio. A
devil's mask with red face, big horns, and human teeth represented the angry demon boss within himself, the slave driver.
When he transformed his studio, Naess decided it was time to
get rid of the slave driver. He buried the devil mask in the
cemetery, next to his parents. They had been driven by the
same internal slave driver they passed on to him. "Let it rest
with them!" Naess has given that aspect of himself a new
name: project manager. He's in charge now.

He enjoys walking out his front door and seeing children
playing. Three- and four-generation families, from newborns
to octogenarians, live on the block. It's a real neighborhood.
"Brooklyn was a 'coming home' to me," Naess said. People of
all races, all colors. I learned how alike we all are."

New York was a "coming home" for Dave and me too.
From our first day here, we felt we belonged to this great, un-
finished city. A week after we arrived, we went to the opera at
Lincoln Center. We were practically intoxicated by the swirl
around us when we left the State Theater. "We don't have to
go home," I said. "We live here."

Appendix

Part One: Suggested Reading

Nonfiction

Anbinder, Tyler. *Five Points: The 19th-Century Neighborhood That Invented Tap Dance, Stole Elections, and Became the World's Most Notorious Slum*. 2001.

Burrows, Edwin G. and Mike Wallace. *Gotham: A History of New York City to 1898*. 1998.

Cantwell, Anne-Marie E. and Diana diZerega Wall. *Unearthing Gotham: The Archaeology of New York City*. 2001.

Cantwell, Mary. *Manhattan, When I Was Young*. 1995.

Caro, Robert A. *The Power Broker: Robert Moses and the Fall of New York*. 1975.

Goodwin, Doris Kearns. *Wait Till Next Year: A Memoir*. 1997.

Jackson, Kenneth T. *The Encyclopedia of New York City*. 1995.

———. *The Neighborhoods of Brooklyn*. 1998.

Kaiser, Charles. *The Gay Metropolis*. 1997.

Klaus, Carl H. *Taking Retirement: A Beginner's Diary*. 1999.

Lopate, Phillip, ed. *Writing New York: A Literary Anthology*. 1998.

McCullough, David. *The Great Bridge: The Epic Story of the Building of the Brooklyn Bridge.* 1972.

Metropolitan Museum of Art. *New York, New York: The City in Art and Literature.* 2000.

———. *New York, New York: The City in Song.* 2000. Compact disc.

Mitchell, Joseph. *Up in the Old Hotel.* 1992.

Rybczynski, Witold. *A Clearing in the Distance: Frederick Law Olmsted and America in the Nineteenth Century.* 1999.

Simon, Kate. *Bronx Primitive: Portraits in a Childhood.* 1982.

Stookey, Lee. *Subway Ceramics: A History and Iconography.* 1993.

Thaxton, John. *New York's 50 Best: Places to Go Birding in and around the Big Apple.* 1998.

Vinton, John. *Take Charge! The Complete Guide to Senior Living in New York City.* 1999.

White, E. B. *Here Is New York.* 1949.

White, Norval and Elliot Willensky. *AIA Guide to New York City,* 4th ed. 2000.

Wolfe, Gerard R. *New York—A Guide to the Metropolis: Walking Tours of Architecture and History,* 2nd ed. 1994.

Fiction

Auster, Paul. *The New York Trilogy: City of Glass; Ghosts; The Locked Room.* 1990.

Bellow, Saul. *Mr. Sammler's Planet.* 1970.

Chabon, Michael. *The Amazing Adventures of Kavalier and Clay.* 2000.

Cunningham, Michael. *The Hours.* 1998.

Doctorow, E. L. *City of God.* 2000.

———. *Ragtime.* 1975.

———. *The Waterworks.* 1994.

Ellison, Ralph. *Invisible Man.* 1952.

Finney, Jack. *Time and Again.* 1970.

Helprin, Mark. *Winter's Tale.* 1983.

James, Henry. *Washington Square.* 1880.

Maxwell, William. *All the Days and Nights.* 1995.

Morrison, Toni. *Jazz.* 1992.

Roth, Henry. *Call It Sleep.* 1934.

Smith, Betty. *A Tree Grows in Brooklyn.* 1943.

Wharton, Edith. *The Age of Innocence.* 1920.

———. *The House of Mirth.* 1905.

———. *Old New York: Four Novellas.* 1924.

Wolfe, Thomas. *The Web and the Rock.* 1939.

Wolfe, Tom. *The Bonfire of the Vanities.* 1987.

Part Two: Crime Statistics

Chapter 1 points out that New York City is safer than many cities with large populations of retirees. This statement is based on a review of the FBI Uniform Crime Reports 2000, the most recent figures available at the time of publication. The following table, "Comparative Crime Rates for Seven Cities," is drawn from the FBI reports for New York City; Phoenix and Scottsdale, Arizona; Palm Springs and San Diego, California; Naples and Orlando, Florida.

To find figures for other cities, and to learn more about crime in the United States, consult the Uniform Crime Reports on the FBI Web site at *www.fbi.gov/ucr/00cius.htm.*

Comparative Crime Rates for Seven Cities
FBI Uniform Crime Reports, 2000

	New York City	Phoenix, Ariz.	Scottsdale, Ariz.	Palm Springs, Calif.	San Diego, Calif.	Naples, Fla.	Orlando, Fla.
Population	7,746,511	1,300,786	214,685	45,192	1,266,132	20,734	190,702
Crimes and Crime Rates							
Murders	673	152	8	2	54	0	21
Murders/100K pop.	9	12	4	4	4	0	11
Forcible Rape	1,630	422	53	25	349	2	141
Rapes/100K pop.	21	32	25	55	28	10	74
Robbery	32,562	3,763	115	114	1,777	16	1,044
Robberies/100K pop.	420	289	54	252	140	77	547
Assault	40,880	5,417	395	317	4,980	58	2,720
Assaults/100K pop	528	416	184	701	393	280	1,426
Burglary	37,112	15,860	2,332	705	6,717	154	3,423
Burglary/100K pop.	479	1,219	1,086	1,560	531	743	1,795
Larceny/Theft	139,664	52,418	5,230	1,718	23,015	768	12,607
Larceny/100K pop.	1,803	4,030	2,436	3,802	1,818	3,704	6,611
Auto theft	35,847	19,466	1,170	357	9,467	49	2,413
Auto theft/100K pop.	463	1,496	545	790	748	236	1,265
Total crimes	288,368	97,498	9,303	3,238	46,359	1,047	22,369
Crimes/100K pop.	3,723	7,495	4,333	7,165	3,661	5,050	11,730

INDEX